First Out in Earnest

Hal S. Gardner
106 - 158 Sqdn

Geo. Dunn DFC LdH
10 76 608 1409 Met Flt

Doms DFC 9 Sqd 158 Sqd
60 Missions

FIRST OUT IN EARNEST

The Remarkable Life of Jo Lancaster DFC

From Bomber Command Pilot to Test Pilot and the Martin-Baker Ejection Seat

DAVID GUNBY

Jo Lancaster
40 & 12 Sqdn

Dave Fellowes LdH
460 SQN RAAF

Frank Tilley
617

John Bell DFC LdH
619 - 617 Sqns

Rusty Waughman DFC AFC LdH
101 (Special Duties) Squadron

Published in 2016 by Fighting High Ltd
www.fightinghigh.com

British Library Cataloguing-in-Publication data. A
CIP record for this title is available from the British
Library.

ISBN – 13: 978-0993212970

Typeset in Adobe Minion 11/17pt
by Alex Szabo-Haslam, www.truthstudio.co.uk

Printed and bound in China by Toppan Leefung.
Front cover design by www.truthstudio.co.uk

Contents

Chapter 1

Childhood

John Oliver Lancaster – known during his early life as 'Ollie' and later, universally, as 'Jo', but by his family always as Oliver – was born in Penrith, in what was then Cumberland, on 4 February 1919. The only son of John and Margaret Lancaster, he was the third of their four children. His family name clearly indicates that on his father's side his ancestral origins lay west of the Pennines, but his immediate ancestors, maternal and paternal, were from Yorkshire. His grandfather, John Lancaster, came from Shipley, a small town north of Bradford, and trained as a cabinetmaker and wood carver, eventually setting up a business in Harrogate, but a wife and growing family led him to seek a more secure job with a railway company. So he moved to Skipton and lived at No. 38 Sackville Street, where his son, also John, was born.

John Lancaster the younger was the fourth of seven children. An elder brother, John, and sister, Ellen, both died of tuberculosis in their teens, while a junior sibling, Frank, ran away from home at the age of sixteen, ending up in California where he established a successful wholesale meat business. He married but remained childless and Jo's father was able to visit him in 1937 when he made a round the world trip on Japanese cargo ships.

Jo's maternal grandparents, the Carters, both died before he was born. But photographs of the family taken in the 1880s and 1890s show his grandfather, Bennett, resembling George Bernard Shaw, a beaming smile behind a big beard. A 'stuff manufacturer', i.e. a manufacturer of fine woollen fabric, in 1881 employing thirty workers, he was also a musician and had an organ installed in his home at 12 Spring Place, Bradford. As a sideline he was secretary at St George's Hall, a large concert hall in the centre of Bradford, where he organised concerts and 'other attractions'. In the 1901 census, living in Addingham, near Skipton, he is described as 'Retired Agent and Sec. Subscription Concerts'. He moved later to Morecambe, where he died in 1912.

Bennett Carter was married twice. In 1860 his first wife, Betsey Green, died in childbirth, and her younger sister, Eleanor, moved in to care for their four children. Marriage to a deceased wife's sister was illegal under the 1835 Marriage Act, and remained so until 1907, but clergy were often willing nonetheless to perform marriages in such circumstances, and in 1865 Bennett and Eleanor were married in Bradford. Seven more children followed, of whom Jo's mother, Margaret, was the youngest, light-heartedly described in the 1881 census as 'pet of the household'. All the children were both musical and artistic, one brother becoming a professional clarinetist, while Jo's mother played the piano and cello, and her eldest brother of the second marriage, Sydney, was a capable painter in oils and watercolours, as well as a good singer and pianist.

Margaret Carter trained as a primary school teacher and taught until her marriage in 1910, first at Dronfield near Sheffield and then at Clapham Common in London. When she and John Lancaster met, he was working as a solicitor's clerk, but he had been deeply affected by the death of his brother and sister and was determined to move to a healthier environment than Bradford. Shortly after their marriage, therefore, they relocated to Penrith, where John set up in business as a coal merchant, furniture remover and storage contractor.

Penrith was then, and remains, a pleasant market town lying astride the main routes to Glasgow, the A6 road link and what was then the LMS railway line from London and the Midlands. To the north-east of Penrith and overlooking the town is a hill topped by a stone structure called the Beacon Pike, a monument that marks the place where fires were lit to warn the townsfolk of the approach of marauding Scots. Beyond the Beacon is the lovely Eden Valley, and beyond that again looms Cross Fell, marking the northern end of the Pennines. To the south-west of the town, following the Eamont Valley, lies Pooley Bridge, Lake Ullswater and the Lake District as a whole.

Like his three sisters, Jo first saw the light of day at 31 Wordsworth Street, one of four parallel streets running steeply up the side of the Beacon. No. 31 was a large, four-storeyed Victorian house, built of stone, gas-lit and heated by coal. The family moved from Wordsworth Street when Jo was about five, but he retains several vivid memories of those early years. One is of horse-drawn hearses climbing Wordsworth Street to the cemetery, and being taught at a very early age to stand to attention on the kerb, and remove his school cap until the hearse went past. He also recalls lorries, manufactured in Glasgow, being driven south through the town on delivery without mudguards or body, each just a bare chassis, with a driver clad in a coat, cap and goggles sitting on a box. He remembers, vividly, the LMS express, the *Royal Scot*, thundering through Penrith station after gaining speed on the descent from Shap Fell, an awe-inspiring sight to a small boy. On one occasion, his father took him to the station, where he walked along the platform to talk to the driver who lifted him up on to the footplate. Not realising that the driver was in charge, Jo was terrified that the engine was going to start up and carry him away.

While living at Wordsworth Street, the Lancasters had the use of Auterstone, an idyllic cottage near Howtown, tucked under Loadpot Fell overlooking Ullswater. And it was perhaps this that prompted the family to move, as they did when Jo was about five, to the village of Stainton, 3 miles west of Penrith. There, John Lancaster had leased for seven years, at £100 a year, a twenty-four-acre farm called Croft House, together with all the farm buildings. With it went the services of a part-time farmhand called Joe Weir who, Jo recalls, spoke a Cumbrian dialect so broad that visitors couldn't understand him, although Jo could perfectly well.

The Lancasters also had the services of a live-in domestic, a local girl, Nelly Hill, a cheerful but boisterous soul who happily did anything that was asked of her for the princely sum of 10s 6d a week, a good going rate for the job at the time.

No. 31 Wordsworth Street had a gas geyser supplying hot water in the bathroom, and mains drainage. Croft House had neither. Lighting was by oil lamps that blackened the ceilings and gave poor light, while water was supplied by a single cold-water tap in the outside washhouse. In the kitchen there was a coal-fired kitchen range with a boiler filled with rainwater next to it. The water was usually brown in colour and often carried the boiled corpses of crickets that had fallen in. In the bedrooms there were marble-top washstands with big bowls and jugs of cold water. Sunday night was bath night. A galvanised tin bath that spent the week hanging on the wall outside the kitchen was brought in close to the kitchen fire. It was Nelly Hill's night off and so the bath was filled with hot water from kettles and from the tank beside the kitchen fire. Use of the bath was by priority of age: his sister Constance went first and Jo last. How his mother and father bathed, he never fathomed.

The sanitary arrangements at Croft House were as primitive as the water supply. Instead of a modern flush toilet there was an outside earth closet 20 yards from the kitchen door. Into it, each morning, was emptied the contents of a slop bucket, containing the contents of the pots that were kept under each bed for overnight use. The earth closet itself was kept sanitary with the ashes from the fireplaces, and with newspaper and carbolic powder in a sprinkler tin.

On the farm the Lancasters raised cows, sheep, chickens and geese, and grew cereals. Even with the services of Joe Weir, it was necessary for all the children to pitch in, and Jo recalls helping to milk the cows, feed the sheep, pigs (a task he disliked) and the chickens and collect the eggs. On occasions the children drank milk directly from the cows, without ill effects, although this would now be anathema for fear of bovine tuberculosis. For someone like Jo, with a growing interest in things mechanical, one of the year's highlights was the arrival of a steam traction engine towing a threshing machine to thresh the corn.

The Lancasters had two ponies: a Shetland called Tinkerbell and a Welsh pony called Gem. The children rode both, while Tinkerbell was also used to pull a pony trap when Mrs Lancaster went shopping. In addition, during the winter months the family also borrowed – for his keep – a horse belonging to the local Territorial regiment, the Westmorland and Cumberland Yeomanry, which used horses only during a summer camp. He was called Fidget, big but very docile, and provided the family with plenty of good riding. Once they went to a meet of the local hunt, but were left miles behind when the hunt galloped off, and so retired from the field.

Although a relatively small village, Stainton was almost self-supporting.

It had fruit and vegetables aplenty from the gardens and farms around, and there was a local butcher who would go to market in Penrith once a week to buy animals for slaughter. At that time refrigerators were virtually non-existent. The village also had its own blacksmith – who was capable of almost anything, including making cartwheels – and also a joiner.

Stainton had a village Institute, a large long wooden building, perhaps an ex-army building from the First World War. It was mostly run and used by the local Women's Institute. Mrs Lancaster soon became its secretary and was heavily involved in organising whist drives, social evenings and concerts, sales of work, and the like. There was always something going on in the Institute. Jo vividly recalls his mother making WI notices using a flat tray with a jelly-like substance in it. Having written the notice, she would place it face down in the jelly and then remove it. Copies could then be made by placing blank paper on the jelly so that the dye would come out on to the paper; these were used to advertise coming events.

In the 1920s, every winter brought a substantial fall of snow and the local boys used to prepare for it by making or updating sledges; Jo's was articulated so that he could steer with his feet. The sledges were constructed out of wood while the blacksmith would fit iron runners for them. There was quite a long hill going down through the village, and because there was so little traffic the sledge owners could sledge safely right through the settlement.

Another winter pastime, when there were hard frosts, was skating. In the fields around the village there were several shallow ponds and on them the local children could skate safely without fear of harm if the ice broke. Farmers, it seems, did not mind the youngsters roaming on their land, whether to skate or, in autumn, to pick mushrooms. The children were brought up to be responsible, to close gates and not to disturb livestock.

Jo's mother had a knee problem caused by a bicycle accident in her girl-hood. Since she should not have been riding the bicycle she told no one, hence her injury received no medical attention. As a consequence she was unable to participate in one of the Lancaster family's major activities, hiking. Some walks were local, but on occasions John Lancaster and his four children would catch a bus to Patterdale, at the head of Ullswater, or some other convenient centre, and go fell walking for the whole day. Clad almost always in plus fours and brandishing a walking stick, John Lancaster would stride out mile after mile. He never owned a car, or indeed drove one. His bicycle or public transport were the alternatives to walking, the pair of Shire horses he owned being used only for pulling coal carts.

Every week, without exception, a large joint of meat was purchased for Sunday dinner. Beef, pork or lamb were standard fare, with chicken, now so commonly eaten, a special treat. On the kitchen range there was always a big earthenware jar called a stockpot, into which bones and odds and ends of meat went. It was hardly ever emptied, Jo recalls, but the contents, used for gravy, tasted good and nobody ever got ill eating them. There was also in the kitchen a large container, always kept full, of parkin, a north-country gingerbread made with oatmeal and treacle. When the farm was not producing its own butter, the Lancasters had a standing order with one of the local farmers for 4lb of it a week. Two 2lb blocks would arrive and Jo and his sisters would plaster it thickly on their bread. When, occasionally, their mother would remonstrate, their father would invariably reply: 'Let them have it. It's good for them'! The medical profession would now say precisely the opposite.

Christmas at Stainton was naturally a special time, and one celebrated by the Lancaster family in a unique way. It always started with the arrival of a big, red, hardbacked mail-order catalogue, detailing everything that Gamage's in Holborn, London, sold. For Jo, the toy section of the catalogue was something to be savoured, with hopes of something from it appearing in his Christmas stocking.

Christmas itself started with the children decorating the tree in the sitting room. Then on Christmas Eve they had a festive tea with Christmas cake and mince pies, the cake – like the Christmas pudding eaten the next day – containing silver threepenny bits, carefully wrapped in greaseproof paper, excitedly searched for by the children. After tea, the four siblings were confined to the dining room while their parents went into the sitting room and put the presents under the tree and their father dressed up as Father Christmas. The sound of their mother playing the piano was their signal to march in line into the sitting room, singing a little ditty that went something like

Come let us sing a merry song
In welcome of a friend
Who always comes to visit us
At every old year's end.

The four children had to march round the tree singing this until the music stopped and would then sit down while their father distributed the presents. The excitement of opening presents over, they went to bed, with the prospect, on Christmas Day itself, of a huge turkey, Christmas puddings and crackers.

Interestingly, though, recalling these Stainton Christmases, Jo emphasises that one of the things he particularly relished was the container in which one of the Christmas treats – tangerines – came. A flat wooden box that came to pieces quite easily, it supplied wood out of which Jo made model aeroplanes. He had not actually seen an aeroplane at that time, but knew what they looked like from pictures in books. Since materials for making models were hard to come by, the tangerine boxes were treasured. Then, one Christmas, Santa Claus brought Jo a real flying model. 'It was a Warneford', he writes, 'with a span of about 24 inches, a stick fuselage, oiled-silk covered flying surfaces, and of course an elastic band motor. Flying this gave me enormous pleasure, and I think that I learned quite a lot too.'

Jo also learned a lot from the two books in the Penrith Public Library on aviation. 'The first', he says,

the title of which I do not remember, gave diagrams and descriptions of the construction of elementary aircraft, and of the arrangement of the flying controls. I remember being surprised when I worked out that to turn left you had to push on the left rudder pedal, which was exactly the opposite to what I did on my home-made go-carts whilst steering with my feet. The second book in the library was Aerobatics by Major Oliver Stewart MC. From this I learned, in theory at least, how to perform aerobatics before I had ever been near an aeroplane.

Stainton had a primary school with a resident schoolmaster, but although there was a tiny Wesleyan chapel, it had no church, so on Sundays the school served as one, the Church of England services being conducted by the vicar from the neighbouring village of Dacre. Remarkably, the school had its own large garden, where the children were taught how to grow fruit and vegetables.

Jo, however, did not attend the Stainton school. Instead, between 1923 and 1931 his schooling was in Penrith, first at the kindergarten in church premises at the foot of Wordsworth Street, then at the Council School and lastly at the local secondary school, the Queen Elizabeth Grammar School – the 'big school'. Boys and girls were educated in separate halves, the girls with their own headmistress and the boys a headmaster with responsibility for the whole school. The headmaster was W.H.B. Leach, nicknamed, for some reason, 'Choll'. He was genial and loved by all, but when he retired he was replaced by a keen young headmaster, H.R.C. Carr. Jo got off to a bad start with Carr because in their classroom there was, in a cupboard, one of the new-fangled wireless sets installed. With Bakelite panels, tuning valves and dials, it had a wire around to the back of the classroom where there was a loudspeaker with a big horn. Jo, like most boys, had a penknife and, larking about one day, pretended to cut the cable to the speaker. Unfortunately, the cable was tender, his knife was sharp, and the cable was actually cut. As a consequence, Jo received six of the best from Carr. He was careful not to tell his parents, since he would probably have suffered further corporal punishment. Mrs Lancaster, former teacher that she was, was very good at maintaining discipline and not averse to taking a riding crop to the young Oliver's backside on occasions or, more frequently, to sending him to bed supperless.

At the Queen Elizabeth Grammar School there was a master called Mr Nicholas – 'Old Nick' – who taught French. He had a large, round, black ebony ruler, Victorian vintage, which he kept in his very deep trouser pocket. He would stand behind a boy in the classroom and while he criticised his work would hit him over the head with it quite hard. Another teacher, Mr Hulton, known for some reason as 'Zan', taught mathematics; his forte was mercilessly pulling a boy's hair and pulling and twisting his ear to drive home the point he was making. Nothing very much like that happened when, later, Jo went to Scarborough High School for Boys, except that a Mr Clark, who taught German and French, would stand in the doorway as the boys filed in or out of the classroom and would randomly slap someone across the back of the head. The boys' aim, naturally, was to get through the door without being the recipient of one of these blows.

With one exception, Jo found it hard to take sports seriously. That exception was cross-country running, over a course of about 4 miles, which he both enjoyed and did well at. He did, however, like scouting, joining the Penrith School troop as soon as he was eleven. They had several camps, and one he particularly remembers – on the shores of Lake Ullswater, just up the road from Penrith – involved trekking all round the lake in a day, something like 30 miles following the shoreline, leaving everybody exhausted. Although later, at Scarborough High School, there was no scout troop, Jo was able to continue his involvement with scouting through a scoutmaster cousin, who lived in Calverley, near Bradford. With his cousin's troop, Jo enjoyed camps in Swaledale and other parts of North Yorkshire.

In January 1931, Jo left Stainton for Ravenscar, near Robin Hood's Bay, where he was to live with his Uncle Sydney, and to attend Scarborough High School. The reason, at this distance, seems extraordinary. It concerned a letter, written in reply to one from a girl whom he had never met.

Jo was, he admits, shy with girls, despite having three sisters. The house seemed to be full of their friends, with whom they always appeared to be giggling and sharing whispered secrets. He hated this and, easily embarrassed and given to blushing, found it all a trial. There was the occasional girl at school he secretly admired, but never admitted this, even to his friends.

At school, the only time the boys and girls saw each other was in morning assembly and in the dining room at lunchtime when names could be put to faces across the hall. But there were a number of girls and boys who lived at Shap and Tebay, to the south of Penrith, who travelled to school by train. They of course knew one another, and one day one of the boys delivered Jo a letter from one of the girls. In due course he replied in the same silly terms as hers. But in it he made an oblique reference to current school tittle-tattle about one of the older boys who had, brazenly it seemed at the time, offered to help a girl who was busy pulling up her stockings. This innocent note had dire consequences, though, because shortly after Christmas Mrs Lancaster took Jo on one side and produced the very letter that he had written.

While Jo never knew precisely what had happened, it seems the girl's mother had found the letter and taken it to the headmaster, Mr Carr, who had given it to Mrs Lancaster, who naturally wanted to know what the veiled reference was about. Once told, she was satisfied that the whole incident was innocent but, nonetheless, Jo learned soon afterwards that in the spring term he would be going to live with his Uncle Sydney at Ravenscar and attending Scarborough High School.

From this interval of time, the incident seems extraordinary. Jo had never spoken to the girl, and didn't even know who she was until she was pointed out to him. Nor did he ever find out what had passed between his parents and the headmaster, but the upshot was that in term times he went to live with his uncle, and very happily too.

As mentioned earlier, Jo's Uncle Sydney, his mother's eldest brother, was talented both artistically and musically. When he left home he had joined his father in running St George's Hall and by 1900 was the manager. Recognising the potential of the cinema, he showed some early films in St George's Hall and in 1902 with two others formed a company called New Century Pictures that by 1930 owned and operated thirty-five cinemas in Bradford, Leeds, Scarborough and elsewhere. At that time all but those in Scarborough, the Londesborough and the Capitol, were sold.

An astute businessman, Sydney Carter also had a financial interest in the Ravenhall Hotel, at Ravenscar, and in 1910 he had bought a fine house, Craghill, overlooking Robin Hood's Bay, and there in the next two years directed and produced four short films, all with local scenarios. One involved the Robin Hood's Bay lifeboat, one of the old rowed-variety, rescuing a fishing boat in distress. Another was about smugglers in Robin Hood's Bay, ending with the smugglers duly caught by the excisemen, while a third concerned two rivals for the heart of a young lady, the one who had been rejected attempting to drown his rival but being foiled by the heroine riding bareback down to the beach and along the sands to save her lover in the nick of time. The fourth was about a little girl who fell down the cliffs and had to be rescued. All of the films, with their conventionally happy endings, were shown fairly widely, from the Midlands to the south of Scotland, but none seem to have survived.

Highly successful as he was in business, Sydney Carter was always held up to Jo's generation as a paragon of virtue in every possible respect, but his reputation suffered within the family when after his wife, Amy, died in 1932, in 1934 he produced a second wife, Elizabeth, complete with a daughter already in her twenties and married. Jo, however, took all this in his stride, with very happy memories both of his uncle and his new aunt. Sydney Carter was a most generous man and Jo's sisters used to join them in spending part of every summer holiday at Ravenscar. He owned a series of yachts, the last a 60-foot converted Brixham trawler, ketch-rigged, called *Gratitude*; aboard her, the Lancaster children spent many enjoyable and fun-filled holidays.

Jo settled in at Scarborough High School for Boys just as contentedly as he did living at Craghill. He quickly made friends with two boys from Ravenscar who travelled with him by train to school. One was Stanley Leake, the son of the local stationmaster and a very good pianist who inspired Jo to take up the piano again. He had had piano lessons for a while in Penrith but was a reluctant pupil, resenting the fact that his lessons were at half past ten on a Saturday morning and that he had to cycle 4 miles to his teacher's house. Hence he did not practise, and only scraped through his lessons because he could read music fairly well. Stanley Leake's prowess, however, encouraged Jo to resume playing, and the two of them would buy from Woolworths, for sixpence, sheet music of the popular songs of the day that they heard on the wireless. Sadly, once he left school, and no longer had access to a piano, Jo's piano playing ended.

It was with Stanley Leake, the stationmaster's son, that Jo had a close encounter with a train on the single-track Scarborough to Whitby line. To the north of Ravenscar station the track went downhill and through a tunnel perhaps half a mile long with a bend at the northern end. Stanley and Jo had often spoken of walking through this tunnel and one Saturday morning in winter, having ascertained that no train was scheduled, they set off. They were only about halfway through when they heard a steam train toot as it entered the tunnel from the northern end, puffing away furiously up the hill. The two boys turned tail and ran, but with no hope of reaching the tunnel entrance before being overtaken by the train, dashed into one of the refuges built into the tunnel wall. As the train went past they were choked with sulphurous fumes and smoke. They covered their ears to muffle the din, but this proved a mistake, since their hands had been rubbed against the sooty walls of the tunnel, so when they emerged from the tunnel they looked, Jo recalls, 'like a couple of Negroes'. He and Stanley set to gathering snow, using it to try to clean off the soot because neither was prepared to tell his family what had happened. The unexpected train was, of course, a goods 'special'.

The other friend was Stephen Birdsall, who lived in a cottage attached to a large farm run by a family called Cross. Jo and Stephen spent many happy hours on the farm, where one of the sons, Arthur Cross, owned several motorbikes. It was there that Jo had his first ride on a motorbike, an ancient Quadrant with long handlebars. Bitten by the motorbike bug, shortly after that he bought a Francis Barnett two-stroke for 15s from one of the chefs at the local Ravenhall Hotel. Jo enjoyed school at Scarborough, and also his free access to his Uncle Sydney's two cinemas, the Londesborough and the Capitol. 'I could take my friends there,' he says. 'All I did was just march straight in, say "Carter", go in and sit down. That was fine.'

Jo lost contact with both Stanley Leake and Stephen Birdsall when he left school, and has no knowledge of what became of the former, save that he died in Norfolk in 2006. The latter, however, joined the Royal Air Force pre-war and when war broke out with Japan, in December 1941, was serving as a wireless operator/air gunner with 100 Squadron, flying antiquated Vickers Vildebeest torpedo bombers in Malaya. Captured when hospitalised after an accident, he spent nearly three years as a prisoner of war in Malaya before being shipped to Japan. Tragically, on 12 September 1944 the ship on which he and 1,158 other British and Australian POWs were travelling to Japan as forced labourers, the *Rakuyo Maru*, was torpedoed by the USS *Sealion*, only fifty prisoners surviving to be picked up by the submarine. Sadly, Warrant Officer Stephen Birdsall was not among them.

Courtesy of his uncle, Jo was made a member of the Scarborough Sailing Club, which brought him the use of a dinghy. In it, on one occasion, he and a friend went out to look at the battleship HMS *Malaya*, anchored off the harbour. Failing to realise how the tides were running they made quick time out to the vessel, but found, when they wanted to return, that a strong tide forced them to sail at a different angle to make the coast, crawling back to Scarborough along the coastline. It was quite late in the evening by the time they reached the harbour after what Jo later saw as a lucky escape from what had been a foolhardy venture. Nor was it Jo's only one, for earlier, while still living at Ravenscar, he had acquired a large rubber inner tube that he took down the cliffs to the sea and launched. Sitting in the tube, he paddled out into the North Sea half a mile or more, and was very fortunate to be able to paddle back without mishap, oblivious of the fact that a tide or offshore wind would have carried him helplessly out to sea.

Early in 1935, worried about her husband's health, Jo's aunt Elizabeth decided that they should move to Scarborough and as a matter of course Jo accompanied them. They lived in an apartment on the Esplanade on the South Bay and one day in July the Cunard liner, *Mauritania*, on her way to Rosyth to be broken up, came right into shore and sounded her horns. Jo, thrilled, was startled to learn that this was for the benefit of his aunt who, prior to coming to Scarborough, had lived on the Wirral and knew a number of the Cunard captains, including the *Mauritania*'s. Another thrill for a teenager with a mechanical bent was the flight up the coast of one of the celebrated German airships, the Graf Zeppelin.

February 1935 brought Jo's sixteenth birthday, entitling him to ride his Francis Barnett motorbike legally for the first time. He was down to sit the Northern Universities School Certificate examinations, and in the run-up to the examinations he locked himself in his bedroom, almost for days on end, studying. The hard work paid off, since he passed with sufficiently good grades to qualify for University of London matriculation. This would have opened the door to sixth-form study, and subsequently university, but this was not possible, financially, for the Lancasters, nor was it a road Jo wished to take. His leaning rather towards things mechanical was emphasised when, on being awarded the fifth-form prize, he chose a book about engineering drawing. Jo wanted, as he himself puts it, 'to go out and get in amongst the oil and cogs and sprockets'. He therefore left school, returned to Stainton, and began looking for employment.

While Jo was at Stainton, two events occurred that served to strengthen even more his determination to take up an engineering career. One was that he met, through his mother's activities in the Women's Institute, a Mrs Robinson and her husband Horace. An engineer, he and his brother had designed and patented a hot-air engine. He had one in his shed, puffing away almost silently charging accumulators through a car dynamo.

Jo was most intrigued by Horace Robinson, by his little toys and gadgets, and by the car that he had designed and built, which had a rear-mounted twin-cylinder two-stroke engine and drove the wheels through a counter- or lay-shaft through 'V' belts. It was a similar system, Jo later noted, to the continuously variable transmission (CVT) used on cars produced in the 1960s by the Dutch company, DAF.

The second event of note was a visit to Penrith of Sir Alan Cobham's Flying Circus. One of the most celebrated English aviation pioneers, Cobham had made several notable long-distance flights, including a cir- cumnavigation of the African continent, landing only on British terri- tory, and a return flight to Australia. In 1932 Cobham had started what he termed National Aviation Day displays, seeking to raise the level of airmindedness. The colloquially labelled 'Cobham's Flying Circus' offered a combination of barnstorming and joyriding, involving a team of up to fourteen aircraft, ranging from single-seaters to modern airliners, and many skilled pilots. The 'Circus' toured the country, calling at hundreds of sites, some of them regular airfields and some, as at Carlton near Penrith, fields cleared for the occurrence. Jo vividly recalls the occasion of his first flight:

> It cost five shillings. I remember it was an Avro 504. I sat in the rear cockpit which had a 'fore and aft' bench-type seat and sat astride this. My fellow passenger was a girl, unknown to me, who just kept her head down and squealed throughout the trip. We went off, and I suppose the whole thing lasted about ten minutes. But on this particular flight the pilot had a piano wire hook on the wing tip and used this to pick up handkerchiefs from the ground. Twelve years later, I was working with Geoffrey Tyson at Saunders Roe and it transpired that he was with Cobham's Circus at this time and that particular trick with picking up bits of cloth was one of the things that he did. So, it's fairly odds on that it was Geoffrey Tyson who took me on my first-ever flight.

One idea Jo entertained was to apply to join the Royal Air Force under the Aircraft Apprentice Scheme, a rigorous three-year training programme for RAF ground crew personnel run at RAF Halton. By some means or other, however, he found the address of the Society of British Aircraft Constructors (SBAC), and wrote to them asking about apprenticeships, receiving a helpful and comprehensive reply. Taking on apprentices at this time, most companies required a premium, which for the Lancasters was out of the question. But, fortunately, two firms, including Armstrong Whitworth, did not, so Jo applied to them and in due course was invited for an interview. Accompanied by his father, he travelled by train from Penrith to Coventry where, for the first time, he saw traffic lights and a Belisha beacon. Jo recalls that as he and his father approached the Armstrong Whitworth works, located at Whitley Aerodrome on the eastern outskirts of Coventry, there was a biplane fighter performing aerobatics overhead. In all probability it was the prototype AW.35 Scimitar, an unsuccessful contender for the Air Ministry's F.7/30 contract, which eventually went to the Gloster Gladiator. It was his first encounter with an Armstrong Whitworth aircraft, and the beginning of an association with the company that would span, although not unbroken, some twenty-seven years.

After the interview, Jo and his father went to Studley, near Redditch, where his sister Margaret was studying horticulture at Studley College, staying a night before taking the train back to Penrith. In due course, a letter of acceptance arrived from Armstrong Whitworth. John Oliver Lancaster was to be apprenticed for a period of five years on a starting wage of a penny-farthing per hour, plus other allowances, including additional payments for piecework. Before he took up the job, however, he had a treat in store, for his oldest sister, Constance, a teacher, took him to Paris, where they stayed in a hotel on the Place de l'Opéra. Apart from a brief call at Boulogne on one occasion when sailing with his uncle in *Gratitude*, this was his first time abroad. Although in the next few years he would fly over it regularly, he would not set foot on continental Europe again until 1951. So it was that in the autumn of 1935 Ollie Lancaster found himself as a sixteen-year-old setting off alone to Coventry and into digs that he had found through the local Coventry newspaper. The accommodation turned out to be less than satisfactory but, luckily, during his first weeks at Armstrong Whitworth, Tony Carpenter, one of the apprentices just finishing his time, told Jo of a vacancy at his digs, which he happily accepted.

Chapter 2

Apprenticeship

In October 1935 the young Ollie Lancaster arrived in Coventry to start his apprenticeship. The aircraft manufacturer for whom he would be working, Armstrong Whitworth – or to give it its full title, 'The Sir W.G. Armstrong Whitworth Aircraft Co. Ltd' – had been founded in 1920, but the ancestry of the company lay in firms established by two of the great engineers of the nineteenth century, William George Armstrong, later Lord Armstrong, and Joseph (later Sir Joseph) Whitworth. Long rival manufacturers, the Armstrongs and Whitworths – giants in heavy engineering, and specialising in guns and ships – had in 1897 formed a joint company, and during the First World War had branched out first into aero-engine aircraft design and manufacture, and later into aircraft manufacture, initially under subcontract to other manufacturers, but eventually producing its own designs. Further amalgamation took place in 1919, when a merger was announced between Armstrong Whitworth and the Siddeley Deasy Motor Car Company, whose managing director, John Siddeley, later Baron Kenilworth, had led his company likewise into aero-engine design and manufacture, and subsequently into the design and manufacture of aircraft. The result of the merger was the Armstrong Whitworth Development Co., under which from 1920 operated Armstrong Siddeley Motors Ltd, car manufacturers, and the Sir W.G. Armstrong Whitworth Aircraft Co. Ltd. Post-war the parent firm, Armstrong Whitworth, was in serious decline as orders for guns and ships dried up, and in 1926 Siddeley bought out the Armstrong Whitworth Development Co., with its car and aircraft subsidiaries, renaming it the Armstrong

Siddeley Development Co.

In 1935, when Ollie Lancaster began his apprenticeship, Armstrong Whitworth's headquarters and works were at Whitley, south of Coventry. Built in 1918 for the Royal Flying Corps, but on decommissioning in 1920 purchased by Armstrong Whitworth, Whitley Abbey, as it was known, comprised three large double hangars with massive wooden latticework roof trusses, built by German prisoners of war, and containing a large machine shop and a detailed fitting shop, inspection room and press shop. There was also a wind tunnel, and in a separate set of buildings the drawing office and the works administration. In addition, there was a further hangar, built of corrugated iron, called the flight shed, which was of particular fascination to the young Ollie Lancaster, since in it were housed aircraft currently undertaking flight trials. Whenever he could he would sneak into the hangar to see what was going on, but was usually spotted and speedily ejected. Ironically, all three prototype aircraft hangared in such seclusion were, or would prove to be, failures, none of them winning Air Ministry contracts.

The oldest of these aircraft was the AW.19, a biplane developed in response to Air Ministry specification G.4/31, which called for a two-/three-seat general purpose aircraft suitable for army cooperation, reconnaissance, day and night bombing, dive-bombing and torpedo-dropping. Not selected to build a prototype, Armstrong Whitworth had nonetheless decided to compete for the contract with a private venture entry. Trials at Martlesham Heath showed the aircraft to be pleasant to fly, but its Tiger engine suffered from persistent overheating. By the time this had been overcome, the contract had already been awarded to Vickers-Armstrongs, whose Wellesley was the only monoplane entry, and the AW.19, returned to Armstrong Whitworth, served as a test bed for development of the Tiger engine until scrapped in 1940.

The second prototype was the AW.23 bomber transport, which had first flown only months before Ollie Lancaster joined Armstrong Whitworth. Competing with Bristol and Handley Page designs under specification C.26/31, the AW.23 was a twin-engined, low-wing monoplane and the only one of the three contenders with a retractable undercarriage. During RAF flight trials it was to perform well and prove pleasant to handle, but the contract eventually went to the Bristol Bombay. After a period in storage the AW. 23 was lent by the Air Ministry to Flight Refuelling Ltd, which used it to demonstrate successfully the technique of air-to-air refuelling. In August 1940 it was to be destroyed in an air raid on Ford Aerodrome, Sussex, which had been Flight Refuelling's base. Ironically, however, as the precursor of its bomber derivative, the AW.38 Whitley, the AW.23 was to prove far more profitable than the Bristol Bombay, which was built only in small numbers, while more than 1,800 Whitleys were constructed.

If the AW.23 proved ultimately fruitful, the third and most recent proto-type housed in the flight hangar in late 1935 was to prove a thorough-going waste of time and effort. An ungainly and, as Jo puts it, 'gawky' machine, the AW.29 single-engined day bomber was built in response to specifica-tion P.27/32, for which the Fairey Battle was also a contender. Overcom-mitment by Armstrong Whitworth to two other large-scale projects – one the Whitley and the other the AW.27 Ensign, a four-engined airliner for Imperial Airways – meant that the construction of the AW.29 took far lon-ger than originally envisaged and by the time it flew, a large Air Ministry contract had already been awarded to Fairey. The AW.29's life was short, for early in the company's flight trials the aircraft had to be landed with the undercarriage retracted. With little incentive to repair it, the AW.29 was eventually scrapped.

One reason for the Air Ministry's preference for the Bristol Bombay over the AW.23 may well have been the Bristol Pegasus engine over the Armstrong Siddeley Tiger. A forceful, even dogmatic, individual, John Siddeley insisted that Armstrong Siddeley engines should be installed in all Armstrong Whitworth aircraft. This was no problem with his earlier, successful radial engines, but the Tiger, used from the AW.19 onwards, proved less than satisfactory, so that while it was fitted to the early marks of Whitley, it was, in the Marks IV, V and VII, replaced by the Rolls-Royce Merlin, providing a critical improvement in performance. Likewise the Ensigns, decidedly underpowered with four 850hp Tiger IX engines, were eventually, during war service, re-engined with American Wright Cyclones of 950hp.

A grass airfield, small and with a hill at the south-west corner, Whitley Abbey had been adequate for the types of aircraft designed and built in the 1920s, but was increasingly unsuitable for the higher-performance aircraft

of the 1930s. When, therefore, in 1938 the Coventry Corporation opened
a municipal airport at Baginton, south of Whitley, Armstrong Whitworth
decided to relocate their main production works there and new, modern and efficient factory buildings were erected. These were gradually
enlarged, and the flight shed, final assembly, spar shop and sub-assembly
sections were all moved from Whitley, followed later by the machine shop,
drawing office and administration section. The wind tunnel remained at
Whitley, but by the outbreak of war little else did.

The standard aircraft engineering apprenticeship was of five years' duration, following two months' probation. The apprentice would first spend
a period in detail fitting, making small parts and learning to use a range
of tools. Then came time in the machine shop, followed by a period in at
least one of three other departments, the first involving the manufacture
of sub-assembly components, the second, the monocoque shop, where
the fuselages were made, and the third the spar shop, where the wings were
constructed. A concluding stint would generally be on the final assembly
line. The fifth and last year was normally spent in the drawing office, but
by 1939, with the prospect of war ever more likely, Jo recalls that he and his
fellow apprentices were living very much for the day, and recognising that
there was more money to be earned working on the shop floor.

In tandem with the development of practical skills, apprentices also
had to undertake theoretical training, and were given one morning and
one afternoon off each week to attend Coventry Technical College. They
were required to pay their own fees, although these were modest, but were
awarded a minimum day rate for attending classes. One September, at
the beginning of the academic year, a moment that Jo recalls is standing
outside the large modern building in which the college was housed, amid
a horde of would-be students, eager to enrol, and hearing one of two old
ladies, standing nearby, say to the other: 'Look at the little bleeders, they all
want to be bloody gaffers.' In 1937 Ollie sat and passed the National Certificate in Mechanical Engineering, the first step towards what the old lady
took to be 'gaffer' status. The next stage was two more years to complete
the Higher National Certificate in Aeronautical Engineering. But by September 1938 Jo's primary interest was no longer in completing his apprenticeship and qualifying as a 'gaffer', but rather on managing to get back

into the newly established Royal Air Force Voluntary Reserve (RAFVR) scheme, from which, as will be related, he had earlier been expelled.

Jo's recollections of life as an apprentice are warm ones. Each apprentice was attached to an old hand who was invariably friendly and helpful. There were no initiation ceremonies, although a good many good-natured practical jokes. Jo recalls one involving a fellow apprentice, Peter Norris, whose mentor wrote him out a requisition order form for a dozen 'lightening holes' and sent him off to the stores. The storekeeper rose to the occasion and gave Peter a trolley with some large round lead weights that were used as ballast in the Hawker Harts being built under contract for Hawkers, and Peter dragged them back to his mate, who quickly put his ruler across them, declared they were the wrong size and sent them back again. Peter, Jo comments, never really realised what it was all about.

Peter Norris and Jo were two of what was an intake of about twenty-five new apprentices starting over a period of a year and who gradually got to know each other and develop in some cases close friendships. There were two apprentices just out of their time whom Jo got to know very well. One was Tony Carpenter, with whom Jo shared lodgings initially. Mad keen to fly, Carpenter was turned down for the RAFVR on account of his defective eyesight. Despite this he gained a civilian pilot's licence and during the war joined the Air Transport Auxiliary, only to lose his life in a 1943 crash taking off from Harwarden in a Wellington. The second apprentice was Ken Oldfield, a hero to the young Ollie because he was, as Jo wanted to be, enrolled in the RAF Class F reserve. Ironically, when war came, and Ken was mobilised, it was discovered, belatedly, that his eyesight was below the required standard for a pilot, so he remained at Armstrong Whitworth, managing a dispersal factory near Northampton. Jo would meet up with him again when, in 1949, he returned to Armstrong Whitworth as a test pilot, to find Ken superintendent of the experimental flight shed at Bitteswell.

One close friendship that young Ollie developed was with fellow apprentice Eric Kelsey. Possessed of a lively wit and a very good mimic, he lived with his parents in Coventry, but was, Jo recalls, a restless soul, not always content with his lot. On one occasion he fell foul of the law when a local policeman with whom he was not on the best of terms caught him riding across a pedestrian area outside a row of shops. For this sin, Eric Norman Kelsey was taken to court and fined 3s 6d. This rated a paragraph in the *Coventry Evening Telegraph*, much to the distress of his mother, who felt he had brought shame on the family. On another occasion, Eric disappeared from Coventry, telling neither Jo nor his parents where he was going. When he returned they found out that he had on impulse gone to Southampton and signed on as a steward on the Cunard White Star liner *Berengaria*. Changing his mind at the last minute, he found himself unable to pay his bill at the seedy little hotel he was staying in, so left hurriedly through a toilet window. Then he applied for a short service commission in the RAF, but to his chagrin was turned down. His application for training in the Volunteer Reserve was more successful, however, and he had almost completed his flying training by the time war broke out.

Eric's wartime career was brief but remarkably varied. One of twelve RAFVR pilots attached to the Fleet Air Arm, he began his service career flying Blackburn Skua dive bombers at Donibristle, before completing a deck-landing course on HMS *Argus*, on which he and his fellow RAFVR pilots sailed round into the Mediterranean, to be landed at Toulon, making their way back to England through France in late 1939. Thereafter the group was sent to RNAS Hatston, in the Orkneys, flying Gloster Gladiators in defence of the naval base at Scapa Flow, and then, bewilderingly, to Aldergrove, flying superannuated Handley Page Heyford bombers undertaking some form of gunnery training. Next stop was 612 Squadron at Digby, flying Spitfires, before yet another posting brought the group back to HMS *Argus*, this time to ferry Hawker Hurricanes to Malta. This was achieved – with the Hurricanes being flown off the *Argus* when within range – but the pilots, expecting to return to Britain, perhaps for further ferrying duties, were instead retained in Malta, joining 261 Squadron. Eric was last seen on 19 January 1941, when, in hot pursuit of a Ju.87 Stuka dive bomber, he flew into the massive box barrage over the Grand Harbour. It was presumed that he was brought down by Malta's anti-aircraft defences.

Another good friend was Handley Rogers, whose father had served in the Royal Flying Corps in the First World War, and who became a commercial pilot post-war, flying with Imperial Airways. It was with Handley Rogers's father that the young Ollie, in company with Handley, had his second flight – this time in a de Havilland Puss Moth – from Anstey to

Croydon. Jo was thrilled to see so many aircraft at close quarters, and particularly to be allowed to board a Handley Page HP.42 Heracles airliner. He also recalls with pleasure that Handley Rogers's father gave him one of his Imperial Airways uniform coats, worn when flying open-cockpit airliners. A navy blue gabardine mackintosh with an oilskin interlining, it proved perfect as outer wear when motorcycling. On the outbreak of war Handley Rogers joined the RAFVR, trained as a pilot and was posted to 149 Squadron at Mildenhall, flying Wellingtons, but his operational career was cut short when he was seriously injured in a flying accident, and when fit again he spent the rest of the war instructing.

Several other apprentices of Jo's vintage also joined the RAFVR. Maurice Butt, like Handley Rogers, was posted to 149 Squadron at Mildenhall, but was shot down in August 1940, and passed the remainder of the war as a POW. Bill Garrioch, from Dublin, flew Wellingtons with 15 Squadron at Wyton and followed Maurice into captivity in February 1941, but Don Tuppen, also operating from Mildenhall with 149 Squadron, was not so lucky, being killed in September 1940. Other former apprentices served on Blenheim squadrons, including 'Bob' Berry, who perished operating with 107 Squadron from Wattisham in June 1941, and Nigel Ashley, with 139 Squadron at Horsham St Faith, who lost his life in December 1940. Yorkshireman Jack Jones, called up at the outbreak of war, was posted to a Blenheim squadron at North Weald and was luckier. Badly injured in a flying accident, he survived the war, to serve as a pilot first with the short-lived British South American Airways, and then with BOAC.

Three other apprentices also served in the armed forces. John Barrett Lennard applied to join the RAFVR, was turned down for pilot training on medical grounds, but qualified as an observer. In 1941, while serving with 40 Squadron, Jo heard on the grapevine that Lennard was with 9 Squadron at Honington. Taking advantage of a night-flying test, Jo and his crew dropped in on him at Honington, and lunched with him in the sergeants' mess. Not long after, in August, Lennard and his fellow crew members were killed when their Wellington failed to return from a raid on Hannover.

At the outbreak of war Peter Cleaver chose not the RAFVR, but the RAF, and trained as an engineering officer at RAF Henlow. Specialising in the recovery and repair of aircraft in the Middle East and East Africa, he had a distinguished wartime and post-war career, in the course of which he completed an MSc degree at the Cranfield College of Aeronautics while still a serving RAF officer. He retired as an air vice marshal.

John May's wartime career was very different. A rugby-playing fanatic, he had some elementary flying instruction before applying to join the RAFVR. Ironically, rejected on account of a heart condition, he signed up instead with the Royal Warwickshire Regiment as a territorial, survived the Dunkirk evacuation, and then enlisted in what was then called the Special Service Battalion at Troon, in Scotland, which became the Commandos, participating in at least two raids, one the highly successful attack on the Lofoten Islands in March 1941. Sadly, John died in the late 1950s of his heart condition.

On taking up his apprenticeship, Ollie Lancaster had to find accommodation. Initially, he took up the offer from Tony Carpenter, mentioned earlier, to share his digs, but when the landlady became ill and could not cope, and they found that a furnished flat was not a practical alternative, Jo went to join John May and Handley Rogers at 47 St Patrick's Road. There were six regulars there, the other three being Ivor Davis, who was selling houses on a large new building estate, Tom Stanley, who was working in the wind tunnel at Armstrong Whitworth, and Arthur Giles, a draftsman with Armstrong Siddeley. The landlords were Mr and Mrs Handley, and Jo remembers them and their son, who lived with them, as tall, thin and very pale. During his time there the lodgers were joined by two RAF men, a sergeant and a corporal, posted in to help set up the Coventry balloon barrage, and it was from them that Jo first heard expressions that were later on to become so familiar, such as 'you've had it' and 'duff gen'.

The trio of apprentices were exuberant, as might be expected in young men of their age, and became something of a trial for the Handleys. There was, for instance, the recurring practical joke involving tomato ketchup. Jo recalls that at dinner in the front room, which was the lodgers' common living and dining space, Arthur Giles always sat with his back to the window and when the food came, usually something with chips, he took the Heinz tomato ketchup bottle and gave it a vigorous shake before plastering his food with sauce. Time and time again – for their fellow-lodger was a slow learner – the apprentices managed to unscrew the top of the bottle, so when he picked it up and shook it, ketchup went all over him and the table. Equally trying for the Handleys was the decision by Handley Rogers, a great admirer of Louis Armstrong, to buy a trumpet and teach himself to play. Jo recalls that one day the tyro trumpeter was sitting practising in his bedroom when an exasperated Mr Handley shouted up the stairs, 'What's this, a bloody soldier's farewell?' The upshot of that and several other episodes was that Ollie, John May, and Handley Rogers were invited to leave.

Unappreciated at St Patrick's Road, the trio quickly found new, and much more congenial, lodgings in Beaconsfield Road with a Mr and Mrs Thackwray and their small son of about six. Mr Thackwray was a dental mechanic and also secretary of the local British Legion, having served in the Royal Army Medical Corps in the First World War. It was at the Thackwrays that, on the morning of 3 September 1939, the three apprentices listened in to hear Prime Minister Neville Chamberlain announce over the radio the outbreak of war, Jo recalling that Mrs Thackwray burst into tears.

The trio's exuberance also found expression outside their lodgings. One night a bunch of apprentices were in the White Lion public house with the bar almost to themselves. John May was admiring the shapely posterior of the Irish barmaid, called Bridie, so the others bet him that he wouldn't go behind the bar and administer a playful slap. Behind the back of the bar was an archway into a dark vestibule. John duly disappeared to carry out this task but never reappeared. Closing time came and he was still missing, and it was not until he returned to their lodgings at four in the morning that they learned what had happened. Apparently the previous night a coin phone box in the dark recess had been rifled and the manager assumed that May, lurking in the shadows, must be the culprit, seized him and called the police, who questioned him for several hours before he convinced them of his innocence.

That Coventry would be one of the Luftwaffe's priority targets when war came is not surprising, given that the city was not only home to Armstrong Siddeley, but also to many of the most famous marques in the motor industry. Local car manufacturers included Triumph, Standard, Riley, Daimler, Alvis, Armstrong Siddeley, Humber, Hillman and eventually Jaguar, while the motorcycle companies included Triumph, Rudge Whitworth, Francis Barnett and Coventry Eagle. Not surprising, either, is how many of the apprentices owned cars or motorcycles. Tony Carpenter had been a motorcycle fiend but by the time Jo met him he had graduated on to a home-made three-wheeler – an Austin Seven chassis with a single wheel at the front – before eventually acquiring a very smart Riley Sprite. John Barrett Lennard's family was well-to-do, and consequently he was in a position to acquire, in 1937, a Morgan 44 sports car. Handley Rogers's father bought him a brand new BSA Empire Star motorbike and Jo took him over to Birmingham to collect it from the factory. On Handley's first trip home to London, however, he was knocked off his motorbike on the Fulham Palace Road and broke an arm. As a consequence he was banned from owning a motorcycle but in due course obtained an elderly Morris Minor.

Ollie himself arrived in Coventry still the possessor of the Francis Barnett two-stroke motorcycle he had bought for 15s at Ravenscar. In September 1937, though, he was able to fulfil a long-held ambition to own a Scott. With a twin two-stroke water-cooled 600cc engine, the TT Replica bought for £22 made what Jo describes as 'a lovely noise' and was very fast. One lunchtime he went out for a spin with his friend Jack Jones, who owned a Velocette. While travelling at what Jack later told him was 70 miles an hour, Jo hit a patch of gravel and came off. Picked up from the side of the road by an ambulance and taken to the Coventry and North Warwickshire Hospital, he was treated for shock and X-rayed for a suspected fracture of the skull. Suffering from severe concussion, he was kept in hospital under observation for three weeks, at the end of which he was discharged but asked, on the way out, to see the lady almoner. In pre-National Health Service days, patients were requested to contribute what they could to the cost of their hospitalisation, and the almoner asked him how much he earned. He told her, and marvelled at her reply, which was to enquire, 'Do you think you could afford twelve and six?' He paid that gladly and still wonders at how little he was asked to contribute to the cost of the ambulance, medical care and three weeks in a hospital – just 12s 6d.

On 25 August 1939, as part of a campaign of violence begun after the United Kingdom government ignored an IRA ultimatum – issued in January, to withdraw all troops from Northern Ireland – IRA terrorists detonated a bomb in an errand boy's bicycle carrier in Broadgate, killing six innocent civilians. But this was not the first IRA bombing in Coventry, for Jo recalls that early in the year the inhabitants of 47 St Patrick's Road were rudely awakened about 6am by a large explosion, followed by the sound of debris landing on the roof: the IRA had detonated a bomb placed in a manhole just down the street.

The Coventry to which Ollie Lancaster moved in 1935, and came to love, was a city with a population of approximately 200,000. The city centre was quite small, comprising as it did the essentially medieval area surrounding the cathedral. It was well furnished with public houses, which Jo appreciated, a particular favourite being the sixteenth-century Golden Cross, standing in the shadow of the cathedral. Another of his favourites was the Coventry Hippodrome, which prior to its replacement by a more modern building in 1937 was still an old-style music hall. It had a bar at the back of the stage and the resident Coventry Hippodrome Orchestra, conducted by Charles Shadwell, which used to broadcast on the wireless every Saturday morning, introduced by the orchestra's signature tune, 'I want to be happy'. There was also an in-house chorus line, the Twelve Zio Angels. When in 1937 Shadwell moved to the BBC to conduct the BBC Variety Orchestra, the Hippodrome Orchestra was taken over by Bill Pethers.

Around the corner from the Hippodrome was the Opera House, which was the home of the Coventry Repertory Company, a theatre company of high standing. Jo himself only attended when, at Christmas, the company put on Victorian melodramas such as *Sweeney Todd*. During these Christmas shows the audience were invited to boo the villains and cheer the heroes and heroines, but Jo recalls that the audience became so vociferous that what should have been a 45-minute show could go on for 2 hours, and that the management had to come on stage and ask the audience to calm down. Coventry also boasted more than forty cinemas at a time when people customarily went to the cinema at least once or twice a week. There were also two roller-skating rinks and two swimming pools. To reach these venues there was a very good public transport system, the Coventry Corporation running a fleet of modern Daimler double-decker buses, as well as the tram system, which reached to the outskirts of the city. For a young person, Coventry had much to offer. It was prosperous, go-ahead, and lively.

Another plus, so far as Ollie Lancaster was concerned, was that Coventry was on the main Birmingham to London railway and that for a very modest 5s 6d, he could make a half-day excursion to London, taking Saturday morning off to catch a train at 10.20am that reached Euston at noon, and left Euston at midnight, to arrive back in Coventry at about 1.40am on Sunday morning. Sometimes travelling down in order to buy motorcycle parts from Pride and Clarks in Stockwell, he more often went in order to see his beloved sister, Con, who was teaching in London. On several occasions she took him to the Gaiety Theatre in the Strand, where the resident company, led by Leslie Henson with Richard Hearne (Mr Pastry), Louise Brown, Florence Desmond and Jo's favourite, Fred Emney, produced a series of immensely popular farces, including three that Jo recalls vividly: *Going Greek*, *Seeing Stars* and *Running Riot*. Little did he know then that five or six years later he would be flying Leslie Henson from RAF Binbrook to Hendon.

When Ollie Lancaster was interviewed for an apprenticeship at Armstrong Whitworth, it was made plain to him that his work would not involve flying. But like so many of those who took up apprenticeships he was determined to fly and, like them, he saw the pathway to qualification as a pilot as joining the Royal Air Force Volunteer Reserve. Formed in July 1936 to provide a reserve of pilots, navigators and wireless operators in the event of war, the RAFVR recruited civilians aged between eighteen and twenty-five, who were trained at Reserve Flying Schools run by civilian contractors, with most instructors members of the Reserve of Air Force Officers who had previously completed a four-year Short Service Commission in the RAF. For young Ollie, the opportunity came when in February 1937 he turned eighteen. He applied, was summoned to the Air Ministry in Ad Astral House, Kingsway, and after an interview and medical that lasted all day, was accepted. Trainees could undertake pilot training on a part-time basis, at weekends, but Jo opted rather for a full-time *ab initio* course, and in early July was sent to No. 6 Elementary and Reserve Flying Training School at Sywell, near Northampton. Run by Brooklands Aviation, 6 ERFTS was housed in a large communal building originally a clubhouse, with the trainees sleeping in chalets that each accommodated six. There were about twenty trainees on the course and, curiously, Jo never encountered any of them again after their flying training was completed. The aircraft employed were de Havilland DH.82 Tiger Moths and

Jo's first flight with his instructor, Flight Lieutenant 'Knocker' West, took place on 6 July. There was a certain amount of competition as to who went solo in the shortest time and Jo took rather longer than average, at 10 hours 25 minutes, because of a tendency to hold off bank in gliding turns, which he recalls as 'a cardinal sin'. Once cured of this, all went well and on 20 July he flew his first solo.

When pupil pilots were sent solo the drill was that the instructor would fly a couple of dual circuits and landings, after which the trainee would taxi back to the take-off point, the instructor would get out and the pupil would complete one solo circuit and landing. Jo, chafing at the bit, was reprimanded afterwards because he opened the throttle to take off before the instructor had had time to get clear of the aircraft and nearly blew him over. His solo flying went well, although he had one close call. Pupil pilots were taught to make engine-off approaches for landing, gliding down slightly on the high side and then side-slipping the surplus height off just over the fence. It was permissible to practise false landings in this way, to be cruising along at 1,500 to 2,000 feet, pick out a suitable field, cut the engine, glide down, make a side-slip approach over the fence and then open the throttle and climb away again. On one occasion at Sywell Jo entered a spin near the airfield at about 3,000 feet. The engine was idling as he spun, but as he recovered he didn't open the engine up again, so did not realise that it had ceased functioning. Only as he glided over the hedge did he realise that the engine had stopped. Jo's reflection on this incident is that it was just as well he did not know this earlier, since he would have felt rather panicky.

Jo finished the course at Sywell at the end of August with a grand total of 52 flying hours and returned in high spirits to Coventry, ready for the next stage in his pilot training, which was to take place at RAF Ansty, 5 miles east of Coventry, but his motorcycle crash delayed this until October. Ansty was the home of No. 9 Elementary and Reserve Flying Training School (ERFTS), which was operated by Air Services Training, based at Hamble, near Southampton, under contract to the RAF. At Ansty, Jo flew both the Avro 643 Cadet – a docile training aircraft whose only defect was the Armstrong Siddeley Genet engine by which it was powered – and the two-seat trainer version of the Hawker Hart day bomber, proudly recalling that he soloed on the latter, a powerful machine with its 525hp

Rolls-Royce Kestrel engine, before he turned nineteen. His flying hours rose steadily, particularly after he discovered that in addition to going to Ansty at weekends, he might turn up on a weekday afternoon, when his instructor, busy with his Short Service Commission pupils, would allot him an aircraft to go off solo. Jo recalls that that was not only great as a way of increasing his flying hours, but also financially, since he made more out of attendance money and travelling expenses than had he been working at Armstrong Whitworth.

All, then, was going well, with a very confident Ollie Lancaster seeing himself as an ace of aces, until a sunny Sunday morning, 10 April 1938. Reporting to Ansty, he was allocated Avro Cadet G–ADTY on which to practise aerobatics. He started the engine, but found that whenever he opened the throttle the engine would cut out. Clearly, there was some-thing wrong with the carburation, which was probably over-rich. Finding, however, that by opening the throttle very slowly the engine did not cut, he decided, foolishly, that he would take off. In a clear blue sky he started doing some aerobatics, but in the course of a slow roll, at 270 degrees with full top rudder, the hand fire extinguisher underneath the instrument panel came out of its clips, fell and jammed behind the rudder bar. Once right side up, but with left rudder jammed on, Jo managed to force the extinguisher partly through the canvas at the side of the fuselage so that he could obtain neutral rudder. The sensible thing to do, given the uncertain behaviour of the engine and the impaired rudder control, would have been to return to Ansty, but instead he landed at nearby Whitley. It being a Sunday morning the place was deserted, save for a groundsman to whom he handed the fire extinguisher before taking off again. Then, compound-ing his errors of judgement, he flew over to where he knew his friend Tony Carpenter kept his own aircraft, the only Dart Flittermouse ultra-light ever built, performed a few aerobatics for his benefit and then carried out a simulated forced landing, which turned into a real forced landing when the engine did not pick up when Jo opened the throttle to go round again. Instead, he ended up crashing the Cadet through a fence. He writes:

> Then came a dreadful silence. I tried to re-gather my wits, and climbed down to the ground. Tony came over, and together we surveyed the sorry scene. Unfortunately both port wings had been

broken by a wooden post, otherwise damage would have been
minimal. As the full significance of what I had done that morning
slowly sank in, I became more and more dismayed. I could now only
foresee the direst consequence, and so it was to prove. Tony drove
me to find the nearest phone box, and I reported to my instructor.
He was Flying Officer Howard, and I had always got along with him
very well. On this occasion, however, his demeanour was distinctly
cool. I gave him what was I think a reasonably truthful and complete
account of the events of that fateful morning, but of course I was at a
total loss to explain why I had taken the decision to land at, and then
take off again, from Whitley. Back at Ansty I was not interviewed by
the Chief Flying Instructor, I was not required to submit a written
report, I was simply told to go home and to report back again in
a week's time. Reporting back, I was sent to see Flight Lieutenant
'Poppy' Pope, the Chief Flying Instructor. Without any other
comment he simply handed me my flying logbook and told me that
I was discharged. In my logbook I found the following endorsement:
'Suspended from further training on account of breach of flying
discipline – aerobatics at low altitude. Crashed aircraft thereby
causing extensive damage to same.'

Dismissed from the RAFVR, John Oliver Lancaster tried everything he
could think of to get reinstated. A letter to Sir Kingsley Wood, the Secretary of State for Air, brought a very courteous reply from his personal secretary but in the negative. An approach was then made, indirectly,
through one of Handley Rogers's uncles, who was a Freemason, to Captain W.F. Strickland, who was the Member of Parliament for Coventry.
Again, nothing came of it. By this time, the RAF had taken over Allesley
Hall, on the northern outskirts of Coventry, as a local RAFVR administrative, social and instructional centre. This was commanded by Squadron Leader 'Jimmy' Riddle, who was sympathetic, but had no more luck
in securing Jo's reinstatement, or even his enlistment for training as a
navigator or wireless operator. Jo became something like an honorary
member – invited to go out to Allesley Hall in the evenings and join the
others – but not one of them.

Ollie Lancaster's chances of service in the RAFVR became even less

likely when in May 1939, in the aftermath of the Munich Crisis, Leslie
Hore-Belisha, the Minister of War, revived the militia, into which, in a
limited form of conscription hitherto unheard of in peacetime, single
men of a certain age were conscripted, to serve for a year before discharge
into the reserve. Just the right age, Jo thus found himself called up in the
first draft, and summoned for interview in Coventry by what he describes
as 'a very puffy major'. Jo's protests that he was a trained engineer and a
trained pilot made no impression, the major simply replying: 'Oh well,
you'll be an absolute dead certainty for the Royal Army Ordnance Corps.'

By the end of August 1939 it was clear that war was inevitable. So on the
nights of Friday, Saturday and Sunday, 1, 2 and 3 September, a group of
about eight apprentices assembled in the Golden Cross, and all got very
merry indeed. It was to be their last time together. Within days all but Peter
Norris and Jo had been called up. They teamed up with two others, one
(Roger Ellis) in a reserved occupation with Alfred Herbert, the machine
tool makers, while Jo continued to lodge, alone, with the Thackwrays. But
the large and rich circle of friends had been broken forever.

TOTAL FLYING.	HOURS	
	DUAL	SOLO
	17.10	15.50
Instrument Flying	01.25	NIL

Proficiency as Pilot

SUSPENDED FROM FURTHER TRAINING ON ACCOUNT OF BREACH OF FLYING DISCIPLINE - AEROBATICS AT LOW ALTITUDE. CRASHED AIRCRAFT THEREBY CAUSING EXTENSIVE DAMAGE TO SAME.

To be Assessed:
As Ab Initio.

~~Exceptional.~~
~~Above Average.~~
Average.
~~Below Average.~~

Any special faults in flying which must be watched :-

[signature]

FLT/LIEUT.

Chief Flying Instructor.

No. 9. E & R.T.F.S.

Date *17.4.38.* WALSGRAVE, COVENTRY School.

Chapter 3

Under Training

When war was declared on 3 September 1939, the three armed forces hastened to set up a combined recruiting centre in Coventry and, naturally, Jo hurried down to join the RAF. The officer in charge of the RAF section, Flying Officer Sparrow, was unhelpful, however, and showed no interest at all in enlisting a semi-trained pilot with a chequered RAFVR history. The naval section was run by Chief Petty Officer Brown, who was far more sympathetic, but unable to assist. Although Jo made no effort to enlist in the army, his earlier conscription into the militia, it seems, had made it the default option and, as a consequence, a short time later he received a letter containing a travel warrant, an advance of pay of 4s, and orders to report to the Budbrooke barracks of the Royal Warwickshire Regiment. Appalled, Jo rushed down to the recruiting centre again, only to find Flying Officer Sparrow as uninterested as before. But he was rescued by Chief Petty Officer Brown, who as a blocking measure signed Jo on for the Royal Navy in an unspecified capacity on deferred service. Subsequently Jo received another letter, informing him that he no longer need report to Budbrooke, and requesting the return of the travel warrant and the 4s advance of pay. Then, eventually, in December 1939 he received a letter from the Air Ministry, stating that he was accepted for service in the Royal Air Force and requiring him to report to No. 2 Reception Centre at Cardington, in Bedfordshire. Early in January he did so, was officially recruited, but then sent back to Armstrong Whitworth on deferred service until May, when he was finally called up.

Once again Jo reported to Cardington, where he was inoculated against sundry diseases, put on a train and sent down to Bexhill, where, after an overnight stay in the Winter Gardens, he was embarked on a train again, this time for Paignton, in Devon, where was situated No. 4 Initial Training Wing. In the ensuing six weeks he and about fifty others of his intake, billeted in the Hydro Hotel, underwent basic training, which included square drill, physical exercises and classroom work covering the theory of flight, engines, meteorology, navigation and signals. The course ended with passing-out exams and various psychological and aptitude tests. These were passed successfully and Jo was posted on 19 August to Desford near Leicester, where there was an Elementary Flying Training School (EFTS) operated by Reid and Sigrist, instrument (and aspiring aircraft) manufacturers, and, reacquainted with that most celebrated of primary trainers, the Tiger Moth, began his flying training. Before they took off for what was customarily a familiarisation flight, however, Jo explained his past history with the RAFVR to his instructor, a Flight Lieutenant Hall. Accordingly, the latter gave Jo the opportunity to demonstrate his flying ability, and on landing commented, 'You haven't forgotten how to fly.' Thereafter, much of the 50 hours' flying instruction was spent practising aerobatics, which Jo enjoyed immensely.

During ground instruction the trainees were told to read the Black Book, which was full of cautionary tales about service personnel and trainees who had misbehaved themselves and what had befallen them. One such involved a certain RAFVR sergeant named Lancaster, and when the penny dropped, and his fellow trainees realised that LAC Lancaster was the offending trainee pilot, he became, as he puts it, 'a bit of a hero really'.

The crisis that started in May 1940 with the blitzkrieg and fall of France, followed by Dunkirk and the Battle of Britain, made little impression on the way of life in the Midlands, Jo recalls. On the night of 25 May a Handley Page Hampden of 106 Squadron had strayed into the Coventry balloon barrage, hit a cable and crashed on the edge of the Coventry cricket ground, about 200 yards from Jo's digs in Beaconsfield Road. Later, visiting Coventry from Desford, he was on a bus when a Junkers Ju.88 slipped unscathed through the balloon barrage to drop a stick of bombs on the Standard Motor Company factory. At Desford, at the height of the Battle of Britain, the ground crews set up a blackboard on which, listening to the radio, they used to keep and update the score relating to Luftwaffe and RAF losses. The only indicator of the direness of the straits the country was in was that some of the Tiger Moths were fitted with practice bomb racks, in case they were needed as a last-ditch defence against invasion barges.

On completion of the course at Desford, trainees were asked to express a preference for fighters or for bombers. Naturally, Jo chose fighters, and in due course was posted to No. 5 Service Flying Training School at RAF Sealand, near Chester, where trainee pilots would fly the advanced trainer, the Miles Master I. Those on Jo's course at Sealand included some interesting individuals. One was Neville Duke, the future test pilot, with whom Jo had trained at Desford, and another, David Barnwell, was the youngest member of a renowned British aviation family. His father was Captain Frank Barnwell, chief designer for the Bristol Aeroplane Company, who had been killed in a flying accident in 1938. Two of David's brothers, Richard and John, were already serving in the RAF, and all three were fated to be killed in action, David on Malta in October 1941. Two were Americans, Galbraith and Mauriello, who were destined to join 71 Squadron, the first of the RAF's so-called 'Eagle Squadrons', fighter squadrons manned by American volunteers. Another, named Bowker, had, like Jo, been dismissed from the RAF, in his case for flying a Hurricane at a dangerously low level, while a pilot named James had flown in the Spanish Civil War, and had a row of medals to show for it. Yet another member of the course was Gordon Brettell, later one of the fifty air force officers shot after the 'Great Escape' from Stalag Luft III.

With a 750-horsepower Rolls-Royce Kestrel engine, constant-speed propeller, retractable undercarriage, and flaps, and with a top speed of some 235mph, the Master provided trainees with a realistic introduction to the fighters they would likely fly on operations – the Spitfire and Hurricane – but also presented them with a major challenge. Among other instructions trainee pilots received was that, in the event of undercarriage trouble, they were to cross the Mersey and land at Speke (now Liverpool Airport). For Jo, such an emergency occurred on his first solo flight, on 11 October 1940, when the undercarriage failed to lower. Remembering the emergency procedure – which was to push a button in the floor and then use the hand pump – he did this, and to his great relief green lights indicated that the undercarriage was down. Further pumping lowered the flaps, and Jo landed safely and taxied in. Several officious individuals rushed out, intent on fining him two and sixpence for taxiing with the flaps down, but were quickly convinced of the reason why he had done so, since it was evident that a hydraulic hose under the engine had burst.

With Liverpool Bay and the Irish Sea close at hand, Sealand was an ideal location for low flying. It was said that previously pilots had flown under the Menai Strait's bridges, hence there was a warning notice that the military were liable to hang cables from the bridges to prevent this. Jo recalls one pilot returning with about 2 inches neatly clipped off the tips of each of the three wooden propeller blades. Asked to account for this by the flight commander he said that he must have raised the tail too high on take-off, whereupon the flight commander, Flight Lieutenant Marsh, ordered the pilot to go and find the broken propeller tips. It so happened that a day or two earlier another aircraft had suffered a broken propeller for some reason, and the pilot took a large lump of broken wooden propeller blade into the flight commander's office. Fortunately, he saw the joke and took the matter no further.

At Sealand the trainees' billets were the original airmen's married quarters, composed of terraces of two up, two down houses. One night there was a noise outside and Jo and others went out to find a twin-engined Blackburn Botha had belly-landed, coming to rest between two rows of houses, without damage either to them or to the pilot.

Down the road from the billets was a little café the trainees used to patronise, run by a dear old lady who would provide 'a good old fry-up of bacon, beans, fried bread, and tomatoes', all for 1s 8d. One Sunday night, Jo and three or four others crossed the bridge over the River Dee into Wales, completely forgetting that in Wales all public houses were closed on Sunday. However, they spotted a British Legion club that was obviously open, presented themselves at the door and were made most welcome, somebody even buying them a drink. Things changed, though, when one of their number won the jackpot on a one-armed bandit. No sooner had he done this than they were approached and ask to pay a visitor subscription!

As part of their training, pupil pilots took it in turns to act as duty pilot, which, involving little more than spending the night in the watch office, was more of a ritual than anything else. On 13 November it was Jo's turn to be duty pilot, and the next morning, rather than sleeping on the day off that went with the overnight watch duty, he took a train down to Coventry and then out to Kenilworth, 4 miles away, where he stayed with some of Handley Rogers's relations who had relocated there. It was 14 November and the night of the big Coventry blitz. Jo recalls that he and his hosts had a grandstand view of it from Kenilworth and it was genuinely awesome. The next day he hitched a lift into Coventry and found the city a shambles. He walked to the station, but was turned back on account of what were said to be nine unexploded bombs, so he trudged through the city, much of which was still in flames, having decided that it would be best to make for Rugby and catch a train there. As he walked a delayed-action bomb went off some 100 yards from him, but eventually he was given a lift by a passing motorcyclist and boarded a train back to Chester and Sealand, fortunately without his absence being noticed.

No. 5 Flying Training School shared facilities at Sealand with No. 30 Maintenance Unit, and the rapid expansion of the latter necessitated the removal, on 17 December, of the Flying Training School to Ternhill near Shrewsbury, where Jo completed his training. 'We were given a bit of leave round about Christmas time,' he says, 'and I went down to my parents at Eastbury, near Newbury, and on New Year's Eve, we could see a tremendous glow in the sky to the east. That was the night that the city of London got fire-bombed.' When training resumed at the beginning of January the airfield was closed for several days, first by heavy snow and then by being completely waterlogged when the thaw came.

It was during Jo's time at Ternhill that his sister, Con, who was teaching at the Royal Normal College and Academy for the Blind in Upper Norwood, London, was evacuated with the school to Rowton Castle, about 6 miles due west of Shrewsbury. Since this was not far from Ternhill, Jo took the opportunity when he could to fly over there and beat the place up. On one occasion he made a parachute out of a handkerchief and some string, with a bottle opener as a stabilising ballast, and wrote a letter that he attached to the bottle opener with an elastic band. He then flew low over the castle and dropped it with great accuracy out of the cockpit window. Not long after, however, his sister decided to join the Auxiliary Territorial Service (ATS), and after a stint in charge of an anti-aircraft battery on the Isle of Sheppey was posted to the Royal Artillery's experimental establishment at

Shoeburyness. Meanwhile, his second sister, Margaret, who had a horticultural degree, was employed in the Dig for Victory campaign, particularly in relation to the allotment in Hyde Park, serving as the technical expert for a campaign fronted by the BBC personality Freddie Grisewood. His third sister, Joan, an artist, joined the Women's Land Army and was involved in growing tomatoes and other vegetables at a nursery in Hertfordshire.

The Miles Master being highly powered for its size, and fully aerobatic, Jo enjoyed himself immensely playing around in the tops of cumulus cloud. He was surprised, however, at how little formation flying was undertaken, his logbook recording only three relatively short flights. This seemed strange, given that for fighter pilots formation flying was important. Not so surprising was that only his group, out of the four into which the course was divided, did any night-flying training, bad weather having so severely restricted flying time that the other groups were unable to fit it in. Jo himself flew at night on two occasions, the first time using glim lights and with six circuits with an instructor followed by three solo. On the second occasion the dimmer hooded gooseneck lights were used, and three circuits were flown with an instructor and six solo. At the conclusion of the course, Jo and his fellow trainees naturally assumed that they would be posted to fighter Operational Training Units (OTUs), but the demand for bomber pilots was such that for some this did not happen. Jo comments:

> Our course at No. 5 SFTS numbered 49 pupils and of those we had one fatality, a chap called Peter Paul, and three were kicked off the course presumably for not being up to it. The course was completed around 15 February 1941 and we were awarded our wings and promoted to Sergeant Pilot. Then three-quarters of the course went off to fighter OTUs. The other quarter, of which I was one, went off to bomber OTUs and about seven of us went to Lossiemouth. Among those I remember were George Bayley, Tommy Young, Charlie Everett, Derek Townshend, Tony Shilleto and Bob Telling.

Of the seven, only Jo would survive the war, Young being killed in action with 7 Squadron in June 1941, Telling with 9 Squadron in January 1942, Bayley in July of that year, while serving with 61 Conversion Unit after

completing a tour of operations with 7 Squadron and earning a DFC, and
Everett with 207 Squadron in August. Derek Townshend, posted as Jo's
second pilot to 40 Squadron, would, in June, fly out to the Middle East to
join 148 Squadron in Egypt, and lose his life in a raid on Crete in October
1941, while Tony Shilleto, posted like Jo to 40 Squadron, would survive two
tours of operations, only to die in a mid-air collision between two OTU
Wellingtons in July 1944.

After his serious crash, Jo had sold his Scott motorcycle, and in 1940,
while still at Armstrong Whitworth before finally being called up, bought
an old Austin Seven saloon, complete with tax and insurance, for £6 10s.
Remarkable in its decor, in that everything inside that was not glass was
painted duck-egg blue, it provided Jo and his friends with a great deal
of fun, and motoring, when petrol could be obtained, at very modest
cost. He recalls that on two occasions the car carried a crew of six, two
of whom had to stand up through the sliding sunshine roof. 'At the time
the police had no problem with this it seems,' he comments. 'Also, we
didn't need a wheel jack. If a wheel had to be changed, two chaps would
lift that corner of the car, whilst a third changed the wheel.' When called
up, Jo had taken the Austin down to Eastbury, in Berkshire – where his
parents, who had moved south from Stainton in 1937, ran the village shop
and post office – and had laid it up. That Christmas, however, he thought
better of this and took it back to Ternhill, only to change his mind again
on learning that he had a posting to Lossiemouth. Not wanting to drive
the Austin Seven to Scotland, he sold it to one of his fellow trainees, Alan
Hendry, who hailed from Lerwick in the Shetland Islands where he was a
budding solicitor and his father and brother were doctors. Alan had not
got the £5 asking price for the car, but as security against future payment
he presented Jo with the Longines watch he had just been given for his
twenty-first birthday. On not hearing from Hendry, Jo made enquiries
and found that in October 1941 he had been killed in a flying accident
at a Spitfire OTU. Jo accordingly kept the watch until, in the 1990s, he
undertook a massive search, found one of Alan Hendry's relatives, and
returned the watch to her.

Jo travelled to Lossiemouth by train, via Edinburgh and Aberdeen, map
reading as he went in order, as he puts it, to 'ensure that the engine driver
knew the way'. At Lossiemouth, known to him hitherto only as the home

of Ramsay MacDonald, the former Labour Prime Minister, the trainees were not housed on station, but billeted in a large detached house that had been requisitioned. Living conditions were spartan in the extreme. Each room had camp beds in it and that was all, while the only heating was by open fires, and trainees were supplied with coal and left to organise the rest for themselves. One had the bright idea of using as a firelighter the candle out of a Very cartridge, put it in a grate and covered it with coal. The result was spectacular but unpleasant; the entire house was filled with acrid red smoke and had to be abandoned for about an hour.

Built in 1937–38 and initially a Service Flying Training School, Lossiemouth, on the Moray Firth, had in April 1940 become No. 20 Operational Training Unit, equipped with Vickers Wellingtons. Nearby, however, was No. 19 Operational Training Unit, equipped with Whitleys, and it seemed to Jo that, having built Whitleys, he should fly them operationally. Accordingly, he sought an appointment with Lossiemouth's station commander, Group Captain Smyth-Piggott, and requested a transfer. Not surprisingly, his request was refused, Smyth-Piggott commenting, 'Oh, we all get to like the Wellingtons.' He was right, in Jo's case, for it was to be the Wellington in which his first tour of operations would be flown, and in which he would, after its completion, instruct others. It was something he never came to regret. Months later, Group Captain Smyth-Piggott's name would crop up in very different circumstances. Jo recalls: 'Whilst at the Rex Ballroom in Cambridge with several pints down me I was dancing with a girl and she asked me my name. Facetiously I answered "Smyth-Piggott", and in a very matter-of-fact way she said, "Oh, you were at Lossiemouth, were you?"'

Despite reaching Lossiemouth in late February, Jo's intake did not fly until the end of March, he being taken up for a first familiarisation flight in a Wellington on the 30th. Of the intervening period he comments: 'I can't remember what on earth we did all that time; obviously we were doing groundwork, there was quite a lot to be done. But six weeks seems an awfully long time. Certainly we didn't have any leave.' Lossiemouth itself Jo found a dull and forbidding place, but fortunately about 4 or 5 miles inland was Elgin, which was rather more cheerful and where the place to congregate and socialise was the not very grand but certainly pleasant Grand Hotel. Whenever they could, however, Jo and his fellow trainees would go into Inverness, which was much more lively. This was made easier by the legacy of £100 that his Uncle Sydney had left to Jo and each of his other nieces and nephews, £35 of which Jo spent on a 1933 Morris Ten bought in Inverness. He ran it for ten years before selling it for £100 to a Rolls-Royce representative at Armstrong Whitworth. Jo remembers the car as reliable in all but one respect:

> This car did not have a conventional petrol pump, but a gadget called a 'petrolift', which was sometimes troublesome. When it stopped working and the engine died, I had to get out, lift the bonnet and hit the petrolift with something hard to make it resume work. On several occasions while with 40 Squadron at Alconbury, after a trip to Cambridge I drove along the long straight A1, repeating this process every five miles or so, whilst four fellow crewmen slept very soundly.

The Wikipedia entry for RAF Lossiemouth comments on its 'location and good weather', noting that on account of the latter, 'many different types of aircraft were frequently diverted to the station'. This may have been so, but it was also true that, situated as it was on the Moray Firth, Lossiemouth was subject to sea mists, which would roll in with little warning, blanketing the base. It was this situation that led to the death of one of those with whom Jo became particularly friendly at Lossiemouth, Sergeant Arthur 'Lofty' Hughes. On 18 April 1941, Hughes – who hailed from Boroughbridge in Yorkshire, and whom Jo had met when he was visiting the town pre-war with fellow apprentice, Jack Jones – was carrying out a series of night circuits and landings with a New Zealander, Sergeant F.S. Hobden. The weather deteriorated and, in trying to land, they approached too low and crashed into a hangar.

The Wellingtons that Jo flew while at Lossiemouth – a mix of Mark IAs and ICs – he describes as 'well used', and indeed most, if not all, were war-weary ex-operational aircraft. The instructors were also ex-operational screened pilots and the instruction they provided seemed to Jo at the time somewhat perfunctory, although later, when himself instructing, he came to see this in a different light. Flying training for the pilots began with familiarisation flights, and then a series of circuits and landings both day and night, dual and solo. The last of these was on 15 April, when pilots were graded as first or second pilot; the first qualified to captain an air-craft. Designated a first pilot, Jo was allocated as his second pilot Derek Townshend. Then came the full crewing-up, which for the Wellingtons at Lossiemouth in this period required two pilots, an observer – who com-bined the roles (later separated) of navigator and bomb aimer – a first wireless operator, second wireless operator (who doubled as front gun-ner) and rear gunner. The process of assembling crews was achieved by a simple method, remarkably original (for its time) and highly successful. Assembling in a hangar all the pilots, along with the observers, wireless operators and air gunners who had been posted in, the powers-that-be simply told crews to form themselves. Jo recalls:

> When we crewed up at Lossiemouth, we aircrew were assembled in
> a hangar in the correct proportions and were told to form ourselves
> into crews. I knew Derek Townshend, of course, who had been
> designated as my 2nd pilot, but knew none of the others, so he and I
> just wandered around looking at brevets before faces. After a few 'Are
> you fixed up?'s, we finally collected a full crew.

In Jo's case, he and Derek Townshend were joined by Canadians Glenn Leitch and Bill Harris as observer and second wireless operator respective-ly, while Jack Crowther, a Welshman, and Keith Coleman, a New Zealand-er, completed the crew as first wireless operator and rear gunner respect-ively. Jo had never met any of them before, nor did they know each other, but they arranged to gather that evening in the Grand Hotel in Elgin. A lively party resulted, and from that time on the crew was a tight and har-monious unit. 'We were,' says Jo, 'as thick as thieves and got on famously.'

At twenty-four Glenn Leitch, the observer, was the oldest member of the crew, and remembered by Jo with affection as 'a very, very lively character who loved England and English beer'. Hailing from Toronto he was guaranteed, if anyone mentioned the word 'Toronto', to immediate-ly respond with 'The Queeeeeen City of the Empire.' Short and stocky, with a mop of wiry hair and a slightly pocked-marked face, he, for some reason that Jo never fathomed, hated policemen in any form, which was ironic given that in civilian life he had been employed in an administrative capacity with the Toronto police. This intense dislike would lead to trouble on more than one occasion, and indirectly to his death.

Jack Crowther, the first wireless operator (as designated then), had been an RAF boy entrant and trained as a ground wireless operator before undertaking aircrew training as a wireless operator/air gunner. The youngest member of the crew, he is remembered by Jo as 'a tallish, slim, snub-nosed little chap, very pleasant, very efficient and very Welsh'. The second wireless operator, Bill Harris, a Canadian from Niagara Falls, occupied the front turret, while in the rear turret was New Zealander, Keith Coleman. The latter had arrived in the United Kingdom in mid-1940 and been posted to a night-fighter squadron at Kirton in Lindsey, equipped with the Boulton Paul Defiant. When Defiants were withdrawn from service he was posted to Bomber Command. Pre-war a representative for the International Harvester Company, he proved to be uncannily accurate as a gunner, Jo recalling an occasion at Alconbury when 40 Squadron was visited by a flat-bed truck with a Wellington two-gun rear turret mounted on the back, fully powered but fitted with a shotgun in place of the Brownings. The squadron gunners were invited to take turns at this, shooting at clay pigeons, while the rest of their crews stood by eagerly watching the prowess of their respective gunners. By a large margin, Keith Coleman was the most accurate.

First flying together on 17 April, although with Jo as second pilot, Sergeant Lancaster and his crew began training for operations, this involving predominantly cross-country flights by day and night during which the crew coordinated their skills, and in particular tested the navigational expertise of Glenn Leitch. He proved efficient and unflappable, as did all the crew. And efficient they had to be, for the lengthy cross-country courses, both over the rugged north of Scotland and out into the Atlantic or the North Sea, were demanding – and potentially fatal, if an engine cut out, since the Pegasus-engined marks of Wellington they were flying, not equipped with feathering propellers, were unable to maintain height on one engine; if one failed, they could do no more than carry out a protracted descent. During Jo's first tour of operations with 40 Squadron, several Wellingtons and their crews would be lost at sea in these circumstances.

A lucky escape from just such a fate was one Jo and his crew observed one morning, while carrying out a cross-country over the North Atlantic. Jo recalls:

One gin clear morning we were doing a day cross-country and
were way up in the north of Scotland. Our route took us over the
island of North Rhona, which is about 50 miles north-west of Cape
Wrath. We were at about 5,000 feet when we saw a Whitley carry out
a belly-landing. North Rhona is a very small and rocky island, but
the Whitley seemed to get down intact. I told the wireless operator
to send a signal to tell Lossiemouth what we'd seen, assuming that
the Whitley was one from Kinloss. Anyway we never heard anymore
about it until many years later in an aviation magazine I found a little
article about it. Apparently it was a Coastal Command Whitley [of
612 Squadron] from Wick carrying out some secret anti-submarine
trials. The RAF subsequently recovered the equipment from it and
later the whole aircraft, which must have been quite a feat.

Besides the day and night cross-country flights, Jo's crew should have
carried out air-to-air firing and bombing exercises. For some reason,
however, both were cancelled, and the crew were posted without completing the full OTU syllabus. All the other crews were transferred to the
Wellington-equipped 3 Group, but Jo's crew were assigned to 40 Squadron.
Ordered to present themselves at Wyton, in Huntingdonshire, where the
squadron was based, they dispersed on leave.

YEAR 1940		AIRCRAFT		PILOT, OR 1ST PILOT	2ND PILOT, PUPIL OR PASSENGER	DUTY (INCLUDING RESULTS AND REMARKS)
MONTH	DATE	Type	No.			
—	—	—	—	—	—	— Totals Brought Forward
AUG	20	DH 82	N6602	F/LT HALL.	SELF	1. AIR EXPERIENCE.
						2A FAMILIARITY WITH COCKPIT LAYOUT
						3. EFFECT OF CONTROLS.
AUG	22	DH 82	N6602	F/LT HALL.	SELF	B. TAXYING.
						4. STRAIGHT & LEVEL FLIGHT.
						5. CLIMBING GLIDING & STALLING.
AUG	24	D.H. 82	N6602	F/LT HALL.	SELF	3. TAXYING
						4. STRAIGHT X LEVEL FLIGHT
						5. CLIMBING GLIDING STALLING.
						6. MEDIUM TURNS
AUG	25	D.H. 82	N6602	F/LT HALL.	SELF	6. MEDIUM TURNS
						7. TAKING OFF INTO WIND
						8. POWERED APPROACH & LANDING
AUG	26.	D.H. 82	N6602	F/LT HALL	SELF	6. MEDIUM TURNS
						7. TAKING OFF INTO WIND
						8. POWERED APPROACH & LANDING
						9. GLIDING APPROACH X LANDING
AUG	27	D.H. 82	N6602	F/LT HALL	SELF	6. MEDIUM TURNS.
						7. TAKING OFF INTO WIND
						8. POWERED APPROACH X LANDING
						9. GLIDING APPROACH X LANDING

GRAND TOTAL [Cols. (1) to (10)]

........9.0.....Hrs.....2.0.......Mins.

TOTALS CARRIED FORWARD

| YEAR | | AIRCRAFT | | PILOT, OR | 2ND PILOT, PUPIL | DUTY |
MONTH	DATE	Type	No.	1ST PILOT	OR PASSENGER	(INCLUDING RESULTS AND REMARKS
—	—	—		—	—	— TOTALS BROUGHT FORWARD
				S/L		Summary for _JUNE_ 19 41 — 1. WELLI
		D.C 'B' FLT.				Unit 40 SQDN Aircraft — 2.
		40 SQDN.				Date 1·6·41 Types — 3.
						Signature _J.O. Lancaster_ — 4.
JULY	1	WELLINGTON	J.2701	SELF.	CREW.	N.F.T
"	2	"	"	SELF.	CREW.	N.F.T.
"	3	" 'S' "		SELF.	CREW.	⑨ OPS. CHERBOURG
"	4	"	"	SELF.	CREW.	N.F.T. & FORMATION.
"	4	" 'S' "		SELF.	CREW.	⑬ OPS. BREST.
"	6	"	"	SELF.	CREW.	N.F.T.
"	6	" 'S' "		SELF.	CREW.	⑬ OPS. MUNSTER.
"	7	"	"	SELF.	CREW.	N.F.T.
"	7	" 'S' "		SELF.	CREW.	⑬ OPS. COLOGNE.
"	9	"	"	SELF	CREW.	N.F.T. HONNINGTON & RETURN
"	9	" 'S' "		SELF.	CREW.	⑬ OPS. OSNABRUCK
"	10	"	"	SELF	CREW.	FROM UPPER HEYFORD.
"	11	"	"	SELF.	CREW.	N.F.T.

GRAND TOTAL (Cols. (1) to (10))

357 Hrs. 15 Mins.

TOTALS CARRIED FORWARD

Chapter 4

No. 40 Squadron

Jo drove down from Lossiemouth to Coventry in his Morris Ten, accompanied as far as Hawick by Tommy Young, whom he had known since Ternhill, then reported as instructed on 6 May at Wyton, along with his crew. There they learned that 40 Squadron was no longer at Wyton, having moved six months earlier to a new satellite airfield at Alconbury, some 6 miles away. Accordingly, the crew drove to Alconbury, where they reported to the commanding officer, Wing Commander Davy, only to find themselves, quite unreasonably, on a charge for reporting late. It was not the most encouraging starts to their posting, nor had the CO made a good impression on the crew. Nor, yet again, was the set-up at Alconbury particularly impressive. Jo recalls:

> Alconbury had three runways but very little else. There were no hangars at all. There was no watch office. There were in fact just about four or five wooden huts to accommodate everybody. The officers' mess was at Upton House, which was about two or three miles up the A1 from Alconbury, whilst the sergeants were in a requisitioned house, Alconbury House, which was within easy walking distance of the airfield. It was a big house and we had one room to our crew. It had six camp beds in it.

No. 40 Squadron, to which Jo and his crew had been posted, had, in the First World War, been a renowned fighter squadron, with aces Mick Mannock, George McElroy, Roderick Dallas and Gwilym Lewis among its most notable members. Its official badge, showing a broom, and its motto, 'hostem a coelo expellere' ('to drive the enemy from the sky') were derived from Mick Mannock's injunction to the pilots in his flight to 'sweep the Hun from the skies'. Disbanded in 1919, 40 Squadron had been re-formed in 1931 as a day bomber squadron, equipped successively with the Fairey Gordon, Hawker Hart and Hawker Hind, and went to France in September 1939 with Fairey Battles. Mercifully withdrawn to Britain to re-equip with Bristol Blenheims in December, the squadron had, nonetheless, like all the Blenheim squadrons in 2 Group, suffered severely during the German blitzkreig of May and June 1940, at one point losing two commanding officers and an acting CO in three weeks. For the rest of the year, heavily engaged in attacks on German airfields and the Channel ports where fleets of invasion barges were being assembled, the squadron was transferred to 3 Group on 1 November 1940, and in January 1941 replaced its Blenheims with Wellingtons, operating solely as a night bomber squadron. Losses had been comparatively light, only one crew failing to return during January and February, with two more lost in March and a further two in April. Things were, however, to change very much for the worse in the months ahead.

In 1941 Bomber Command still followed the practice, later abandoned, of allocating new crews to an experienced pilot, with the original first pilot now acting as second pilot, and the original second pilot moved to another crew. In the case of Sergeant Lancaster's crew this meant the departure of Derek Townshend, who was made second pilot to Pilot Officer F.J. 'Stainless' Steel, a New Zealander, taking the place of Sergeant Jim Taylor, who became the captain of Jo's crew. Jim was married, and despite the fact that the RAF frowned upon wives living close to their husband's operational stations, his wife Barbara resided in digs in St Ives, where Jim when not on duty would visit her on his motorbike. The crew also spent time with Jim and his wife on occasions, swimming and basking in the sun on the banks of the River Ouse.

Jo's crew first flew with Jim Taylor on 8 May, when they made two cross-country flights, one in daylight and the other at night, each of about 2 hours. Next day they carried out a night-flying test (NFT) and flew their first operation that night, one of eleven crews operating. The other ten, experienced, carried out an attack on the German city of Mannheim, but as was customary, a 'freshman' crew was allocated a relatively undemanding target, in this case invasion barges at Calais. All went smoothly, the squadron Operational Record Book (ORB) noting that 'A high level attack was made from 13,000 feet. 2 SBCs [small bomb containers] and 6 x 500 lb bombs being dropped. The bombs were seen to burst near the entrance to the docks and several fires were started.' The crew of T2701 'S' arrived back at Alconbury at 1.15am. in high spirits, Jo recalls, 'hooting only 29 more to do'.

The crew's second operation, the next night, was to a far more testing target: Hamburg. No. 40 Squadron supplied twelve crews as part of a Bomber Command force of ninety-two carrying out the third attack on the city in a week. Conditions were good, and major fires were started, the ORB reporting that Sergeant Taylor's crew dropped its load of seven 500lb general purpose bombs from 15,000 feet, the bombs bursting 'just beyond the aiming point', starting two fires. In squadron terms, however, the raid had been much less than successful, since four of the twelve Wellingtons had to abandon their task for a variety of reasons, while of the eight that did bomb, three were attacked by night fighters, two were shot down, and the third, badly damaged, made an emergency landing at Marham, the rear gunner dead and the wireless operator severely wounded. Both crews lost were experienced, that of New Zealander Sergeant Finlayson – who had been with the squadron since September 1940 – on its twenty-seventh operation. With twenty-eight operations of their tour still to be flown, and evidence that even the most experienced were not immune, Jo and his fellow crew members were in a sober frame of mind, something that was reinforced, in his case, by being detailed to attend the funeral at Marham of Sergeant Martin, the rear gunner.

By the end of May, Jim Taylor and his colleagues had flown two further operations, one – to Hannover – proving abortive when cloud prevented the identification of the target, the crew eventually bombing flak units and searchlights near Osnabrück. The other, on 27 May, was unusual in all respects, since it was a 6-hour daylight search for the German cruiser *Prinz Eugen* (or 'Prince Engler', as the 40 Squadron ORB has it), the companion of the *Bismarck*, sunk that morning. Bomber Command put up fifty-two Wellingtons and twelve Stirlings in an attempt to locate the German

cruiser, 40 Squadron supplying ten crews. The search was fruitless, however, and the *Prinz Eugen* was able to slip unobserved into Brest on 1 June.

During June Jo and his crew continued to fly under the cool and experi -
enced Jim Taylor, completing four further operations, two to Düsseldorf early in the month, and two late in the month to Cologne. All were
uneventful, although on the morning of 3 June, the faithful T2701 touched
down at Mildenhall, fog at Alconbury making landing there hazardous,
as witness the crash on landing of Sergeant Sargent and his crew, all but
the rear gunner being killed. On the night of 11 June, industrial haze over
Düsseldorf made visibility so poor that the ninety-two Wellingtons and
six Stirlings were prevented from bombing with any degree of accuracy,
the most that Taylor and his crew could report being that its nine 500lb
bombs fell on an 'unidentified part of the town'. Six Wellingtons were
lost, two of them from 40 Squadron, one to a night fighter and the other,
captained by Squadron Leader Mark Redgrave, the B Flight commander,
crashing on a sandbank in the Scheldt estuary when damaged by flak and
blinded by searchlights and taking evasive action at low level. Redgrave
and his crew survived and were taken prisoner. Those of the other missing
Wellington did not. Squadron Leader Redgrave's successor was Squadron
Leader Reg Weighill, who arrived on 25 June.

In all, five 40 Squadron Wellingtons were lost in June, four of them to
enemy action, while a sixth was badly damaged in a night-fighter attack over
Rotterdam on 12/13 June, the second pilot and front gunner being wounded.
The second pilot was Tony Shilleto, who had trained with Jo at Lossiemouth.
Happily, his wounds were not serious, and he soon rejoined the squadron.
In June, also, Derek Townshend, who had been Jo's second pilot at Lossie-
mouth, left Wyton for the Middle East, in one of two crews posted there by
way of reinforcement. On 29/30 October, his 148 Squadron Wellington was
shot down during a raid on Cania in Crete, with only the captain, Flight
Lieutenant Canton, himself formerly with 40 Squadron, surviving.

On 28 June the squadron Operations Record Book, Form 540, notes
that 'Sergeant Taylor, having completed his tour of operational duty, left
the Squadron on posting to No.11 O.T.U., Bassingbourn.' What the ORB
does not register is that, as a consequence, Sergeant Lancaster was promoted to first pilot and captain. Provided with a second pilot, Pilot Officer
Slater – who had arrived from 23 OTU with a new crew on 23 June –

Sergeant Lancaster's crew, as now they were, flew their first operation on 2/3 July, a 'freshman' attack on the docks at Cherbourg. On debriefing Jo's crew reported that 'Against slight searchlight and flak activity and on a quiet target' they had dropped their mixed load of incendiaries and 500lb bombs in the dock area, 'resulting in a vivid white explosion and fires. The latter being visible for 25/30 miles away.'

Two nights later they operated again, this time against Brest, where the *Prinz Eugen* had taken refuge. Smokescreens made target identification difficult, but Jo's crew claimed to have succeeded in picking up the outline of the docks through the smoke and to have seen the bombs burst. They also reported a Wellington going down in flames. This was in fact a Whitley, the only aircraft lost out of a mixed force of eighty-eight Wellingtons and Whitleys. Two nights later again, on 6/7 July, the target was Münster, attacked by forty-nine Wellingtons, of which 40 Squadron supplied eleven. It was not a good night for the crews, since four had to abandon their task for a variety of reasons, most failures of equipment, while a fifth was shot down with only the wireless operator surviving. Jo's crew reported that on arrival the target was a 'mass of flames', which made the location of the aiming point difficult, but nonetheless felt that the bomb load 'burst on or near the aiming point'.

At this point in the war, the German defence against Bomber Command depended on what was known as the Kammhuber Line. Named after its originator, Generalleutnant Josef Kammhuber, the system involved a series of radar stations with overlapping coverage, layered three deep from Denmark to the middle of France, each covering a zone about 32 kilometres long (north–south) and 20 kilometres wide (east–west). Each control centre was known as a Himmelbett (canopy bed) zone, and consisted of a Freya radar, with a range of about 100 kilometres, a 'master searchlight' governed by the radar, and a number of manually controlled searchlights throughout the cell. Each cell was also assigned a primary and a backup night fighter. When an RAF bomber crossed the Kammhuber Line, Freya radar operators directed the master searchlight to illuminate the bomber, the manually operated searchlights picked it up and coned it, holding it while night fighters attacked it. Since at this time Bomber Command was despatching aircraft individually – not, as later, as part of a massed

bomber stream – this meant that Himmelbett centres were dealing only
with small numbers of aircraft at once, and sometimes only one, making
interception easier.

For Jo and his crew, therefore, making life difficult for the searchlight
crews was a task of some importance, and they waged their own personal
war against the searchlight system. He writes:

> During this 1941 period we had to negotiate a wide belt of very efficient
> searchlights – 'the Kammhuber Line' – which stretched down through
> Holland and Belgium. This caused us considerable disquiet. For our
> revenge, when the target was in the Ruhr area, we often retained one
> of our 500lb HE bombs and, on the return leg, made a careful run up
> on one of the searchlights. They must have been able to hear it coming,
> because invariably the light went out before we saw the bomb burst.
> We normally carried a few empty bottles which the second pilot would
> drop down the flare chute and when I'd been a second pilot I'd taken
> great satisfaction in dropping bricks, marked 'London Brick Company',
> taken from a pile adjacent to our dispersal pan.

On 7/8 July 40 Squadron contributed 11 of 114 Wellingtons for a raid on
Cologne. In near perfect weather the bombing was accurate and concentrated, and the Cologne authorities rated it the heaviest and most
destructive raid of 1941. Returning 40 Squadron crews were upbeat about
the results of the raid, although noting the heavy flak and searchlight
defences. The ORB records that Sergeant Lancaster's crew bombed from
12,000 feet, and that the bomb load of nine 500lb bombs 'fell on the west
side of the river, resulting in a large flash, black smoke and red flame'. It
also notes 'considerable flak when aircraft caught in S/L'. Pencilled notes
in Jo's logbook documents that the crew flew east of the city, turned and
made a timed run in, lining up the railway bridge over the Rhine, and hit
both the Hohenzollern bridge and the station immediately to the west
of the river. Just as Glenn Leitch was jubilantly reporting that the nine
500lb bombs had straddled the target, T2801 was coned. Jo comments:
'We were at 10,000 feet. I immediately headed south, losing height to gain
speed, and threw the thing about as violently as I could, accompanied by
encouraging shouts such as "Go it Ollie" from the crew, and we emerged

into calmer waters unscathed.'

On 9/10 July the target was Osnabrück, 40 Squadron putting up ten of the fifty-seven Wellingtons despatched. No reports from returning crews are included in the ORB, since heavy fog meant that the aircraft were diverted to airfields further west, most landing at Upper Heyford and crews there being debriefed. Everitt and Middlebrook's *The Bomber Command War Diaries* records that aircrews reported loads that 'burst in target area' causing 'several fires', but Osnabrück records state that no bombs fell on the city and only a few in neighbouring villages, where one death was reported. Again 40 Squadron lost one aircraft and, as with the loss on the 6/7 July attack, it was a crew whose pilot was new to captaincy. Jo's most vivid memory of this raid is of his crew lying stripped to their underwear alongside T2801 next morning, sunbathing at Upper Heyford while waiting for fog to clear at Alconbury. He flew the Wellington back to Alconbury barefoot, and remembers that the rudder bar felt most uncomfortable.

The Osnabrück raid was the last on which Pilot Officer Slater was second pilot, the ORB recording on 7 July that a crew drawn from volunteers from several other teams, including Slater as second pilot, were to be posted to the Middle East. They were given leave, with orders to report to Harwell on the 15th. Operating from Malta with 38 Squadron, the crew would, in October, rejoin 40 Squadron on its arrival on the island. In place of Pilot Officer Slater, Jo's crew received as second pilot Sergeant Gordon Byrne, whom Jo calls 'a very bright lad'.

It was about this time that all crews were issued with what Jo describes as 'little yellow skull caps with tapes hanging down the side'. 'These,' he adds, 'were the product of somebody's fertile brain, the idea being that we would be easily spotted bobbing about in the water from a search plane. In point of fact they were quite useless. I have a photograph somewhere of a few of the crew modelling these. There was a good deal of hilarity but I don't think anyone ever wore them.'

After Osnabrück, the crew did not operate again for nearly a fortnight, the reason being that Jo and Gordon Byrne were posted, on the 13th, to Wyton for a week's course with No. 4 Blind Approach Training Flight (BATF), while the rest of the crew were kept occupied (pointlessly in the case of observer Glenn Leitch) by a posting to a short refresher gunnery course at Newmarket. Jo recalls that pilots

learnt how to use the SBA, Standard Beam Approach, which was a
system based on the pre-war Lorenz system. It was a radio beam and
on one side you received a Morse letter N ('dar dit') and on the other
you received letter A ('dit dar') and when you were on the beam itself
these two interlocked to give you a continuous note. It was a very
long-winded tedious business establishing yourself on this beam and
it was totally unsuited for operational use. Later on these beams were
put out from various places on the coast. I think they were called Z
beams at the time. The idea was that we could home onto them in
returning aircraft, but this never appealed to me because they could
lead to some congestion.

During their absence B Flight had lost yet another flight commander, and
in somewhat odd circumstances. On 16 July Squadron Leader Weighill's
crew were one of nine detailed to attack Hamburg. The weather was bad
and the raid unsuccessful, several aircrews reporting that they were unable
to locate the target. Two did not return. New Zealander Sergeant Tony
Bird and his crew were shot down by a night fighter and crashed into the
sea off the Dutch coast as they made their way back to Alconbury. Squadron Leader Weighill's machine, however, crashed near Great Yarmouth
some half an hour after take-off, diving into the ground from low level
after being seen circling the area, some 60 miles north of the designated
flight path. No explanation for the crash could be determined, although
it was felt possible that the pilots were blinded by searchlights. Jo, though,
recalls that he and others speculated as to a different cause, related to the
second pilot, Sergeant Raymond Hesketh. The latter joined the squadron in mid-April, flew three operations as second pilot, the last on 11/12
May, and then disappeared from the squadron records until captaining a
crew on 13/14 June, detailed to attack Bologne, but turning back when his
aircraft would not climb beyond 6,000 feet. By the end of the month six
further operations had been essayed, but three had been abandoned, one
owing to 'an apparent shortage of petrol due to a faulty gauge', a second
due to bad weather (which forced others to turn back also) and a third to
intercom failure. Jo also recalls that on another occasion, not mentioned
in the ORB, the undercarriage of Hesketh's aircraft was retracted while
taxying, and it may have been this, rather than the aborted operations,

which led to Hesketh being relieved of his captaincy and made second pilot to Squadron Leader Weighill.

Squadron Leader Weighill's replacement as B Flight commander was Squadron Leader Alan Martin, who on Malta in 1940 had been one of the pilots flying the famed Gladiators, 'Faith', 'Hope' and 'Charity'.

On 22 July, back at Alconbury, the crew found themselves on the Battle Order for that night, the target Mannheim. The raid was a small one, only twenty-eight Wellingtons being detailed, eight of them from 40 Squadron. The weather was bad, with thunderstorms, while haze over the target made bombing difficult for the five crews who reached Mannheim. For the first time, however, the trusty T2701 let Jo's crew down, the starboard engine misfiring and the gyro malfunctioning, so the operation was aborted over the North Sea, the aircraft landing at Alconbury with bombs aboard after a flight of some 90 minutes. It was fortunate that the engine did not fail completely, for as Jo comments, while

> the Pegasus XVIII engine was very reliable, this was just as well, because at 965 hp each, and having non-feathering props, the Wellington IC was really under-powered and could only manage a protracted descent on one engine – even if the Pilots' Notes said otherwise! A fairly regular event was for a valve rocker box to come adrift, which effectively put that cylinder out and resulted in quite unpleasant vibration.

It may have been just such a problem that the airmen had experienced. But whatever the reason, it was clearly quickly remedied, since the next morning they found themselves detailed, in T2701, as one of six crews to take part in an ambitious daylight raid on the battlecruisers *Scharnhorst* and *Gneisenau*, and the cruiser *Prinz Eugen* at Brest. Only the day prior to the raid, however, it had been discovered that the *Scharnhorst* had been moved to La Pallice and accordingly the plan was modified, with fifteen Halifaxes sent to La Pallice, unescorted, while a mixed force of Fortresses, Hampdens and Wellingtons attacked Brest. In the face of fierce fighter attacks and some flak the Halifaxes pressed home their assault with great determination, and five armour-piercing bombs hit the *Scharnhorst*, causing damage that took four months to repair. The cost was heavy, though, five Halifaxes being shot down and all the remainder damaged.

At Brest the results were less satisfactory, just six unconfirmed hits being claimed on the *Gneisenau*, but the losses were again heavy. The plan called for a preliminary raid by three RAF Fortresses of 90 Squadron, bombing from 30,000 feet. This, it was hoped, would draw up German fighters prematurely, while the second phase – an attack by eighteen Hampdens escorted by three squadrons of Spitfires with long-range tanks – would complete the process of 'drawing up', allowing the main force of seventy-nine Wellingtons to strike unescorted. What seemed viable on paper, however, proved not so in actuality. The Luftwaffe was not tempted to engage the Fortresses, and although the Hampden's were assaulted, and two shot down, the German fighters were still up in strength when the unescorted Wellingtons arrived.

To the force of seventy-nine Wellingtons, 40 Squadron contributed six, which were to operate in two Vics of three, the first led by Squadron Leader Stickley, the A Flight commander, and the second, in which T2701 was the left-hand machine, by Sergeant Morris. Some crews had participated in formation flying practice on the 19th, but Jo's was not one of them, and the operation itself was the first occasion on which he flew in formation in a Wellington. On the run-up to bomb, in a cloudless sky, both Vic formations were subject to heavy flak, Sergeant 'Pat' Pattison, wireless operator in Sergeant Morris's aircraft, later recalling that 'Flak was frightening enough at night with a flash and a thump, but in daytime the black menacing cloud which followed each flash was terrifying in itself and seemed to envelop the whole formation.'[1] The flak was accurate, and one of the Wellingtons in the first Vic – captained by New Zealander Sergeant Mervyn Evans, DFM – received a direct hit and went down in flames, crashing in the town, while a second – flown by another New Zealander, Pilot Officer Alex Greer – was also hit. The second Vic got off more lightly, although all three were damaged, the right-hand Wellington piloted by a third New Zealander, Sergeant Trevor Bagnall, significantly.

After bombing, the five remaining aircraft came under sustained fighter attack, and the two aircraft in the first Vic became separated. Pilot Officer Greer's Wellington was raked with machine-gun and cannon fire that killed the second pilot, Australian Sergeant Holliday, and wounded the rear gunner, Sergeant Gould, whose turret was put out of action. In a second assault the wireless operator Sergeant Hobbs, who was manning a beam gun, was wounded in the head and legs and knocked out, but in a third attack the German pilot gave the front gunner an opportunity to get in three bursts, which sent the fighter down in flames.

Meanwhile, the second Vic, which remained intact, also came under fighter attack, Sergeant Morris's crew reporting that 'Near Porspoder Me.109 which was attacking two Wellingtons on starboard bow turned off and approached our aircraft from that direction but did not fire. Our front gunner fired 100 rds which were seen to enter enemy amidships. Enemy suddenly went into a spin and pilot seen to bail out and land in sea 5 miles off shore.' Since Keith Coleman, Jo's rear gunner, and Bill Crowther – manning with second pilot Gordon Byrne the beam guns mounted for this operation – also fired on the fighter, credit for its destruction was shared.

Ten out of the seventy-nine Wellingtons were shot down, and unfortunately the results of bombing so steadfastly carried out were disappointing, with neither *Gneisenau* nor *Prinz Eugen* being hit, although a large merchant ship in the harbour was. One clue to the lack of success may be found in Jo's crew's report that 'The bombs seen to fall in town itself, this aircraft being on left of formation.' Bombing in Vics of three, and in relatively open formation, only the lead aircraft could aim precisely at the ships they had come to sink.

The fighters seen off, Jo's aircrew headed north across the Channel. He recalls:

On the way home we saw a Wimpy, with its starboard engine on fire, ditch some miles off the Brittany coast. As his dinghy was stowed in the starboard engine nacelle, it was obvious that this would have been burnt. I thought of dropping them our dinghy, but decided this wasn't practicable, because it would almost certainly have finished up wrapped around our tailplane. Instead we sent a radio report, though we never heard whether our valiant air-sea rescue chaps were able to snatch them back. Short of fuel, we made for St. Eval, in Cornwall, as did a number of other aircraft, mostly well shot-up and carrying dead and wounded. It was a fair shambles, and we all had to muck in together to help as best we could. Our little trio came through without casualty, though the aircraft were in a bit of a mess. Mine had the main hydraulic system completely out of action and was well perforated. One small piece of shrapnel came through the windscreen. I found it on the cockpit floor and keep it as a little memento.

Pilot Officer Greer's aircraft, which also landed at St Eval, was even more shot up, returning with the hydraulics damaged, wheels and flaps down and the bomb doors open.

Not counting the aborted trip to Mannheim on 22 July, the Brest raid was the crew's fifteenth, and by far the most 'dicey' to date. The sixteenth turned out to be chancy too, though for other reasons, and came on the night of 30/31 July when they went to Cologne, part of a mixed force of 116 Wellingtons, Hampdens, Halifaxes and Stirlings. Bad weather hampered target identification, with eight- to nine-tenths cumulus cloud up to 13,000 feet and icing affecting several crews, two of which had to turn back, unable to climb above the cloud. The most that those who did bomb could claim was that they believed that Cologne had been hit, Sergeant Lancaster's crew reporting that 'On E.T.A. numerous fires, flares and bombs seen. Bombed between two sets of fires which seemed to indicate the two ports of Cologne on either side of the river. Results not satisfactorily observed. Very little heavy flak and not many searchlights but a lot of tracer.' The reality was that crews, many like Jo's, bombing on estimated time of arrival (ETA), had very little chance of hitting the target accurately and the Cologne authorities reported that the city was hit by just 3 high-explosive and 300 incendiary bombs, causing no casualties and damaging just six buildings.

This was a result typical of those achieved in less than ideal conditions during 1941, as was demonstrated when the celebrated Butt Report was delivered in September. Analysing photos taken during June and July by bombers equipped with cameras activated by the bomb-release mechanism, David Bensusan-Butt, a civil servant in the War Cabinet Secretariat, had concluded that

  1. Of those aircraft recorded as attacking their target, only one in three got within 5 miles [8 kilometres].
  2. Over the French ports, the proportion was two in three; over

Germany as a whole, the proportion was one in four; over the Ruhr it was only one in ten.

3. In the full moon, the proportion was two in five; in the new moon it was only one in fifteen.

Since these figures related only to aircraft recorded as actually attacking the target, Butt concluded that the proportion of the total sorties that reached within 5 miles of the designated aiming point was less than one-third. The Directorate of Bombing Operations attempted to counter the report with its own analysis, released in September, which argued that, based on damage inflicted on British cities by the Luftwaffe, the RAF could destroy the forty-three German towns with a population of more than 100,000 with a force of 4,000 bombers. Post-war studies, however, confirmed Butt's assessment, showing that 49% of RAF Bomber Command's bombs dropped between May 1940 and May 1941 fell in open country.

The ORB report focuses on the results of bombing that night. But Jo recollects what the ORB does not state, which was that R1168 'B' – which Jo and his crew were flying that night while their regular mount was under repair – very nearly did not return from Cologne. He recalls:

Ice protection on the Wellington IC consisted of alcohol sprays for the props and engine air intakes, and alternate hot air for the carburettors. The wing leading edges were smeared with a substance popularly known as 'snowdrop grease', which looked like marzipan, and which, of course, frequently got knocked about by refuelling hoses. I have no idea of the effectiveness of this treatment, but it was never used later in the war. On the night of 30 July 1941, while on the way home from Cologne in Wimpy R1168, 'B', I handed over control to my second pilot, Gordon Byrne, and took up station in the astrodome. We flew into cloud and when it became clear from the turbulence and St. Elmo's fire, that we'd entered a cu-nimb. electrical storm, I instructed Gordon to select carburettor hot air and to turn 180 degrees to get out of it. When the starboard engine began to surge I decided to go forward and resume control. As I passed the wireless operator he was out of his seat, recoiling from his equipment, which was all aglow. Having changed places with Gordon again, I found he had not selected carb. hot air, and had not turned through 180 degrees. This totally uncharacteristic stupidity was undoubtedly the result of his not having a serviceable oxygen tube, even though we were only at about 10–11,000 ft. Things then started happening very quickly. The whole aircraft was aglow, it was extremely turbulent, lightning was lighting up the inside of the cloud, and after wild surging the starboard engine died – shortly followed by the port engine. The aircraft was difficult to control and must have been badly iced up. Then there was a colossal bang and a blinding flash – obviously a lightning strike. I had to turn the lights up full and even then it seemed a long time before I could see the instruments clearly. As we rapidly lost height we heard the unmistakable sound of flak, too close for comfort, and could see signs of searchlights playing on the cloud base not far below. By this time – naturally – the crew had taken up their bale-out positions. We were all waiting, putting off the evil moment until the last possible second, when, having lost height down to about 3,000 ft, the starboard engine suddenly showed signs of interest again. As I nursed it back to full chat, hey presto, the port engine recovered its senses too, and we were soon able to start gaining height. The jubilation which erupted was soon flattened, however, when there was no reply from Keith in the rear turret. We thought he must have baled out. Then, as I sent Gordon down to the rear to have a look, Keith came back on the intercom. He explained that as he prepared to abandon ship, parachute pack clipped on his chest and turret turned to port beam ready to fall out backwards, he could see the altimeter which formed part of the oxygen regulator. As all was silent on the intercom, he deduced that the rest of us had departed, but as there was still three or four thousand feet showing and the kite was quite steady – or at least right side up – he decided to stay until the last moment too. Then he heard one engine going again, then two, and his altimeter started to show a profit. Checking further, he discovered, just as Gordon banged on his turret from inside the fuselage, that in putting on his parachute pack he'd inadvertently pulled out his intercom plug.

By now Sergeant Lancaster's crew were one of the more senior on the squadron, and life had settled into a familiar routine. Jo remembers:

> In retrospect it all now seems to have been very casual. By mid-
> morning each day we would know if ops were on or off. It was
> commonly said that if one visited the bar of The George Hotel in
> Huntingdon at lunchtime, the Senior Intelligence Officer, Sqn Ldr
> Chamberlain, was certain to be there, and could be relied upon to
> disclose the 'Target for Tonight'. I never personally tested this, but I
> believe it to be true.

It was in Huntingdon one night that Glenn Leitch, with his dislike of
policemen, got the crew into some strife. Jo relates:

> He got us into trouble on one occasion in Huntingdon. When it
> was a stand down night it was full of air force chaps from 15 and
> 40 Squadrons, all with several pints of beer consumed. There was a
> poor RAF service police sergeant called Sergeant Marks, whose job it
> was to control Huntingdon and of course Glenn used to insult him
> terribly, tell him to 'get some in'. On this occasion Sergeant Marks
> reported the whole crew to the CO, Wing Commander Stickley, and
> we were hauled up in front of him and lightly admonished.

If the crew was rostered to operate that night, a night-flying test (NFT)
would be carried out, this usually including

> most of the ground as well as air crew, and invariably consisted of
> a beat-up at nought feet up one side of the Bedford Canals, two
> of which run dead straight between Chatteris and King's Lynn, and
> back down the other. We gleefully terrorised the Land Army girls and
> others working in the fields, and sometimes landed at neighbouring
> airfields to pay social calls on friends and perhaps join them for
> lunch.
>   Quite often we landed at another station; sometimes there was an
> official reason, but others it was just a social call. On one occasion,
> for instance, we landed at Honington and had lunch with John
> Barrett Lennard, ex-Armstrong Whitworth. After Jim Taylor left us to

instruct at Bassingbourn, we also visited him a couple of times.

An NFT also required the testing of the radio:

> The radio was the TR9, and it was next to useless. But we went
> through this ritual every time, calling up Wyton, since Alconbury
> did not have a receiving unit. We were required to say everything
> twice: 'Hello Pioneer, Hello Pioneer, this is Cayman S for sugar, this is
> Cayman S for sugar, how are you receiving me? How are you receiving
> me? Over to you, Over.' Then an almost unintelligible response would
> come, not really very useful for passing any information on. You
> would then say, 'Hello Pioneer, Hello Pioneer, this is Cayman S for
> sugar, this is Cayman S for sugar, receiving you strength nine.' At that
> time strength was rated up to ten as opposed to five at the present
> time. Of course, they were hardly intelligible but we always reported
> strength nine.

'The TR9 did improve a bit later on,' Jo notes, 'but at that time it was
hardly ever used for landing, which was done visually with Aldis lamps.'

The latitude allowed to crews in the early years of Bomber Command
was considerable, Jo recalling that 'there was no specified or mandatory
route to or from a target, and no specified take off time or time over target, it being largely left to the individual crews to plan their own route'.
He continues:

> Most of our operations on this tour came in the summer with long
> days and very short hours of darkness and often it was getting light as
> we crossed the enemy coast on the way home. One morning the sun
> was almost up as we hurried across Belgium, and we passed a Dornier
> going the opposite way, only about 500 yards away – presumably on
> his way home too. With dawn breaking before we got to the English
> coast I would go down low over the sea and Glenn, with his very
> difficult job almost finished, would come up forward and stand
> beside me while we would have a cigarette and a cup of tea out of
> a thermos. We used the compass as an ashtray and we didn't tackle
> the tea earlier because we couldn't afford to be taken short on the

journey. We would cruise in over the coast to a very tranquil scene and the world below us just waking up after a good night's sleep. We would look for Ely Cathedral sticking up out of the morning mist and cruise gently past it and on to Alconbury, the night's work done.

Reflecting on the strengths and weaknesses of the Wellington IC, Jo comments:

Normal maximum bomb load was nine 500lb, or nine SBCs (Small Bomb Containers) housing 81 x 4lb incendiary bombs. The maximum standard fuel load was 750 gallons, though on some occasions we were fitted with two 140-gallon overload tanks in the bomb bay. We could not carry full internal fuel with a full bombload, so a balance was decided according to the distance to target. In each wing were six fuel cells and a tank in the nacelle. The pilot's fuel control consisted of an on/off cock for each wing tank group, and a cross-feed cock. There was a panel with (I think) 12 contents gauges – one for each cell – and all hopelessly inaccurate. It was quite impossible to judge the fuel situation, so a system was evolved whereby the cock on the port engine nacelle tank could be turned on or off from the fuselage by manipulating two wires which emerged from the wing root. This tank could then be turned off during flight until, hopefully well on the way home, one engine cut, whereupon the pilot opened the cross-feed, while the second pilot hastily turned on the nacelle tank; we then knew we had 40 minutes in which to get down.

The cabin heater was a liquid heat transfer system from an exhaust pipe muff to a radiator which heated air before it was fed into the cabin. Even when it was working properly it was very ineffective, but it was so unreliable, due to a tendency to boil dry, that it was generally given up as a hopeless job. Instead we wore marvellous wool/silk mixture 'Long John' underpants and long-sleeved vests, silk gloves, and full inner and outer Sidcot-type flying suits. The gunners wore electrically heated Irvin suits. Even so, we were often extremely cold for many long hours.

The flap lever was undoubtedly responsible for a number of crashes from the overshoot condition. This lever was next to, and resembled, the undercarriage lever. It was very light in operation, and unless extreme care and finesse were exercised to make very small and momentary 'up' selections, the flaps were liable to retract almost instantaneously, with probably catastrophic results. Eventually a restrictor device was introduced on the flap lever to at least partially remedy this. The pilot's seat I recall as being very comfortable. One particularly good feature, never to be repeated, was a large adjustable support pad which supported each knee. Although our aircraft were fitted with an early form of auto-pilot, like the cabin heater this never worked for long, and we had to 'pole' the aircraft manually for long weary hours, so a comfortable seat position was most welcome.

From the first Jo's crew had been a harmonious and cohesive unit, both in the air and on the ground. As Jo recalls, sharing a room at Alconbury House they benefited from being a mixed commonwealth crew, since

Keith Coleman used to receive from New Zealand abundant supplies of tinned butter and tins of Nescafe mixed with condensed milk. Glenn Leitch and Bill Harris received from Canada tins of peanut butter and hundreds of cigarettes. We all smoked heavily, and cigarettes were in short supply, so Canada kept us all well supplied, while all we needed for supper was a loaf of bread and some hot water.

As good crews did, they socialised together, with some hilarious incidents, as Jo recollects:

One of our favourite outings was to a little pub in a mining village north of Coventry called Bedworth. The pub was called Hit or Miss and the attraction there was a blind pianist who was very, very good. We used to thoroughly enjoy a good singsong there and then carry on to Nuneaton or Hinckley where there were other attractive places of entertainment. The landlord and landlady of the Hit or Miss were 'Dickey Bow' Richards and his wife Maybelle. They moved to a large pub in Nuneaton called The Nags Head and from Alconbury I and the crew used to drive over to Nuneaton, where we'd walk into The Nags Head, they would give us a key and say 'Go and enjoy yourself

boys.' So off we'd go around Nuneaton, come back at all hours
and let ourselves into the pub. They'd allocated us beds and in the
morning we'd get up and help ourselves to breakfast and [go] on our
way. How was that for hospitality and trust?

Alconbury was astride the A1, the great north road down to
London, and it was easy to go and stand there and hitch a ride,
since almost everybody stopped to pick up hitchhikers. In London
we sometimes made a beeline for The Hammersmith Palais. But
if it was daytime we would go to The Beaver Club, tucked away in
Trafalgar Square, which was intended for the Canadian forces, while
if we had to stay the night we would go to Russell Square, where The
Russell Hotel had also been taken over for the benefit of Canadian
personnel. The fact that only two of us were Canadians didn't seem
to matter.

Walking around the West End in the blackouts at that time of course
we were constantly being propositioned by ladies of the night and
Glenn being Glenn he used to frequently engage them in conversation
just for fun. On one occasion he did this and we wandered on a few
paces. He shortly caught us up laughing his head off and said that
he'd beaten her down to three and sixpence. On another occasion in
response to her proposition we insisted that we all came and that didn't
seem a very good idea to her at all. So eventually she said, 'Well, you
can all come if you buy a bottle of whisky.' To which we said, 'Don't
be silly, where can you buy whisky at this time of night? In fact, where
can you buy whisky at any time of night?' She led us through some
little backstreets and alleys somewhere around The Regent Palace
Hotel, and knocked on a door. It opened revealing a little bar. She was
obviously well known and said what she wanted. They produced a
bottle of whisky at a reasonable price and off we set. We emerged into
Regent Street, not quite knowing what was going to happen next and
she rushed onto the road and hollered a taxi which came along. She
rattled off an address to the taxi driver, we opened a door and pushed
her in, shut the door and said 'OK driver, carry on.' Off he went with
her shrieking in the back and we disappeared with the bottle of whisky.
I don't know what we did with it because none of us drank whisky
anyway.

On the nights when we went to Cambridge we had two favourite pubs there, The Volunteer and The Baron of Beef. The latter, by Magdalen Bridge, was our favourite. There were three barmaids, Stella, Bella, and Daphne, and they also had a radiogram on which they played a 78 of Artie Shaw's rendition of 'Begin the Beguine'. It had come out in 1938, but this was the first time I had ever heard it, which greatly surprised Glenn and Bill Harris. Having drunk our fill at The Baron of Beef we would come outside and turn right, over the bridge, where it became a ritual that we would offer Glenn £5 to jump in. When we finished our tour we took this same route again and Glenn was intent on jumping in for nothing. We had to physically restrain him. Beyond the bridge we would continue up the hill and turn right to The Rex Ballroom, where there was music and more drink. I remember standing there one night swaying gently on the side of the dance-floor when there was a loud thud, and looking down beside me I saw a prostrate airman, who had fallen off the balcony. I watched, bemused, as he was carted away. We found out the next day that the individual concerned had been posted to 40 Squadron that day. I think he recovered and rejoined the Squadron.

The evening's entertainment over, we would usually make our way to the railway station where the RTO, Railway Transport Officer, had a large building in the station yard equipped with bunks for servicemen who were having problems on their travels. We didn't bother the RTO, but made a beeline for the hut, climbed into bunks, spent the night there and set off early in the morning. Heading out of Cambridge towards Huntingdon we usually encountered the milkman and we would buy a bottle of milk to drink to take the nasty taste away. We knew that in due course, and it always happened, a lorry would come along belonging to Short Brothers. At the time 15 Squadron at Wyton had just converted to Short Stirlings and the working party from Shorts based at Wyton chose to live in Cambridge and commute every day. Of course they always stopped and picked us up and took us to Wyton. There we would get the service bus from Wyton round to Alconbury just in time for the half-past nine parade.

The Volunteer was right in the centre of Cambridge and particularly

famous for the ritual of the landlord at closing time. It was a seething
mass of uniforms, mostly air force, and he would look around the
room and pick out the highest rank that he could see, which might
perhaps even be a Group Captain, and he would bawl out, 'Piss off
all Group Captains', gradually working his way down the ranks,
always loudly cheered by the lower ranks who were still there.

The need to let off steam when not on operations was common to most
crews, and Jo vividly recalls the effective party trick of a New Zealand
pilot, Ken Jenner, who in a crowded bar would move to the corner of the
room with a soda syphon down his tunic, double up, squeeze the bulb of
the syphon, and thus appear to be throwing up. As those around him drew
back in distaste, Jenner would straighten up, grinning, and produce the
soda syphon from inside his tunic.

The closeness and rapport of the six-man aircrew was replicated among
the ground crew, since each crew were allotted their own aircraft and the
luxury of their own individual ground crew, one fitter IIE to each engine,
and two fitter IIAs for the airframe. Jo remembers:

Here again, a tremendous team spirit, pride, loyalty and mutual
confidence was engendered. On one occasion on run-up prior to
an op, there was a massive mag. drop on the port engine. The fitter
who 'owned' that engine, Cyril Bell, fell upon it in an absolute frenzy.
This was high summer, and the nights were short, so when the time
came when it was too late to start, we scrubbed. By that time Cyril
was literally in tears. He ignored 'Chiefy's' order to pack it in, and
continued his frantic efforts to rectify the defect – which was in no
way due to faulty maintenance – through the night.

One day in mid-July, Sergeant Lancaster was summoned to the Orderly
Room, presented with a form and told to fill it in. It was an application for
a commission. His account of what ensued is as follows:

I hadn't asked for a commission but I was to fill it in and that
was that. So I filled it in and in due course was summoned for an
interview by the station commander at Wyton, the much-liked Group

Captain 'Pussy' Foster. When I went in he had all my records out on his desk in front of him, including, apparently, the business about me being kicked out of the VR and he said 'What's all this?' I told him and he roared with laughter and presumably signed on the dotted line. That was all that happened in that interview.

The next step was an interview in London. I had to go down by train and my crew inevitably came to see me off. We called in at The George in Huntingdon for a quick one on the way to the station and the quick one had turned into several when closing time came. So I arrived at the station rather worse for wear and managed to get a train to London, arriving about two in the morning I suppose. There was an air raid alert on with sporadic bombs dropping around the place. In the blackout I managed to find one of the canteens or hostels that were run by The Church Army, the Salvation Army and various other organisations and I got a bed there. The next morning I found there was no mirror and no washing facilities, and I had a hangover. Anyway I did my best and presented myself for the interview. There were three large highly ranked gentlemen sitting there asking me questions which I did my best to answer and that was that. I returned to Alconbury and resumed my routine.

We were due for leave and I had my car then, and we were issued with petrol coupons for leave depending on where you were going. I gave a bogus address, some people I had vaguely met in Shrewsbury, and off I went on leave, going nowhere near Shrewsbury. But when I came back off leave, they said 'Why aren't you an officer?' Apparently they'd sent a telegram to this address in Shrewsbury saying 'commission granted, endeavour to return as Pilot Officer'. So post haste I was off to Cambridge to get myself measured for a uniform. In due course the uniform was ready and off I went to Cambridge again, complete with crew, entered the shop as a Sergeant and came out as a Pilot Officer. Glenn was walking ahead of me making sure that everybody saluted me. Much later on the C.O. [then Wing Commander Stickley] told me that when word came from London that my commission was granted they added the comment that they recommended that I be sent on a PT course!

Jo notes that as a sergeant pilot, and captain of a Wellington, bombing far-flung targets, he was paid the princely sum of £8 8s a fortnight. When he was commissioned his pay actually decreased slightly, a pilot officer's rate then being about 10s 6d a day.

Jo's promotion to pilot officer became official on 6 August, when the ORB noted that Sergeant Lancaster of B Flight had been granted a commission. This required a change of accommodation, and he moved into the hut complex in the grounds of Upton House, where he shared a hut with three others, the longest-standing being New Zealander Pilot Officer Jack Field, who had been posted in only a fortnight after Jo. The other beds were filled by a succession of officer aircrew, of whom Jo only remembers two – Flying Officer William Wright and Pilot Officer J.H.S. 'Bottle' Bebbington – air gunners who, at thirty-one and thirty respectively, seemed 'old' to Jo. Wright, whom Jo recollects primarily for his habit, on returning from an operation, of sitting up writing letters where other aircrew were eager to sleep, was on squadron just over a month before he was killed. Bebbington – who arrived within days of Wright being killed and was still on squadron when Jo was posted – went out to Malta, but drowned when, in November, his aircraft had to ditch in the Mediterranean after engine failure.

One curious incident that Jo recalls from the officers' mess in Upton House occurred sometime in August or September, when for several nights in a row, as they listened to the six o'clock news, a ghostly voice came through behind the BBC announcer, saying 'Lies – all lies.' He has never seen mention of it anywhere, but swears it happened.

Following their leave, Jo and his crew did not operate again until the night of 12 August, when the target was Hannover. A force of seventy-eight Wellingtons and Hampdens was detailed, with 40 Squadron supplying nine of the sixty-five Wellingtons. The raid was significant in that it was the second occasion on which the new navigational aid, Gee, was employed, four aircraft from 215 Squadron using the equipment. One was lost, but fortunately the Germans did not learn anything of the still highly secret device. Of the 40 Squadron crews, seven bombed the target, one bombed Schiphol airfield south of Amsterdam when the port engine gave trouble, while the ninth (Pilot Officer Lancaster) was forced to turn back when ten-tenths cumulo-nimbus cloud to over 15,000 feet was encountered. The bomb load was brought back.

Two of the 40 Squadron crews had a more memorable night. Sergeant Stephens and his airmen had abandoned their primary task when the port engine was damaged by flak over Holland and turned back, bombing Schiphol airfield south of Amsterdam, en route. Losing height, the aircraft crossed the English coast, only to be warned that Alconbury and Wyton were under attack. Suddenly a Ju.88 closed, and with a short burst disabled the remaining engine. Pat Pattison writes:

> At this time I estimated our height at around 1,500 ft and we were in a dive heading for the town of Huntingdon. The skipper shouted 'Brace yourselves for a crash-landing, there's a large meadow almost directly below us.' I unplugged my intercom and scrambled back to my position at the wireless desk. The front gunner crawled out of his turret and standing in the gangway held on to a strap on my right and braced his feet against the geodetic structure. The silence was frightening; only the swish of the aircraft gliding down and occasional heavy breathing over the intercom. I could hear prayers being murmured and I joined in. Then a bump, a blinding flash and we hit the deck, heaps of earth ploughed into the aircraft as we bellied along for what seemed an eternity, then suddenly we had stopped.[2]

Unharmed, the crew ran clear, then turned to look back, to see the Wellington 'majestic on her belly, but miraculously in one piece'; so much so, indeed, that it was recovered a week later, repaired and returned to service. What followed had elements of *Dad's Army* farce about it:

> Through the gloom we saw a squad car heading across the field towards us. It stopped about 10 yards in front of us, and three or four helmeted soldiers jumped out with rifles trained on us, an officer stepped forward with a pistol pointed at us, and shouted 'Achtung. Hands above your heads.' We all started to laugh and the skipper tried to explain that we were RAF, but the officer was not convinced even when we pointed to our faithful old Wimpy displaying the RAF roundels.[3]

It took a phone call to Alconbury from the police station to convince their Home Guard captors, who then plied the crew with hot tea and rum.

Pilot Officer Arthur Fitch and his crew were also surprised by a Ju.88, but near Nijmegen, en route home after bombing. In the first attack, from astern and below, the rear turret was put out of action and the second pilot (Pilot Officer Derek Hutt) wounded. In two further attacks both the front and rear gunners (Sergeants J.C. Beauchamp and W.P. Hudson) were also wounded, Sergeant Beauchamp nonetheless engaging the German fighter, and Fitch, whose peacetime vocation was that of a Church of England priest, finally shaking off the night fighter by diving into cloud.

On 12 July there had been a visit to Wyton by 'the father of the Royal Air Force', Lord Trenchard, and all the aircrew from Alconbury joined 15 Squadron to hear an address from him. Jo recalls that 'we were drawn up on three sides of a square on the tarmac with a dais for Lord Trenchard to address us. The great man duly appeared, got up on the dais and said "Come on in, come in", and waved us into a rabble in front of him. The Station Warrant Officer must have had a fit I should think when that happened.'

On 16 August, Alconbury itself was visited by the Secretary of State for Air, Sir Archibald Sinclair, and his under-secretary, Sir Hugh Seely. They attended the briefing of crews for a raid on Duisburg, dined in the officers' mess at Upton House, saw the crews take off and stayed for the debriefing. No. 40 Squadron supplied nine of the fifty-four Wellingtons despatched, one of them being Jo's. Returning crews reported heavy flak and searchlight defences, but most were able to identify the marshalling yards, which were the target. One, however, were forced by intense flak to abort the attack and bombed Essen instead, while another (led by Pilot Officer Lancaster), who took off an hour later than any other crew, were unable to identify the target because of industrial haze and bombed what was thought to be Oberhausen, some 8 kilometres north-west of Duisburg. Night fighters were active, two attacks being repelled, one resulting in the shooting down by Flight Lieutenant Healey, the squadron's gunnery officer, of an Me.110, which was seen to crash.

Two nights later, Duisburg was again the target, with 40 Squadron despatching another nine crews as part of a Wellington force of forty-one. Bomber Command reported good bombing results in clear weather, but it was not a stellar performance from the 40 Squadron crews, only four of them confident that they had identified and bombed the marshalling yards, Jo Lancaster's crew one of these. Two others were foiled by haze, one set course incorrectly and bombed what was thought to be Antwerp, while two found they were unable to maintain height, and bombed targets of opportunity, one an unnamed airfield and the other Emmerich.

On 25 August, ten crews were briefed for an attack on Karlsruhe as part of a small force of thirty-seven Wellingtons and twelve Stirlings. The raid was a failure, with severe electrical storms forcing most aircraft to turn back, and only one, captained by Gordon Byrne, Jo's former second pilot, felt confident they had located and bombed the target. Two crews failed to return, one captained by Squadron Leader Martin. For Jo's aircrew, however, the flight ended just 8 minutes after take-off, as Jo recalls:

> On 25 August, in T2701, 'S', we suffered our only true engine failure. With a full bomb load we had just taken off from Alconbury and were climbing away at about 750 ft, when I noticed that we'd lost all oil pressure on the port engine. Oil was streaming from the engine and it shortly seized up. Fortunately, we were just able to make it to neighbouring Wyton, where we landed out of the twilight, unannounced and unscathed; a main oil pipe had fractured.

They were extremely lucky. At 750 feet, with an engine out, and a full bomb load that could not be jettisoned at that height, the crew of T2701 would have had to carry out an extremely hazardous crash-landing had not there been an airfield nearby. They might well not have survived.

On 28 August the target was again Duisburg, with Bomber Command despatching 118 bombers, the bulk of them Wellingtons, but including Hampdens, Stirlings, Halifaxes and Manchesters. In good weather with clear conditions, crews, including Jo's, reported that they had identified and bombed the target. One aircraft failed to return, however, and another crashed at Wyton attempting an emergency landing after just 15 minutes in the air. It was T2701, Jo's regular mount, but being flown that night, for some reason, by Pilot Officer Fitch and his crew. Like Jo's aircrew three nights earlier, they had an engine fail soon after take-off, made for nearby Wyton, crashed with a full bomb load, but survived. For Jo and his crew the loss of T2701 felt personal.

Mid-August brought two crew changes to Jo's team, one routine and one not. The latter change was occasioned by illness, front gunner and second wireless operator Bill Harris developing pleurisy and being admitted to the RAF Hospital at Ely. The severity of his illness meant that there was no hope of his rejoining the crew before they completed their tour, and he was subsequently repatriated to Canada. Later commissioned, he would die in July 1944 in a crash on take-off at Goose Bay, Labrador, in a Lockheed Hudson of a Royal Canadian Air Force maritime reconnaissance squadron. Bill's stand-in replacement for five operations was Sergeant Roy Leggett, whose crew had been broken up following the illness of their skipper, New Zealander Sergeant Derek Jannings, and then, from 7 September to the end of their tour, by Sergeant Davidson.

The routine change was that of second pilot, with Gordon Byrne replaced by Sergeant George Bateman, whom Jo recollects as 'a rather timid, sensitive type whom I personally considered totally unsuited for the job'. How unsuitable is demonstrated by the second pilot's handling of one of his tasks, turning on the nacelle tanks when the main tanks were running low. As with all his second pilots, Jo had given Bateman a thorough demonstration of where to find the two wires protruding from the wing roots and how to pull them to effect the fuel cross-over. Jo remembers:

> On the very first occasion, 16 August to Duisburg, when I yelled for him to turn the tank on, after a long interval he said he couldn't find the wires! I had to hastily get the Wireless Operator back there to do it. Naturally, I was somewhat displeased and later gave George another thorough demonstration. The next op was again to Duisburg, on 18 August, and when this time I called for him to turn on the tank, George said, 'It is on – it's been on all the time.' When I asked why he hadn't told me, he said, 'I was afraid you'd be cross'! With finger nails bitten down to the wrists, we thankfully slid into Wyton. We found that the tank, in fact, was not turned on, and the next day there was not enough fuel left in the main tanks to even taxi.

On the last night in August, Jo's crew was one of seven detailed to participate in a raid on Cologne. Bomber Command despatched a total of 103 bombers, but the weather was bad and less than half of the force bombed, and almost all of them on ETA, like Jo's crew, the ORB noting that they 'bombed concentration of searchlights'. Little damage was caused, and with one German civilian killed as against twenty-one aircrew, with three others as prisoners of war, the balance was decidedly in favour of the Germans.

On 2 September Pilot Officer Lancaster and his airmen were detailed as part of a nine-strong 40 Squadron contribution to an attack on Frankfurt by a mixed force of 126, predominantly Wellingtons. Four bombers went down, one of them from 40 Squadron, skippered by Pilot Officer Fitch, who in a brief operational career had already faced a night-fighter attack and a crash-landing. This time Fitch lost his life, as did his wireless operator, Sergeant Robertson, who remained at his set, transmitting until the moment of impact, when the aircraft was forced to ditch in the North Sea because of engine failure. The rest of the crew survived.

No. 40 Squadron despatched two 'freshmen' crews to Boulogne on 7 September, four more experienced aircrews to Kiel, and three of the most seasoned to Berlin. Among the latter – and part of what was for the time a large force of 197, comprising all types of night bomber then in service – were Pilot Officer Lancaster and his men in Z8859, 'S'. The weather was clear over the target and, by 1941 standards, the attack was successful, with considerable damage inflicted on areas in the north and east of the city. Having bombed effectively, Jo and his crew turned for home, but a big change in the forecast winds meant they drifted north and over ten-tenths cloud flew back over Hamburg, Bremen, Wilhelmshaven and Emden. Jo recalls:

This route provided almost continuous flak. Eventually, down on our port side, there appeared a small gap in the cloud below, and through it we could unmistakeably identify the causeway which crosses the entrance to the Zuider Zee. Just as we were all distracted by this sudden glimpse, a great shower of red tracer shot just over the top of us, followed by an Me.110. We quickly went into a tight defensive left-hand turn. The Me.110 went round in a wide left-hand turn and tried another attack. We went into a steep spiral dive, and in attempting to follow us the 110 presented a view of its belly to Keith, who raked it from end to end. It disappeared vertically into cloud at about 4,000ft. Now the limit in speed of a Wimpy IC was 266 mph – officially. In the recovery from our dive, our airspeed was indicated as 330 mph! We sustained no damage, either from the 110's efforts or by having exceeded our 'limiting speed' by 25%, and arrived back at Alconbury after eight and a quarter hours in the air without overload tanks.

The Me.110 was officially claimed as 'damaged', and it seems this was accurate, since no night-fighter loss on that night can be clearly linked to this attack. It is just possible, however, that their opponent was a Bf.110 of 1./NJG3, which crashed on landing at Emelage/Balum bei Vechta, killing both crew.

The trip to Berlin was the longest Jo and his airmen had undertaken to date. Another long flight was scheduled on 10 September, this time to Turin, a target that Bomber Command had not visited since the previous winter. No. 40 Squadron detailed eight crews, but although Bomber Command reported good results in the face of slight opposition, the result for the squadron was a fiasco. Only two crews – one of them that of Squadron Leader Kirby-Green, the new B Flight commander – actually reached Turin and bombed; the others abandoned the operation for a variety of reasons. One aircraft had intercom failure, a second a faulty gyro compass, a third elevator problems, while two others had the port engine fade when switching to overload tanks. One of the crews turning back was that captained by Wing Commander Laurie Stickley, who had succeeded Wing Commander Davy as CO of 40 Squadron on 23 August. Another was Pilot Officer Lancaster's, which reported on return after 2 hours 35 minutes that the aircraft would not climb above 11,000 feet, insufficient to enable a crossing of the Alps.

On 12 September three freshmen crews were sent to bomb Cherbourg while six experienced aircrews were part of a 130-strong force sent to Frankfurt. Thick cloud prevented accurate bombing, or the identification of the designated aiming point, but the 40 Squadron airmen felt that they were 'definitely' over Frankfurt. On debriefing, Jo's crew reported that they were unable to obtain a pinpoint, but that there was 'intense searchlight activity on DR point', at which they bombed from 16,500 feet, seeing 'one large flash reflected in the cloud'. Frankfurt records show that

75 high-explosive bombs hit the city, and 650 incendiaries, causing major fires, but Mainz, 20 miles away, also reported heavy bombing.

After Frankfurt came Hamburg, Jo and his crew joining seven other experienced crews on 15 September as 40 Squadron's contribution to a force of 169 given railway stations and shipyards as aiming points. The weather was good, with clear visibility, although some crews reported that identification of the bombing point was hampered by searchlight glare. Hamburg reported heavy bomb damage, with a number of large fires, nearly 1,500 citizens bombed out, 82 killed and 229 injured. Of the 40 Squadron aircrews, however, three failed to bomb Hamburg, two were unable to locate the city and a third turned back because of concerns about fuel consumption. Of these, two bombed Bremen and the third Bremerhaven. Jo's crew reported that the target was identified by the river and that there were no fires seen when they arrived, to bomb from 18,000 feet. 'Bursts were observed about ½ mile N. of aiming point. Four or five good fires started.'

On 17 September 40 Squadron supplied what was, for 1941, the large number of eleven of the small force of thirty-eight Wellingtons that bombed Karlsruhe, but Pilot Officer Lancaster's crew was not detailed. Two nights later, though, they were among the eight crews detailed to bomb the Baltic port of Stettin, in doing so penetrating further east into Germany than the squadron had hitherto been. Bomber Command reported that only sixty of the seventy-two crews detailed found the city, and very few of them located and bombed the individual targets they had, optimistically, been allocated. But seven of 40's eight crews found and bombed the target; the eighth, captained by Jo's former second pilot, Gordon Byrne, had to turn back after being hit by flak over Heligoland, which in retaliation they bombed. Jo recalls:

> The longest op we did was in Wimpy Z8859, 'S', on 29 September, to Stettin. This time we had overload tanks and were airborne for nine hours and five minutes. There was little opposition over the target, and we made four 'practice bombing range' type run-ups before Glenn, our navigator cum bomb aimer, was satisfied that he had got it all exactly right.

On debriefing, the crew reported that the bombs, three SBCs (small bomb containers) and 3 x 250-pounders, had been seen to burst immediately west of the aiming point on an existing fire.

It was on return from Stettin that Jo found that he had no hydraulics. Either the engine-driven pump had failed or the hydraulics had leaked. Using the reserve system, with its separate fluid reservoir and a hand pump, he was able to get the undercarriage down and locked, but found that he had insufficient fluid to operate the flaps. He comments:

> I don't think that I had been faced with a flap-less landing before, and they were not on the OTU syllabus. It is really a matter of common sense – to approach low, using power to keep the airspeed just above the stall, and to cut it as soon as you reach the threshold. On this occasion the aircraft was, of course, very light – hardly any fuel – and no bombs. That makes it much easier.

It was on the Stettin raid that, irritated by being admonished for not making routine W/T contact calls, Flight Sergeant Hennigan, DFM, who had been Squadron Leader Kirby-Green's wireless operator on a first tour of operations, decided to make a point. Jo recollects:

> The next time out, to Stettin, from over the target he tapped out a request for a QDM (course to steer for base). This would normally only be requested when within about 100 miles of home. On receipt of his QDM he acknowledged and added that he would call again in four hours, which caused a lot of mystification.

After Stettin, 40 Squadron did not operate again until 3 October, when twelve crews were detailed to bomb the docks at Rotterdam. In good weather, and with little flak to distract them, all claimed to have bombed accurately, Pilot Officer Lancaster's crew reporting that although the first two bombs hit the water, the remainder fell across the docks. With a total flight time of just 2 hours 45 minutes, it had been one of the easier of the crew's operations, even if on return seventeen flak holes were found in the aircraft, while Jo recalls how uncomfortable it was flying at altitude with a head cold.

Bad weather then intervened, Bomber Command undertaking no operational flying until 10 October, when raids were made on a range of Channel ports. No. 40 Squadron despatched three freshmen crews to Dunkirk, including that of the new A Flight commander, Squadron Leader Bill Craigen. The next night, however, a record thirteen crews were sent to Emden, as part of a twenty-seven-strong bomber force. The weather was dismal and aircrews reported ten-tenths cloud, which prevented the identification of aiming points. Crews recounted that they had 'bombed on a medium sized fire close to Emden', 'bombed estimated position of Emden' and 'bombed concentration of flak and searchlights, believed Emden'. Jo and his crew had no better luck, simply announcing that they had 'bombed flarepath in DR position. Burst seen in area of lights.'

On the Emden raid Jo had a new second pilot, Sergeant Cooper, George Bateman having been promoted to captain after an unusual ten operations as second pilot. Convinced that Bateman lacked the confidence and the judgement required of the captain of a bomber crew, Jo had several times urged Squadron Leader Kirby-Green, the B Flight commander, not to promote him, but had been told that the shortage of experienced pilots meant that Bateman had to be entrusted with a crew. Over Emden the new crew encountered the same conditions as had frustrated others, reporting that they had 'bombed on DR position after locating bend in the river 3½ miles W of Emden'.

On 12 October three crews were briefed for attacks on Bremen and nine (including Pilot Officer Lancaster's) on Nuremberg. The ORB notes, however, that 'One machine, P/O Lancaster, failed to take off', and Jo explains why: on taxying out to take off, George Bateman clipped the front turret of Jo's aircraft with his wingtip, rendering it unserviceable. Sadly, but almost inevitably, Bateman's crew did not return. Last heard from at 22.00 hours signalling 'task abandoned', the crew of X9822 were probably in the Wellington seen by Squadron Leader Craigen going down in flames. Commenting on the loss, the ORB stated: 'Sgt Bateman was only carrying out his second operation as captain, but he had had an excellent record as a second pilot, and was extremely keen, as indeed were his whole crew.' Keen perhaps Bateman was, but his record as second pilot had been sub-standard, and Jo, reading the ORB comment, wondered – and still wonders – whether the eulogistic comment by the squadron adjutant was a sign of a guilty conscience.

It was, maybe, fortunate that Jo's aircraft was prevented from taking off for Nuremberg, for the operation proved both frustrating and costly. Of the 82 Wellingtons in the 152-strong bomber force five were lost, and one of those was that of New Zealander Pilot Officer Jack Field and his crew. They had joined 40 Squadron only three weeks after Jo, and were flying their twenty-eighth operation, Field described in the ORB as 'one of the squadron's best pilots at the present time', and his observer, Australian Pilot Officer Eric Sugg, as 'particularly able'. After commissioning and shifting to Upton House, Jo had shared a hut with Jack Field, and recalls a prank in which he and others wrecked Field's bed with him still asleep in it. Field's Wellington was shot down over Belgium by a night fighter on the outward journey, crashing near Dinant.

Sadly, the raid, the first on Nuremberg, was a complete failure. Although crews reported fires started, Nuremberg records detail only a few bombs falling in the city, with one person killed and six injured. On the other hand many bombs fell on Schwabach, 10 miles south of Nuremberg, and the village of Lauingen, on the Danube 65 miles from Nuremberg, was heavily bombed, as was Lauffen, 95 miles west of the target. As Martin Middlebrook and Chris Everitt put it in their account of this raid:

> It is significant that both Lauingen and Lauffen were situated on wide rivers, as was Nuremberg, and it was probably this factor that persuaded a few hopelessly lost crews who were navigating on dead reckoning that they had found Nuremberg. Other crews were then attracted to the scenes of the bombing and joined in. These errors illustrate the navigation difficulties experienced by crews in changeable wind conditions when flying to inland targets, albeit they are extreme examples of such error.[4]

The ORB indicates that the eight crews who took off for Nuremberg did no better than crews in other squadrons. Three had to abandon the operation because of a variety of mechanical defects, and of the five who bombed, none was certain that they had found Nuremberg, not even Squadron Leader Kirby-Green's, who circled the target area for 90 minutes yet were still unable to obtain a pinpoint, and could only maintain that bombs were seen to burst 'among buildings'.

Two nights later, Bomber Command again targeted Nuremberg, but with even worse results. The weather was appalling, with severe icing and thick cloud, and only fourteen of the eighty aircrews despatched claimed to have bombed the city, and only one to have positively identified its target. Of the twelve crews sent from Alconbury, seven abandoned the operation because of the weather and two due to mechanical failure, one being Jo's, who turned back when it was found the microphone lead to Keith Coleman's helmet was unserviceable. Guided by Glenn Leitch, however, they located and bombed Ostend. The three remaining crews failed to return, one lost without trace and presumably either shot down over the North Sea or brought down by icing, and the other two over Germany. With a 25% loss rate, it had been a bad night for 40 Squadron, one of the worst during a difficult year.

With the second Nuremberg raid Jo and his crew completed the requisite thirty operations of their tour, but on 16 October, with the squadron having lost six crews out of sixteen in a week, they flew an additional operation to make up the squadron numbers. That night Bomber Command returned to Duisburg, despatching ninety-five aircraft, eight of them detailed for searchlight suppression duties. As over Nuremberg, thick cloud cover prevented accurate target identification, and only two of the seven 40 Squadron crews were confident they had located and bombed the city. Three others bombed on ETA or dead reckoning, one being Jo's, who reported on return that they had 'bombed a concentration of searchlights and flak in DR position'. Again, a crew failed to return, this time that of Squadron Leader Kirby-Green, Jo's flight commander, the fourth B Flight commander to be lost since he joined the squadron in May. The only crew member to survive when their Wellington was hit by flak – which killed the rear gunner and made the aircraft uncontrollable – was Tom Kirby-Green, who was imprisoned in Stalag Luft III, where in March 1944 he would be one of the fifty air force officers shot in the aftermath of the 'Great Escape'. Jo remembers Kirby-Green as 'a rather flamboyant character. He was very fond of Carmen Miranda, had loads of 78 records of her and I never established whether he was in fact any relation to a pre-war aviatrix called Mrs Kirby-Green.' Kirby-Green's flamboyance was not diminished during his time in Stalag Luft III, a fellow inmate recalling entering the hut they were to share and seeing 'this great 6ft 4in man with a beard lying on a top bunk wearing a kaftan and reading Proust'.

Duisburg was the last operation of Pilot Officer Lancaster and his regular crew, who had completed thirty operations and were on 23 October declared 'operationally tour-expired'. This meant that what had been a very close-knit crew was broken up on posting to operational training units. Jo was to join No. 22 Operational Training Unit at Wellesbourne Mountford, near Stratford-upon-Avon, training Wellington pilots. Glenn Leitch was first posted to No. 18 (Polish) OTU at Bramcote, a unit which, as its title makes clear, was devoted to training Polish Air Force bomber crews, also on Wellingtons. He did not enjoy the posting, where he was one of a very few, if not the only member, of the RCAF on station, and was very glad when he was transferred in July to the newly opened RAF station at Gaydon, a satellite of No. 12 OTU at Chipping Warden, training mainly Canadian, Czech and New Zealand pilots and providing short navigation courses. There, sadly, he 'fell into bad company' as Jo puts it, and was court-martialled, which prevented him being posted for a second tour, as they both hoped, as Jo's navigator. Instead, he was sent to a Canadian unit, No. 429 Squadron, operating Wellington Xs as part of the Canadian No. 6 Group of Bomber Command. Operating from East Moor in Yorkshire, on 11 June 1943 he and his crew were shot down by a night fighter while outward bound to bomb Düsseldorf. Only the pilot survived. Glenn Leitch is buried in Eindhoven, in the Netherlands.

Jack Crowther, the wireless operator, was posted to yet another operational training unit, No. 15 at Harwell, where Jo lost touch with him. Only in 1997 did Jo learn that Jack had flown a second tour of operations on Halifaxes with 51 Squadron, been commissioned and awarded the DFC. As an ex-Boy Entrant Jack had stayed in the RAF until 1954, when he emigrated to Canada and joined the RCAF. There, in the 1990s, with the help of a Canadian friend trawling through Crowther families in Canada, Jo tracked down Jack's widow, whom he later met, to learn that Jack had died just two years earlier.

Keith Coleman, the New Zealand rear gunner, was not posted to an operational training unit, but instead opted, for personal reasons, to stay with 40 Squadron, which was about to be sent to Malta. As rear gunner to a fellow New Zealander – Flight Lieutenant Jim 'Stainless' Steel, himself flying a second tour with 40 Squadron – he would complete a second tour operating from Malta and Egypt and be awarded the DFM, the citation stating:

> As air gunner this airman has completed 50 sorties, including raids on Germany, as well as on targets in Italy and Libya. Throughout he has always shown the greatest keenness to engage the enemy.

Posted back to the UK, Keith was repatriated to New Zealand in 1942, where he was commissioned and retrained as a pilot. In the late 1980s, he and Jo re-established contact, and in 1990 he and his wife Clare visited the UK. It was forty-nine years since they had last seen each other. The trip coincided with the fiftieth anniversary of the Battle of Britain and Keith asked if Jo could obtain tickets for the service in Westminster Cathedral. With some wangling, Jo managed to do this. In 1994 Jo visited New Zealand for the first and only time, and stayed for two months, enjoying the hospitality of the Coleman family and several other Kiwis. Then, in 2004, apparently on the spur of the moment, Keith decided to attend the ceremonies in Normandy to mark the sixtieth anniversary of D-Day. Afterwards he became confused as to his transport back to the UK, found himself at a French Air Force base, and, famously, was given a lift to Paris with the French President, who sent Keith a bottle of wine with his compliments. Keith finally made his way back to the UK and stayed a few days with his daughter Sue, and with Jo. This was the last time they met. Keith died in May 2010.

Asked to reflect on his first tour of operations, Jo sums up:

> When we arrived at Alconbury we had already got to know each other rather well. We enjoyed each other's company and, I think, had total confidence in each other's abilities. I think that we all liked Jim Taylor, and had full confidence in him. He did a very good job in introducing us to the little matter of bombing Germany from a Wellington IC. In the eight trips that we did with him we didn't have any real 'shakey dos', and morale remained pretty high. During post ops interrogation we were offered real Royal Navy rum with which we could lace our mugs of tea, and by the time we made our way across the fields back to Alconbury House we were usually very 'happy', proclaiming things

like 'Only 26 more to go!', and greeting a poor old resident donkey! As I said, I felt total confidence in Jim, and do not recall ever having any doubts or apprehension. When I took over as skipper I felt that I had the full confidence of my crew from the start, which made me feel proud. We were a good team and I think that we all felt strongly that we could not let each other down. We did inevitably have our 'shakey dos', but everyone always remained calm and rational, so confidence and morale never really suffered. When we were safely back on the ground and had had time to unwind a bit we usually managed to have a good laugh about it!

Personally I came to have a period of apprehension before an op, the degree depending to some extent on what the night's target was, but as soon as my crew were all assembled and I saw them being their usual selves, cheerful and confident, how could I let them down? I am sure that the possibility of not making it was never, ever, discussed. I think that it may be some kind of self-protection instinct, but inwardly I don't think that I ever considered the possibility that I might be killed. I always thought that the worst thing would be to end up in prison camp. Little did I know at the time that only 10% of those missing survived to become Prisoners of War! When close friends and colleagues failed to return I never ever saw any tears or histrionics. Usually there would be very little conversation for an hour or two, then gradually back to normal. The 'committee of adjustment', consisting of the adjutant, the padre and a sergeant from the orderly room, lost no time in clearing out the personal effects of the missing, and their beds would probably be re-occupied within a day.

How lucky were Jo and his crew to survive a first tour in 1941? The 40 Squadron statistics for the period from May to October make it clear that they were very lucky. While they were on squadron twenty-four crews were lost, the equivalent of one and a half times the squadron establishment of sixteen crews. Some were operating for the first time under a new captain, or early in their tours, others were highly experienced and close to being tour expired. Others again, including four of the flight commanders lost, were flying second tours. A few captains were clearly not up to the task, others early identified as above average. Most crews perished due to enemy action, to flak or night fighters, but several failed to return because of the inability of the Wellington IC to maintain height on one engine, and one crashed on landing, killing all but the rear gunner. The loss rate was particularly heavy towards the end of Jo's tour, as witness the fact that to bring the squadron up to strength for deployment to Malta, which took place within days of Jo's posting, six complete crews had to be brought in. Jo and his crew were very skilled, of course, and a cohesive and efficient unit, but they were also very fortunate.

Ironically, because of the stress and chaos associated with despatching the squadron on detachment to Malta (a 'detachment' that lasted not the expected two to three months, but until 40 Squadron was disbanded in Egypt in 1947), Jo did not receive the obligatory end of tour assessment that would have rated his performance as 'below average', 'average', 'above average' or 'exceptional'. It is hard to believe, however, that had Wing Commander Stickley found the time to complete the assessment, it would not have read 'above average'. His later flying career suggests nothing less.

Chapter 5

Instructing

Jo's tour of operations with 40 Squadron completed, he went on leave to
his parents' home at Eastbury. Then, as ordered, he reported on 23 October to No. 22 Operational Training Unit at Wellesbourne Mountford,
some 3 miles north-east of Stratford-upon-Avon. Formed on 14 April 1941
in No. 6 Group, to train night bomber pilots, No. 22 OTU was equipped
with what Jo calls 'very clapped out Wellington ICs'. Allotted to A Flight,
which was the conversion flight, Jo found himself instructing pilots fresh
out of Flying Training School – where they had flown Airspeed Oxfords or
Avro Ansons – in the art of flying Wellingtons. Interestingly, of the pupil
pilots he taught, perhaps 60% were Canadian and about 20% Australian.

By a curious coincidence, the officer commanding A Flight, Squadron
Leader E.J. Little, had been a flight commander with 40 Squadron until
late April 1941. 'Sam' to his friends and peers, but by those who served
under him nicknamed 'Daddy', Little was deeply religious and a Method-
ist lay preacher, his nickname deriving, it seems, from his earnest attempts
to limit his crews' drinking and socialising in the interests of optimal
operational fitness. After a posting in July 1942 as chief flying instructor at
No. 11 OTU, first at Bassingbourn and then at Westcott – where he would
have found himself dealing with a high proportion of hard-drinking New
Zealanders – Sam Little took command of 623 Squadron at Downham
Market on 18 August. His period in command was brief. Flying the inadequate Short Stirling, on 31 August 623 Squadron lost three aircraft in a
raid on Berlin. One was that of 'Daddy' Little. He and his crew all perished.

Jo found Sam Little 'something of an oddball', and his replacement as officer commanding A Flight, Squadron Leader Bob Barrell, 'a great improvement'. Later, as Wing Commander R.G. Barrell, DSO, DFC and bar, the latter had a distinguished period commanding 7 Squadron of the Pathfinder Force at Oakington, before losing his life on 24/25 June 1943 when his parachute failed to deploy as he baled out of his stricken Lancaster, the first to be lost by 7 Squadron.

The instructors' sleeping accommodation at Wellesbourne Mountford was in wooden huts, two to a room, and Jo found himself sharing with Pilot Officer W.A. 'Bill' Fullerton, DFM. Bill, who had completed a tour of operations on Whitleys with 58 Squadron, was a licentiate of the Royal Academy of Music and a gifted pianist, equally at home with the classics or the popular songs of the day. He had a girlfriend, Cora Brickwood, in Coventry, and when Jo was off to spend an evening with friends there, he would give Bill a lift, enabling him to spend time with her.

Two other A Flight instructors were Bob Hickling and Hugh 'Dusty' Miller, a New Zealander in the RAF. Serving with 77 Squadron, in November 1940 the latter had been lost over the North Sea in his Whitley and finally ditched near a small ship, to find that he was only about 8 miles off the Northumberland coast. Tony Hughes, the last of the instructors, Jo remembers as 'just about the only ex 4 Group pilot there who had not received a gong'. He comments:

> The instructors had mostly come from 4 Group and having completed a tour on Whitleys it seems they automatically got a DFC or a DFM. On 40 Squadron (and I think it was the same throughout 3 Group) there were only about six medals dished out when I was there and in each case it was the result of somebody having a very, very sticky time.

'I'm not trying to detract from the 4 Group chaps,' he continues, 'they were jolly good chaps and it's not sour grapes. It's just a case of how things worked in different groups.'

The process of converting incoming pilots to the Wellington was undertaken with pairs of pupils, and for Jo this began with spending an hour with each, 'going round the aircraft, making sure that they knew where

everything was and what it did, although they were supposed to have
already learnt all this in the Chief Ground Instructor's (CGI) instructional
fuselage'. This would be followed by a careful explanation of procedures,
before instruction in the air began. Jo remarks:

> With one pupil in the astrodome, I would demonstrate one circuit
> and landing to the other, who was in the right hand seat, then change
> places with him and talk him through a few circuits and landings.
> Then the pupils would change places, and we would repeat the
> process. The whole purpose was to teach them to take off and land,
> and once they had observed me doing so, I would take over the right
> hand seat, and it would be the pupil in the left hand seat who landed
> the aircraft. Perched on a temporary right hand seat, the instructor
> had duplicate flying controls and throttles only, and the seat had
> to be folded up to enable first pilot occupants to change over. This
> could be tricky, while the installation of the duplicate flying controls
> made entry and exit via the forward hatch very difficult indeed. Only
> when they were confident and competent would we repeat much
> the same procedure at night. On completion of that, they moved to
> the navigation flight at Atherstone to embark on cross-country and
> practice bombing exercises.

The daily routine on the Wellington conversion flight involved 3-hour
stints, Jo usually flying two in a 24-hour period. This was not especially
onerous, but for him a particular bête noire was the night flying:

> This was in the depths of winter and the night flying schedule was
> divided into four three-hour stints. You can imagine that the midnight
> to 3 am or 3 am to 6 am stints were very unpopular. It was dreadful
> to have to get out of bed and go and do three hours of circuits and
> bumps. On top of that during night flying you had to take your turn
> as ACP, i.e. Aerodrome Control Pilot, when you were out at the end of
> the runway by the threshold with a landline to the watch office and an
> Aldis lamp to signal the aircraft to take off. They would signal when
> they were flying on the down-wind leg on the downward identity light
> and you would give them a green to continue their final approach.

This was a pretty miserable and tedious job.

Although instructing was clearly not as dangerous as flying on operations, it was far from hazard-free, with its combination of inexperienced aircrew and worn-out aircraft. There had been two 22 OTU crashes with fatalities in the month preceding Jo's arrival at Wellesbourne Mountford, and on the night of 7 December there were two more. The weather was bad, with snow and heavy icing, and it was when flying into a snowstorm that a crew from E Flight, captained by a screened pilot, Pilot Officer W.J. Turner, DFM, lost engine power, lost height rapidly and at 18.15 hours crashed into a tree about a mile from the runway. Three, including Pilot Officer Turner, were killed, and the other two crew members severely injured. Ten minutes later there was a second crash when a Wellington of A Flight, captained by Sergeant J.H.A. Cox, found itself landing slightly off the centre line of the runway and began to overshoot. In very poor visibility the aircraft flew into Loxley Hill just south of the airfield. All the crew were injured, two fatally. That the hill posed a hazard was highlighted in a 6 Group report on Wellesbourne Mountford, compiled in the summer of 1942, which noted that only one of three runways was much use, one being too short for night flying, and another dangerous because it led directly towards high ground.

Early on 3 January there was yet another fatal accident. Wellington X9640 of B Flight, carrying a screened pilot, Flight Sergeant G.M. Bigglestone, two pupil pilots and two support crew, suffered port engine failure and on approach to land at 01.05 hours, crash-landed with its wheels retracted, short of the runway, skidded across a field and into a river bank. In the crash the cables supplying power to the base were severed, plunging it into darkness. Two of the crew, including the pilot, were killed instantly, and a third succumbed to his injuries less than 48 hours later.

This crash was one of the two that Jo witnessed. The second occurred just a week later, on the night of 14 January:

I think it was a nine to midnight stint and there was a very hard frost. One of my fellow instructors on A Flight, Flight Sergeant Brian Farmborough, went off. We had a TR9 radio on which he could talk to the watch office. It didn't work very well but we gathered that his artificial horizon was not working. I think it was his artificial horizon, anyway he had instrument trouble. Although the weather was clear it was very dark and he made various attempts to land but eventually spun in and crashed on the far end of the aerodrome. Of course they were all killed.

The subsequent inquiry of the crash established that both the air speed indicator and the artificial horizon of the elderly Wellington IC had been unserviceable, perhaps because iced up, and that in difficult conditions the Wellington had stalled in circuit, spun and crashed near Charlecote, just north of the airfield. 'There were always accidents happening,' Jo comments, 'quite a number of them fatal.'

There were indeed. On 28 January another Wellington on a night cross-country exercise lost power and at 22.20 hours crashed on high ground some 3 miles south-east of the airfield, killing the pilot and injuring the other six airmen aboard. On 3 March, again at night, yet another Wellington had engine problems, but the captain, Squadron Leader Burgis, took the prudent step of ordering the crew to bale out, leaving the Wellington to crash near Yattendon. Then a fortnight later, landing at 22.00 hours after night-flying training, Sergeant Jardine's Wellington swung off the flare path and struck the corner of No. 9 hangar. Luckily no one was injured, either on the aircraft or in the hangar, although the A Flight crew room was wrecked.

Engine failure or not, landings at night were clearly the most hazardous element in crew training. On 27 March a Wellington overshot on landing and finished up, wrecked, in a hedge. All aboard escaped unscathed. On 8 April another crew were not so fortunate when, on a night exercise at 2,000 feet, an engine cut out in turbulent conditions. The pilot instructor, New Zealander Pilot Officer John Warnock, attempted a forced landing, but the Wellington hit a tree at Great Coxwell. He and two others were killed instantly, and a fourth crew member died of his injuries.

The crashes continued, even as the weather improved. On 28 April Canadian Sergeant Schweitzer and two fellow airmen died when he lost control in a turn while carrying out circuits and landings, the Wellington crashing near the airfield and exploding. On 5 May another crew carrying out night-flying practice stalled and crashed when going round again after overshooting. Three of the five-man crew died instantly as the air-craft burned, while a fourth, rescued by the station medical officer, Squadron Leader George Mogg, later died of his injuries. For his efforts, carried out with complete disregard for his own safety, Mogg was awarded the George Medal. On 19 July Mogg was again involved in rescue efforts when a Wellington flying down the flarepath at 400 feet, suddenly dived into the ground and finished up on fire in the River Dene. On this occasion Squadron Leader Mogg recovered the body of the Canadian pilot, Pilot Officer J.W.M. Harley.

Although most of the accidents that occurred during Jo's time at Wellesbourne Mountford happened in crashes on or near the airfield, there were other fatalities through crews getting lost while on night cross-country or navigation exercises. On 8 February, Sergeant L.G.J. Mizen and crew, three of the six Canadians, took off on a day navigational exercise. The wireless failed, preventing the crew obtaining fixes, and in bad weather they over-flew the Isle of Man and failed to recognise the southern coast of Scotland. Turning east, they flew into high ground at Ireby, between Cockermouth and Carlisle in Cumbria, only the rear gunner surviving. On 7 May, Sergeant J.C. Wood and his predominantly Canadian crew took off to carry out a night cross-country and were last heard of at 02.17 hours, reporting an imminent forced-landing. They probably came down in the Irish Sea, no trace of them or their aircraft being found. Another night cross-country, on 6 July, brought more Canadian deaths when Sergeant J.S. Kemp and his all-Canadian crew crashed on Waen Rhydd, in the Brecon Beacons, 4 miles south of Talybont. Like Sergeant Mizen and his crew, they had no doubt become lost, and made the cardinal mistake of descending in cloud to establish their position.

In all, during Jo's time with 22 OTU, the fourteen crashes involving crews from Wellesbourne Mountford resulted in thirty-eight deaths, while other crashes associated with crews operating from Stratford resulted in sixteen more over the same period.

Jo barely recalls Wing Commander Harman, the chief flying instructor at Wellesbourne Mountford when he was posted in, but vividly remembers his successor, Wing Commander Hughie Edwards, who had been awarded the Victoria Cross for his leadership of a low-level daylight raid by

Blenheims on Bremen in April 1941. An Australian and a regular RAF officer, he seemed to Jo friendly and approachable, and also receptive to the
latter's enquiry about taking an instructor's course at the Central Flying
School, Upavon. With Hughie Edwards's endorsement of the application,
Jo was successful, and on 12 April 1942 began the three-week course. He
had undertaken the course realising that he was not a born instructor, that
he was good at demonstrating what to do, but not good at explaining. At
its conclusion he was more certain than ever that instructing was not for
him, and certain also that he did not like the Airspeed Oxford that he had
been flying at Upavon.

On the other hand he found 'some interesting chaps' also taking the
course. One was Flying Officer Ivor Broom, who had been a sergeant pilot
with 107 Squadron on Malta flying suicidal anti-shipping operations in
Blenheims. When all the squadron's officers had been lost, he was told by
Air Vice Marshal Lloyd, the AOC Malta, to 'Move into the officers' mess.
We will sort the paperwork out later.' Broom would stay in the RAF post-
war and retire as Air Marshal Sir Ivor Broom. Another later to achieve
fame was the then Pilot Officer T.G. 'Hamish' Mahaddie, subsequently
famous as Group Captain Mahaddie of the Pathfinder Force. A somewhat
mysterious figure was a Dutch civilian named Vos, who, Jo recalls, 'used
to get very annoyed when they'd spell his name as "Voss", with two ss:
he said "No, one s, Vos; two sses is German".' Piet Vos, Fokker engineer
and member of the Fokker board of directors, had escaped to Britain in
1941 aboard a Fokker G.1 fighter flown by test pilot Hidde Leegstra. To
do this the pair had surreptitiously had to acquire additional fuel for the
supposed test flight and en route duck into clouds to deter the trailing
Luftwaffe aircraft from following. Lastly, there was Roy Lawson, who had
trained with Jo at Ternhill, but as a fighter pilot. He took his Upavon
course on the Miles Master III, Jo on one occasion managing to hitch a
ride with him. Posted to Malta, Lawson would die late in December while
serving with 249 Squadron.

During the winter of 1941–42, a group of Training Command instructors came through as pupil pilots to convert to Wellingtons prior to going
on to bomber operations and for Jo and his fellow instructors 'they were a
great relief because they already knew perfectly well how to fly and were no
problem at all'. One whom Jo particularly recalls was Desmond Plunkett,

who a few months later was shot down and taken prisoner. Sent to Stalag Luft III, Sagan, he was there put in charge of forging travel documents and making maps for escapees. Another coming through as a pupil at that time was Wing Commander Lord Carlow, or to give him his full name George Lionel Seymour Dawson-Damer, Viscount Carlow. A keen book collector and typographer who knew many of the leading literary figures of his day, Carlow had, in 1936, established the Corvinus Press, which published new work by such luminaries as T.E. Lawrence, James Joyce, Edmund Blunden and H.E. Bates. Carlow would be killed in a flying accident in April 1944. But Jo remembers him primarily for a coincidence:

> Curiously, while we had Lord Carlow in the mess one of the intelligence officers had a bull terrier who was called Carlo. He was not very fond of other dogs but human beings could do no wrong and he was a great pet of everybody in the mess. I took him flying once. He was a big lump; we had to heave him bodily up the ladder into the nose of the Wellington and he just stood there and looked bored the whole time.

On 1 July 1942 the basic petrol ration was abolished, which meant no private motoring at all was possible. So after coming back from the OTU instructors' course at Upavon Jo took leave and drove his car down to his parents' home at Eastbury, near Lambourn, where they were running the post office and village shop, and laid it up. Strangely, the petrol ration for motorcycles continued for a time, so Jo took himself off to Coventry, where he acquired an old Rex Acme motorbike, which had an outside flywheel and exposed primary chain ('We used to rattle along fine,' he comments) and used it until the late summer when the petrol ration for motorbikes was also abolished. While still mobile, however, he visited Cambridge and looked up an old friend from 5 FTS days, George Bayley, who was flying Stirlings on the Stirling Conversion Unit at Waterbeach. Jo recalls:

> We had a night out in Cambridge and stayed the night in one of the colleges, with which he had some connection. The next day we were out at Waterbeach where I had a couple of flights with him in a Stirling. I was most amused by the Stirling because it had the throttles

in the centre of the panel unlike the Wellington and these were huge levers almost like a signal box. George got on the end of the runway and opened up three engines almost to full throttle and then as the aircraft rolled forward and tried to swing he gradually opened up the other throttle to counteract the swing and off we went into the wide blue yonder. But whilst I was there, there was obviously some panic, something was brewing. There was a lot of tight security so I headed off back on my Rex Acme to Wellesbourne and sure enough there were extra guards on the gate. When we got in there was a lot of speculation about what was to happen. What did happen of course was the first of the 'Thousand bomber' raids.

The brainchild of Air Chief Marshal Sir Arthur Harris, who had taken over as Air Officer Commanding-in-Chief of Bomber Command in February 1942, the so-called 'Thousand Bomber' raids of May and June 1942 were designed to demonstrate in unmistakable fashion the destructive capability of Bomber Command, and thereby to secure for it the resources that Harris fervently believed would materially hasten the end of the war. In order to despatch the symbolically effective 1,000 bombers for the first of these raids, on Cologne on the last night in May, Harris had to call on all Bomber Command training units to supply crews. No. 22 Operational Training Unit put up a total of 33 aircraft, 12 operating from Wellesbourne Mountford, 11 from the satellite airfield at Stratford, and 10 from Elsham Wolds in Lincolnshire, where 103 Squadron was based. 'We didn't know what the target was until the briefing,' Jo says.

Security was very good indeed. I was given a screened navigator, Flight Sergeant Joe Hart, and a screened wireless operator, Flight Sergeant Harrison, plus two Canadian pupil air gunners, one of whom became so excited over the target that he asked if he could spray his guns about. I told him to look inconspicuous. Our aircraft, Z9932 'X', was one normally engaged on dual circuits and bumps training. It still had its dual controls fitted which made entry and exit rather difficult – particularly if one was in a hurry. We took off in rain but on the return trip the weather was fine, as with dawn breaking, we cruised back towards Wellesbourne Mountford at about

1,000ft. The W/Op, Flight Sergeant Harrison, came up forward to sit
beside me and we were enjoying a cigarette when – I think almost
simultaneously – we saw the starboard engine oil pressure gauge
drop abruptly to zero. Fortunately Harrison was a very experienced
Wimpy man and knew exactly what to do. He dashed aft and started
to transfer oil from the 14 gallon reserve tank by hand-pump and the
oil pressure quickly recovered. The engine had drunk its normal oil
capacity of 17 gallons in less than five hours' flying. Two nights later
we took the same aircraft to Essen, but this time we didn't wait for the
starboard engine to consume all its oil before replenishment.

Of the thirty-three aircraft sent to Cologne, four failed to return. One was
captained by a South African in the RAF, Flight Lieutenant Alwyn Ham-
man, DFC and bar. From his aircraft only the screened wireless operator
survived. The second, from which no one escaped, was captained by a
New Zealander, Flying Officer Harold Blake, who had been instructing at
No. 20 OTU, Lossiemouth, when called on to lead a Wellesbourne crew.
There were no survivors, either, from the crew of Flight Sergeant C.J.
Edwards, or from the Wellington captained by Jo's friend and roommate,
Bill Fullerton. Only recently married to his fiancée, Cora, he and his crew
were shot down, outward bound over Holland at 23.40 hours, by a night
fighter.

The first 'Thousand Bomber' raid was a great success, both in terms
of the destruction wrought, and as a public relations exercise. The second, targeting Essen, was far less effective, low cloud and haze preventing
accurate bombing. In fact, the neighbouring cities of Duisburg, Mülheim
and Oberhausen were more heavily bombed than Essen itself. For No. 22
OTU, however, the raid was in one respect more satisfactory than that
on Cologne, with none of the thirty-four Wellingtons despatched failing
to return. The third and last, to Bremen on 25 June, also found the target
obscured by cloud. But Gee-equipped aircraft marked the target effectively, and substantial damage was caused. Of the Wellingtons and Whitleys of
the operational training units, just over 11% were lost. This included two
of the twelve Wellingtons sent from Wellesbourne, although the crew of
one of them, which had ditched in the North Sea 60 miles off Yarmouth,
was rescued after five days in a dinghy. Jo was to have participated in this

raid also, but as the Wellington was lined up to take off the intercom system went dead, and the wireless operator was unable to fix the problem. The summer night being so short there was no time to have the fault rectified, and accordingly they were scrubbed from the operation.

Recognising that he was not by nature cut out for instructing, Jo had become somewhat disillusioned with life at the OTU, as had Joe Hart, with whom he had been crewed for the 'Thousand Bomber' raids, so they decided that they would go together to Alconbury and offer their services to 156 Squadron, the unit formed out of the skeletal Home Echelon of 40 Squadron after its departure for Malta. 'It had Hercules-engined Wellington IIIs,' Jo says,

> and a very nice aircraft too. So on 28 June we flew off to Alconbury
> and got an audience with the CO, Wing Commander Price, who
> said he'd be very glad to have us and would 'do what he can'. But
> nothing happened and I learnt later that he'd got the chop not very
> long afterwards. Much later still I discovered that Joe Hart had in
> fact gone back on ops with 156 Squadron with another Wellesbourne
> screen[ed] pilot, George Hookway. Unfortunately on an Essen raid in
> March 1943 they were both killed.

On 15 July 1942 Jo was posted, but not to an operational squadron. No. 28 OTU at Wymeswold, just east of Loughborough, had opened on 16 May and Jo found himself one of a small nucleus of aircrew sent to get it under way. Several became Jo's close friends, including Squadron Leader Peter Way from No. 21 OTU, Moreton-in-Marsh, and Fred Drury and Jack Stevens, who came from No. 15 OTU, Harwell. Another instructor was Flight Lieutenant David Penman, DSO, DFC, one of the few to survive the low-level, deep-penetration raid on Augsburg in April 1942. Penman came from 97 Squadron, where he had been flying Lancasters, and Jo wondered how he now felt about flying clapped-out Wellington ICs. Another of the founding aircrew was John Edward Terence 'Sandy' Mansfield, so nicknamed because he was the heir to Lord Sandhurst. 'He had', Jo recalls, 'done a tour as an observer on 149 Squadron in 3 Group and after my time on 12 Squadron he joined it as bombing leader, and

I saw quite a bit of him after the war at 12 Squadron reunions.' Jo also remembers 'Sandy' Mansfield as proving himself 'always without equal in the silly competition of who could sink a pint of beer fastest. He was really quite outstanding in this.' The late Lord Sandhurst's *Daily Telegraph* obituary (6 July 2002) elaborates, noting his 'ability to down a pint of beer while upside down with his legs hooked over the bar for support'. 'We all got on together famously,' Jo adds, 'and went around en bloc visiting the local towns and the country pubs. We explored Nottingham and Leicester and Loughborough, delighted to find that Loughborough still had an old fashioned music hall with a bar at the back of the stalls. It was great fun there.'

Being among the first to arrive at Wymeswold, Jo and his fellow instructors were initially assigned to ferry in the OTU's complement of Wellington ICs, most of them from other OTUs but some from operational squadrons. His first flight from Wymeswold, thus, was to Chipping Warden on 28 July, while the following day to Chipping Warden again, followed by Honington, Waddington and Litchfield. His logbook reveals, however, that he did not undertake his first flight as an instructor with a trainee crew until 22 August, with the first day cross-country flown on 28 August and the night flying, circuits and landings using a dual-control aircraft, on 8 September. He comments:

> The complement of aircraft gradually built up, and other instructors were posted in, so in due course training operations started with a vengeance. By September and October we were working very hard. In addition to the training programme a crew would occasionally be detailed to participate in one of the Bomber Command operations and join in the main force or occasionally (this was somebody else's good idea) a thing called 'moling', whereby an aircraft went out on its own with the intention of staying under cloud cover the whole time. It was really just a nuisance operation but it was highly dangerous because with the prevailing weather moving from west to east there was always a danger that a clearance would come along behind the aircraft and it would be trapped by the clearance; that wouldn't be funny at all.

Fortunately, Jo was never tasked with one of these hazardous operations.

It was during his months at Wymeswold that Ollie Lancaster acquired the nickname 'Jo', derived of course from his initials, by which thereafter he was generally known, although his old friends continued to call him 'Ollie'. It was also at this time that he met the then Group Captain (but later Air Vice Marshal) Donald Bennett. The Australian Dictionary of National Biography notes that Bennett 'possessed an impatient, dictatorial and pedantic style of command which, while sometimes most effective, inevitably made him enemies'. Jo's experience, however, was quite different:

> It must have been when I was on leave from Wymeswold, in August or September '42. As I sometimes did, I went on a quick tour of old friends and acquaintances in the Cambridge area, being dropped off at Wyton. I made my way to the guardroom and stood outside, waiting for a lift or a bus ride into Huntingdon. Along came a large American-type car driven by a Group Captain, with a lady beside him on the large bench seat, and I was offered a lift. I was about to get into the back seat when he suggested that instead I join him and his wife in the front. His wife slid along a bit, and the three of us drove off happily into Huntingdon. It was a little while before I realised that this was indeed Don Bennett, recently posted in to Wyton to set up 8 Group Pathfinder Force. What a nice man!

Another memory of his days at Wymeswold remains equally vivid in Jo's memory:

> When the basic petrol ration for cars was discontinued completely I knew Jack Stevens had a motorbike and I used to go into Nottingham with him. I was on the pillion one night and we had a nice evening out during which we met another member of our staff at Wymeswold, a chap called Foster. He was the navigation leader and he hadn't got any transport back to the station. So we all three went back on Jack's motorbike. I was tail end Charley, there was a very bright moon shining from the port beam and I was highly amused at sitting there looking at our shadow, with the three figures crouched in line astern, speeding along.

During Jo's seven months at Wellesbourne Mountford, there had been a succession of crashes, many involving fatalities. At Wymeswold, however, luck seemed to smile on screened and trainee aircrew alike, since during July, August and September, despite the increasing tempo of training, no serious accident occurred. This changed, though, on 7 October, as Jo recalls:

> One of the screened pilots was a Warrant Officer Tony Gee, a very good chap. He was flying along at about 1,500 feet on a lovely sunny summer's afternoon and suddenly the aircraft just dived into the ground. Everybody was killed and nobody ever really established what was the problem. It was all a bit disquieting really.

Recording the loss – in which Gee, a trainee pilot, Sergeant Barker, and a screened wireless operator, Flight Sergeant Jones, were killed – Bill Chorley notes that the Wellington was being flown to provide the trainee with dual and right-hand seat flying experience, and that 'Shortly before 1608, the Wellington was seen jettisoning fuel; it then crashed at Woodhouse Eaves, 3 miles S from Loughborough, Leicestershire. At the Court of Inquiry a rigger suggested that there may have been extensive stripping of fabric from a vital area of the starboard wing.'[1]

The next day, Jo was detailed to carry out a five-hour cross-country training flight with a pupil crew. He writes:

> As usual the cabin heating was not working, it was a very cold trip and I got back late afternoon, to find I was detailed with another crew in another aircraft on a bullseye [an exercise to simulate an operational sortie, often to provide ground units, such as the Observer Corps, with training in detection and identification]. I didn't have time to go to my billet to get any warm underclothes, there wasn't a proper meal laid on for me and off I launched on this bullseye which was going to be about a five hour flight with a completely trainee crew, no screened wireless operator, no screened navigator. We were up somewhere near the Mull of Galloway when the wireless operator reported his radio completely out of action. We were in severe icing conditions (there hadn't been a proper briefing beforehand so I hadn't had proper weather information on the route) and I was very concerned about

how we were going to find our way back to Wymeswold without a wireless working. It was exceedingly cold because yet again the cabin heating system wasn't working, and I was very cold because I didn't have proper underclothing. So I decided to pack it in after a couple of hours or so and return to Wymeswold.

In those days the only means of navigation you had, apart from dead reckoning by the navigator and the wireless operator and his radio, were beacons on the ground. There were two kinds. The red ones, called Pundits, were attached to airfields and would be in one of three positions which were varied from night to night. The others, white Occults, were usually in the same place but very widely spaced. These flashing beacons flashed two Morse letters and the navigator was armed with information about them, which varied from day to day, as did the positions of the Pundits. Thus if you saw a red Pundit flashing two letters you knew what station it was attached to and where the station was in relation to it. I found myself hungry, weary, very cold, flying in icing conditions with a navigator who was a beginner whose capabilities I did not know, and a wireless operator of whose capabilities I was equally ignorant, but who in any case declared his radio unserviceable. So where were we? I decided that I was going to retrieve the situation rather than prolong things and then have to let down through cloud not knowing where on earth we were. So many lives had been lost doing that. So we about turned, and let down in clearer weather over the east of the country and found our way back without the help of the radio.

'It's by doing things like that,' Jo adds, 'that I'm still alive to tell the tale.'

Despite making such an eminently prudent decision, Jo found himself called to account for it. He recalls:

The next day I was hauled in front of the Chief Flying Instructor whom I had never spoken to before. Wing Commander Foord-Kelcey was a regular RAF officer, but had nothing by way of decorations to indicate that he'd ever done anything worthwhile on operations in his life. He laid into me about cancelling this bullseye. I explained all the circumstances but he demanded to see my log book and in it I had stuck a little cartoon taken out of a Flight magazine some time before. It was by a well-known cartoonist of the time called Brockbank. The caption was 'All the way from Hamburg on one engine'. It was of course of a cheerful little chap sitting astride just one engine to the astonishment of an airman standing by. Foord-Kelcey got all umpty about this and said, 'Did you come back from Hamburg on one engine?' I said 'No, of course not, Sir.' Anyway I began to lose my rag after a while and was a bit insubordinate.

Perhaps not surprisingly, very shortly after this testy interview Jo found himself posted to 150 Squadron at Snaith. 'No doubt', Jo comments, 'Foord-Kelcey thought he was doing something nasty to me but in point of fact it was very welcome.' He had had his fill of instructing, and was eager to return to operational flying.

On arrival at Snaith, near Goole in South Yorkshire, Jo found that the commanding officer, Wing Commander Carter, was not expecting him and that, with no crew available, he was surplus to requirements. Nonetheless, he was allocated an aircraft and made two or three flights, one of them at night, to familiarise himself with the Hercules-engined Wellington III – 'quite a hot ship', Jo recollects. Then, still surplus to requirements, Jo was asked by the CO what he wanted to do. Jo's reponse was immediate and decisive: he wanted to fly his namesake, the Lancaster, equipped with the new navigational aid, Gee. How that was arranged, Jo never knew, but within a week of being sent to Snaith, he received another posting, to 12 Squadron at Wickenby in Lincolnshire.

YEAR		AIRCRAFT		PILOT, OR 1ST PILOT	2ND PILOT, PUPIL OR PASSENGER	DUTY (INCLUDING RESULTS AND REMARKS)
MONTH	DATE	Type	No.			
—	—	—	—	—	—	TOTALS BROUGHT FORWARD
MAY	12	WELLINGTON	Z.8782	SELF.	SGT. GERVIN.	DUAL.
"	27	STIRLING	R.9304	P/O BAYLEY.	SELF.	DUAL & TEST TO 20000'
"	27	" "	R.9304	SELF.	P/O BAYLEY.	WATERBEACH — WYTON & RETURN.
"	28	WELLINGTON	X.9932	SELF.	CREW.	N.F.T.
"	29	"	X.9932	SELF.	CREW.	N.F.T.
"	29	"	X.9932	SELF	CREW.	W/T TEST.
"	30	"	R.1522	SELF		A/C TEST.
"	30	" 'S'	X.9932	SELF.	CREW.	(32) OPS. COLOGNE.

(signature) F/O

O.C. B FLT.

SUMMARY FOR ...MAY... 1942		AIRCRAFT TYPES.
UNIT .....22 O.T.U.....		1. WELLINGTON
DATE .....1/6/42....... 19.....		2. STIRLING
SIGNATURE ...J.C.Lancaster...		3.
		4.

JUNE	1	WELLINGTON	X.9932	SELF.	F/SGT. HARRISON.	CONSUMPTION TEST.
"	1	" 'S'	X.9932.	SELF.	CREW.	(33) OPS. ESSEN.
"	3	"	R.1711.	SELF.	P/O FRIEND	AIR TEST.
"	3	"	R.1711.	SELF.	SGT. BURRILL.	DUAL.
"	4	ANSON.	AX.258	SELF.	CREW.	CROSS-COUNTRY.
"	6	WELLINGTON	DV.491	SELF.	SGT. WEBSTER.	A/C TEST.
"	7	"	W.5669	SELF.	P/O MOULD.	TO SATELLITE.
"	7	"	X.9932	SELF.		FROM SATELLITE.

GRAND TOTAL [Cols. (1) to (10)]
715 Hrs. 50 Mins.

TOTALS CARRIED FORWARD

YEAR 1943		AIRCRAFT		PILOT, OR 1ST PILOT	2ND PILOT, PUPIL OR PASSENGER	DUTY (INCLUDING RESULTS AND REMARKS
MONTH	DATE	Type	No.			
—	—	—	—	—	—	— TOTALS BROUGHT FORW
JAN.	2.	LANCASTER	R. 4366	SELF.	CREW.	N.F.T. AND FORMATION LANDED AT DIGBY.
"	2.	"	R 4366.	SELF.	CREW.	DIGBY - BASE.
"	3	"	R 4366	SELF.	CREW	FIGHTER AFFILIATION AT Do
"	4	"	W 4791	SELF.	CREW.	OPS. ESSEN. SPECIAL HIGH ALTITUDE 22000'. ABANDON W/OP UNCONSCIOUS. REAR TURRET
"	8	"	R 4366	SELF.	CREW. �37	OPS. HAUGSUND FIORD. 6 x 1500 VEG. BFX DYCE LANDED LOSSIEMOUTH
"	9.	"	R 4366.	SELF.	CREW	LOSSIEMOUTH - BASE.
"	20	"	V 4794.	SELF.	F/LT. NODEN CREW.	TO ELSHAM & RETURN.
"	21	OXFORD.	V.4146.	SELF.	P/O. WOOLLAND.	TO WYMESWOLD & RETURN AND S.B.A.
"	23	LANCASTER	W 4991	SELF P/O MARSHALL N. F/S N'KENNA W. P/O CRIMMONS G.	SGT RAMSEY B. �38 SGT. PEARN. E SGT. WILD M.U.	OPS. DÜSSELDORF. 1 x 4000 lbs. 12 x S.B.C.
"	24.	"	R 4366	SELF.	CREW P/O GREY.	AIRCRAFT TEST CONSUMPTION TEST (OIL

GRAND TOTAL [Cols. (1) to (10)]

948 Hrs. 40 Mins.

TOTALS CARRIED FORWAR

Chapter 6

No. 12 Squadron

After the briefest and most pointless of postings to 150 Squadron at Snaith, on 29 October Jo Lancaster found himself en route by train to join 12 Squadron at Wickenby, some 7 miles north-west of Lincoln. He remembers the day vividly:

> I arrived at Snelland, which was the local station, about a mile
> and a half from the airfield, on one late October evening. It was
> overcast, rather dark, drizzly and misty and I was pointed up a
> lane for directions to the airfield. Up I trudged in this mist and
> eventually became aware of the dark outline of the odd Wellington
> and realised I was on the perimeter track: so much for security. I
> walked around the perimeter track and eventually found my way to
> the officers' mess, which was completely deserted. There was no mess
> secretary anywhere so I went in the anteroom, sat down and made
> myself comfortable. Eventually in walked a Wing Commander, who
> introduced himself in a New Zealand accent as Wing Commander
> Dabinett. I introduced myself and he walked over to the fireplace,
> turned his back to the fire, squatted down and let out a right
> uproarious fart. That was my introduction to the Commanding
> Officer of 12 Squadron (and Station Commander, Wickenby)
> universally known as 'Dabs'.

No. 12 Squadron had been formed in 1915 as a corps reconnaissance squadron, serving as such on the Western Front until converting to Bristol

Fighters in April 1918. Disbanded in December of that year, it was re-formed in 1923 as a day bomber squadron equipped successively with the DH9a, Fairey Fawn, Fairey Fox, Hawker Hart and Hind and, at the outbreak of war, the Fairey Battle. Flying the latter as part of the Advance Air Striking Force in France, it was all but wiped out in attempting to stem the German blitzkreig of May–June 1940 before the survivors were withdrawn to England to re-equip, in August 1940, with the Merlin-engined Wellington II. In August 1942, re-equipment with the Hercules-engined Wellington III had begun, but when Jo arrived at Wickenby the squadron was still operating a mix of the two. Nor was the conversion to the Wellington III to be completed, since it had already been decided that 12 Squadron would convert to the Avro Lancaster.

Jo had had a brief acquaintance with the Wellington III at Snaith and found it a delight after the IC. It introduced a number of improvements, based on operational experience with the earlier marks, including a more efficient de-icing system on the wings, and windscreen wipers. It also had a four-gun rear turret fitted, although still equipped with the .303 Browning machine gun. What most distinguished the Mark III, however, were the two 1,495hp Bristol Hercules XI engines, which provided almost 50% more power than the Pegasus engines of the Wellington IC, and some 40% more than the Rolls-Royce Merlin Xs of the Wellington II. But, crucially, the Mark III was fitted with featherable de Havilland hydromatic propellers, giving the pilot confidence that in the event of an engine failure, height could be maintained on the remaining engine.

Wickenby was a recently built RAF station, having only opened in September 1942 as a satellite of Binbrook when 12 Squadron – which had been based at the latter since July 1940 – moved there to allow Binbrook to be provided with concrete runways. The airfield followed the standard Bomber Command layout, having three concrete runways and a perimeter track with thirty-six aircraft dispersals around it. The administrative and domestic buildings were mostly Nissen huts. Jo remembers them well:

All the station buildings of course were temporary structures; we slept in Nissen huts, the officers four to a hut, with a pretty ineffective stove standing in the middle. The huts consisted of two shells of

corrugated iron and mice used to get in between them. You could
hear them scampering around inside and you could lean out of the
bed and thump the side: there'd be silence for a minute or so and off
they'd go again.

The toilet facilities were pretty primitive there. Outside each group
of huts was a bathhouse, which was very cold, bleak and damp.
Usually there was no hot water and the toilet facilities were pretty
gruesome too. The batman, one between two of us, used to bring us
a tin of warm water in the morning and we'd have a tin wash stand
each and that was the only way we managed to do our toilet, scrub
our teeth and so on. It was fairly primitive and I don't know whether
we were very hygienic all the time.

The messes were of single course brick with asbestos roofs over
steel trusses. On the occasion when we weren't flying but aircraft were
going on ops the regular thing was they would climb up overhead
and time themselves to pass over Sheringham on the Norfolk coast
at a given height at a given time. The result was that the sky of
Lincolnshire was full of Lancs climbing up and the Nissen huts used
to literally buzz with vibration.

On arrival at Wickenby, Jo found himself allocated to B Flight, under
Squadron Leader E.I.J. 'Dinger' Bell, taking over a Wellington crew from
the former flight commander, Squadron Leader D.D. Haig, who had been
posted sick with sinus problems. The navigator was Flight Sergeant R.A.
Marshall, known from his initials as 'Ram'. 'He was', Jo says, 'an ex-Warder
from Exeter prison and he looked like it. He always carried a .38 revolv-
er with him on operations.' The wireless operator, Flight Sergeant P.H.
'Paddy' McKenna, was an Irishman from Dublin, and had joined the RAF
pre-war. The rear gunner was Sergeant S.C. Marsh, while according to
the 12 Squadron ORB, Squadron Leader Haig's bomb aimer – who also
occupied the front turret as required – was a Canadian butcher from
Guelph, Ontario, Flight Sergeant Bill Crimmins. In fact the latter was an
air gunner, and it seems likely that while Crimmins did indeed man the
front turret as required, the bomb aiming would have been done by 'Ram'
Marshall, who had trained as an observer, combining the roles of bomb
aimer and navigator. When Jo took over the crew, however, Bill Crimmins

was on commissioning leave and for the first of the three operations flown with a Wellington crew of five, Jo had a stand-in bomb aimer, Sergeant Alexander. His place was then taken by Sergeant J.E. Ramsey, who would remain with the crew until the end of Jo's tour in early April 1943, Crimmins replacing Sergeant Marsh when the Lancaster crew was assembled.

After one or two flights during which he and his crew became accustomed to each other, Jo found himself and them detailed to operate for the first time on 3 November, when four crews, including one from A Flight flying a Wellington II, were allotted to carry out 'gardening' (i.e. mine-laying) in Quiberon Bay, Brittany, near the islands of Houat and Hoëdic in the approaches to Saint-Nazaire. The flight path lay over the Breton peninsula, and Jo elected to cross it at low level. 'It was a dark night,' he says, 'but you could see the ground fairly well. I remember distinctly seeing a chap on the ground with some sort of hurricane lamp and he swung it round in a circle as we flashed past.' The dropping zone was located by a timed run from Belle Isle further offshore, and the two 1,500lb mines were laid accurately by Sergeant Alexander without opposition. The trip took just under five hours, and on return they and the other three crews operating were diverted to Chivenor because Wickenby was fogbound.

On the 7th they were again on the Battle Order for mining, this time as one of five crews detailed to lay mines off the Frisian island of Terschelling in the approaches to Emden. In hazy conditions the mines were again laid accurately, and without opposition, this time by Sergeant Ramsey, who was to be Jo's regular bomb aimer henceforth.

Two nights later Jo and his crew flew their final Wellington operation, which was also the last by the squadron, save for three individual mine-laying sorties by A Flight crews in Wellington IIs. The target was Hamburg, and 12 Squadron's nine aircrews were part of a force of 213 bombers, predominantly Wellingtons, but also including Stirlings, Halifaxes and Lancasters. The weather was very bad, crews reporting ten-tenths cloud and icing, and the eight 12 Squadron crews that bombed all did so on ETA. An inaccurate wind forecast, however, played havoc with navigation, and many bomb loads fell into open country or the River Elbe. Several fires were started, three of them major, but the fifteen aircraft that failed to return – representing a loss rate of 7% – were a heavy price to pay for small success. On arrival back the now Flying Officer Lancaster and his crew could only report '10/10ths cloud bad vis. Bombed target ETA. Location unknown.' Two crews landed away from base, Jo's at Coltishall after making landfall on the north Norfolk coast in poor weather.

With B Flight stood down from operations, the lengthy process of conversion to the Lancaster began, the first aircraft being flown in by Air Transport Auxiliary pilots on 8 November, with all the Wellington IIIs on charge being flown to Blyton on the 10th, to equip 199 Squadron, formed just two days earlier. Two dual-control Lancasters and instructors were due on the 12th, but bad weather forced a postponement. Two aircraft on loan from No. 1656 Conversion Unit, with their instructors – Flying Officer Graham and Flight Sergeant Fahey from 460 Squadron – arrived on the 13th, when, the ORB tells us, 'Lectures on the new aircraft were commenced for aircrew.' The next day ten air gunners were posted in from No. 2 Air Gunnery School, Dalcross, 'for mid upper gunner duties with Lancaster aircraft', with ten flight engineers turning up two days later, and fourteen more air gunners on 21 November. By this time A Flight had also been stood down from operations, and on 20 November two more pilot instructors had arrived, the ORB noting that 'Flying Officer Southgate and Flying Officer Crossley were attached to the Squadron from 103 Squadron for flying instructor duties on Lancaster aircraft for the conversion of A Flight to these aircraft.'

While this was going on, however, six complete Wellington crews were being posted to 199 Squadron, being, as the ORB puts it, 'surplus to the requirements of the squadron'. Since all were recent arrivals, it seems they were selected on account of their relative inexperience, operationally. In their place, sent from 199 Squadron – so the 12 Squadron ORB claims – were four crews captained by pilots beginning their second (and in one case third) tour. Their exodus from 199 Squadron (where they can only have been posted nominally, since they had never actually arrived and were not mentioned in the newly formed squadron's ORB) left Squadron Leader Blomfield – who was posted from 12 Squadron to command the new unit – very short of experienced crews, and 12 Squadron with a strong core of second-tour captains.

Flight Lieutenant David Villiers was one of the four highly experienced pilots who joined 12 Squadron on 7 November. The others were Flying

Officer Ken Stammers, inevitably nicknamed 'Kay' on account of the glamorous tennis star of the 1930s, Pilot Officer R.K. 'Ray' Kitney and Pilot Officer R.F. 'Bob' Noden. Jo particularly recollects his first meeting with the last-named:

> I remember him presenting himself for the first time in the B Flight office in a brand-spanking-new greatcoat and service hat with the stiffener still in, a little military moustache, looking a little older than the general run; I thought what a sprog he looked. But when he took his greatcoat off he had a DFM and later on we discovered that he was really on his third tour because he had done one tour in 3 Group and then was pushed off out to the Middle East with 37 Squadron, where he had completed a second tour. After that, if my memory serves me right, he spent some time instructing Turkish pilots. It was generally assumed that the posting to 12 Squadron had been some kind of administrative error, but Bob didn't complain. Anyway he succeeded in doing a very good third tour and when he'd finished we persuaded him to climb up in the rafters in the officers' mess and inscribe the ceiling with 'third tour Noden'. Lots of things were inscribed up there.

For Jo the process of conversion to the Lancaster began on 15 November, when he was taken up for a 2¼-hour familiarisation and dual flight by Flying Officer Graham. This was followed up by a 20-minute check-out the following day, evidently successful, since the same day he flew his first solo, lasting 3 hours. His first flight with his full crew took place on 21 November, when they spent 2 hours 20 minutes' local flying, and the next day they carried a 2½-hour cross-country flight employing Gee. Night-flying training began on the 23rd, and Jo's first night solo was on the 27th, when his full crew flew with him.

The Wellington had a crew of five, the Lancaster seven, and so the Wellington crew of Lancaster, Marshall, McKenna, Ramsay and Crimmins was expanded by the addition of a flight engineer, Sergeant Harry 'Tich' Pearn, and a mid-upper gunner, Sergeant P. Wild, inevitably nicknamed 'Jimmy' after Jimmy Wilde, the celebrated Welsh boxer who became the first world champion in the flyweight division. The airmen quickly became, Jo says, an efficient unit, with high morale and complete confidence in each other and their 'skipper', but never the tight-knit group off-duty that his 40 Squadron crew had been. In part this was because neither Ram Marshall nor Paddy McKenna were what Jo terms 'party animals', and in part also because Jo was an officer, promoted on 20 December to flight lieutenant rank. Another factor was the sense of cohesion in the officers' mess created by the several enjoyable mess parties held during the nearly two months of conversion to Lancasters. A key element in the success of these mess parties was the CO. Jo comments:

> Dabs was a New Zealander; he'd joined the RAF pre-war and somewhere along the line he put up a bit of a black officially by becoming involved with a ranker WAAF named Connie. However, they eventually got married and she was demobbed. He had her installed at Wickenby. Dabs was really quite a lively chap. He was of an age rather past operational flying, and while I was at Wickenby he didn't do any flying on his own account but did do the odd operation as second pilot even though he wasn't supposed to.
>
> Although he didn't lead from the front Dabs was still well respected and well liked. He had a large American car and every so often he would invite a few of us to leap into it, and off we'd go to Grimsby or somewhere else, and have a nice evening out. I remember one occasion when he went on ops with Pilot Officer Dougie Hagerman. I was not flying; I was in the mess anteroom with two WAAF officers and we had the radio tuned into, I think, 31 metres where we could get the aircraft radio traffic such as it was. We heard Hagerman call up, joining the circuit, and they were told to circle at something like two thousand feet. This instruction was followed by a New Zealand voice saying 'Well, f*** me sideways.' He was quite unmistakable.

'Dabs' Dabinett was definitely a 'party animal', with one of the most popular pastimes in the mess a particular favourite of his: Lie Dice. Jo explains:

> Lie Dice was played with a set of 5 poker dice and a suitable cup or similar, under which it was possible to keep them hidden. A player would shake them in the cup and then throw them, but keeping them hidden from the other players. He would then peep at what he had

thrown and pass them on, hidden, declaring, say, 'two pairs'. The next player could either accept this, in which case he could re-throw and declare a higher set, or disbelieve and expose the dice. If the two pairs were there, he lost, and if not, the previous player lost. At Wickenby we each started with 6 'lives' (matches), and whenever a player had lost all six, he bought a round of half-pints and started with 6 again. They would have big schools of this. The bar was run by a Corporal and the poor chap was kept up to all hours of the night and morning during these sessions.

Alongside the mess parties, however, went a great deal of hard work, since for the seven-man crews there was much to learn about the Lancaster aircraft. The mid-upper gunners, for instance, attended lectures on the Frazer-Nash F.N.50 turret, while the wireless operators were inducted into the intricacies of two electronic countermeasures, 'Tinsel' and 'Mandrel'. The first involved a microphone placed in a bomber's engine bay record-ing the deafening engine roar for transmission by the wireless operator on to German ground-to-air frequencies, making communication between night fighters and their controllers impossible. The second, 'Mandrel', had the capacity to jam the German long-range radar called Freya. Wireless operators also needed to be au fait with the R1355 radio receiver for Gee, the navigational aid that had come into use earlier in 1942, and navigators with the Type 62 Indicator Unit, which displayed the readings from the Gee transmitter stations. Finally, there was, for all crews, the tedious but potentially life-saving dinghy drill.

In late November and early December bad weather significantly cur-tailed conversion. Even so the first air-to-air firing began on 7 December, and the first bombing practice the following day. Cross-country flights of up to 9 hours followed, and bullseyes, a particularly busy day being 23 December, when the ORB recorded: 'Night flying training was arranged and carried out, consisting of the following exercises: 3 cross country trips, 2 cross country and Infra Red practices combined, 2 cross coun-try and practice bombing sorties combined, and 1 practice bombing and photography sortie.' 'Infra Red practices' involved making a bombing run, using only a camera, over a target at which was installed an infra-red light, visible only to the camera. From the film, the degree of accuracy could be determined. It was usually conducted in conjunction with a cross-country or bullseye exercise.

One feature of the conversion process that the ORB does not mention, but which Jo remembers vividly, is the low-level formation practice carried out on four occasions between 10 December and the end of the month. To him, and to others, this seemed ominous, suggesting that Bomber Command had in mind a repeat of the raid of 17 April 1942, in which twelve Lancasters drawn from 44 and 97 Squadrons had made a low-level daylight attack on the MAN diesel engine factory at Augsburg, deep in southern Germany. Seven of the twelve Lancasters were lost and the rest returned more or less damaged. Fortunately, if Bomber Command HQ had a repeat in mind, it never eventuated.

Another vivid memory is of an occasion when Jo and his flight engineer, Tich Pearn, were carrying out a flight test and he feathered three engines and flew low over Wickenby with only the port inner engine running. 'For Tich it was', says Jo, 'quite spectacular'.

During the six weeks of conversions there were several successful mess parties, as Jo recalls:

It seemed to be that as soon as there was £50 in the mess fund it was time to organise a party and it usually finished up with the fund being £50 in debt. But these parties seemed to occur about every three or four weeks and were jolly good dos. My B flight commander, 'Dinger' Bell, was usually the MC and generally it started with all the assembled company sitting cross-legged in lines facing each other. Each would be presented with a half a pint of beer and there'd be a relay race, as one drank it and banged his glass down the next one started. Of course, we would have one of these relays and then someone would declare a false start or some other foul and there would have to be a re-run. By the time that was over, the party was getting under way nicely. In the early days there the Officers' Mess didn't have a piano. The Sergeants' Mess had one provided from official sources through the PSI, the Public Services Institute, but the officers were supposed to buy their own. On one occasion we should have all been court martialled as a gang of drunken officers dashed into the holy of holies, the Sergeants' Mess, grabbed the piano,

pushed it out the door, up the slope, down the road, and down into
the Officers' Mess. Fortunately soon after that we managed to get a
piano from somewhere, though Bill was about the only chap who
could play it.

'Bill' was Pilot Officer W.A. Allinson, navigator in Squadron Leader David
Villiers's crew, who was in great demand as a pianist not only in the mess
but also in the local pub, the White Hart at Lissington. Jo remembers: 'On
the piano in the pub was a name plate, the maker probably Weber, with
the name Berlin. With the landlord's permission this was unscrewed from
the piano and screwed onto the side of David Villiers' 'V Victor', where it
paid several return visits to Berlin. When they finished their tour David
and Bill took it off the aircraft and put it back on the piano.'

It was intended that 12 Squadron should be fully operational by New
Year's Day 1943, but in fact it was ready to operate almost a week earlier,
the ORB noting on 27 December that 'The squadron was now ready for
operations with 24 crews converted to Lancaster aircraft, and operations
were scheduled to begin on 28th December.' The next day sixteen aircraft were prepared, but bad weather necessitated a cancellation, as it did
the following day, when six aircraft were preparing for gardening sorties. With the weather continuing to frustrate attempts to carry out a first
Lancaster operation, the squadron was stood down, and it was not until
2 January that another weather-frustrated attempt was made. Thus it was
3 January when the first Lancaster operation was carried out, with ten
Lancasters despatched to lay mines off La Rochelle. All returned safely.
Jo and his crew were not detailed for that operation, which was carried
out in good visibility without opposition, but were on the Battle Order
for the second Lancaster raid, to Essen on the 4th. Just four 12 Squadron
crews were assigned, part of a small Bomber Command force of Lancasters, together with Mosquitoes of the Pathfinder Force, whose role was to
employ a new blind-bombing device called Oboe. The device, which was
installed in an aircraft but controlled from ground stations in England,
enabled an aircraft to maintain an accurate course, and also allowed the
ground stations to signal the moment when its bombs should be released.
The system had limitations, the greatest of which was that it was a line-

John Oliver Lancaster in an obligatory sailor suit photo, circa 1924.
(All pictures are courtesy of Jo Lancaster unless otherwise indicated.)

Jo, astride Tinkerbell, with his cousin Joan and her dog Ranter, Cumberland 1929.

Apprentices Jo Lancaster and Eric Kelsey on Jo's Scott motorcycle, Coventry, 1937.

Apprentice, Armstrong Whitworth, New Year's Day 1939.

Sergeant Jim Taylor and crew, Alconbury, May 1941. Left to right, Glen Leitch, Jo, Keith Coleman, Bill Harris, Jack Crowther, Jim Taylor.

Wellington IC T2701 'S', Alconbury.

On approach to Alconbury, summer 1941.

En route to Brest, 24 July 1941. Sergeant Morris leads in 'C', with, on his right, Sergeant Bagnall in 'R'.

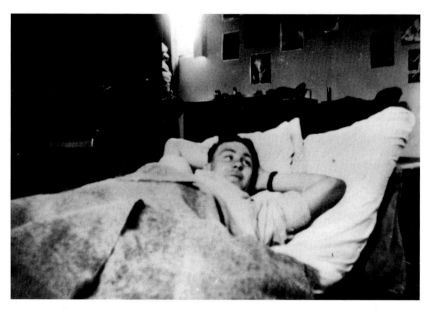

Pilot Officer Jack Field, RNZAF, Officers' Quarters, Upton House, Summer 1941.

Newly commissioned Pilot Officer Lancaster, Alconbury, August 1941.

Flight Lieutenant Lancaster, tour expired, Wickenby, April 1943.

Jo astride a 4000 lb 'Cookie' with regular Lancaster W4791 'W', Wickenby.

Flight Lieutenant Lancaster and crew in front of W4791: Wickenby. Left to right, Sergeant 'Ram' Ramsey (front gunner/bomb aimer), Sergeant 'Jimmy' Wilde (mid-upper gunner), Flying Officer 'Griff' Griffiths (navigator), Flight Lieutenant Jo Lancaster (pilot), Sergeant Harry 'Tich' Pearn (flight engineer), Flying Officer Gordon Fisher RCAF (Wop), Flying Officer Bill Hill (rear gunner). The paint damage on the fuselage was caused by leakage of windscreen de-icing fluid, possibly as a result of overfilling.

The paint damage on the fuselage was caused by leakage of windscreen de-icing fluid, possibly as a result of overfilling.

Overload trials of the SRA1, Cowes, 1948. Jo Lancaster at the controls.

Armstrong Whitworth AW 52 Flying Wing. *(IWM ATP 16936B)*

Jo disembarking from Armstrong Whitworth's DH891 Rapide G-AEML communications aircraft.

Jo Lancaster in the cockpit of a Meteor, Baginton.

Test Pilot Team, Baginton, 1956, with the last production Meteor NF14. Left to right, Eric Franklin, Bill Else, Jim McCowan (rear), Jo Lancaster, Martin Walton.

Jo welcomed at Birmingham airport on return from tropical trials in the Argosy, 4 November 1959: left to right, unknown, Jo, E.D. Keen (Chief Designer) and H.M. Woodhams (Managing Director).

Jo and Honor Frost, noted underwater archaeologist, Tartus, Syria, 1963.

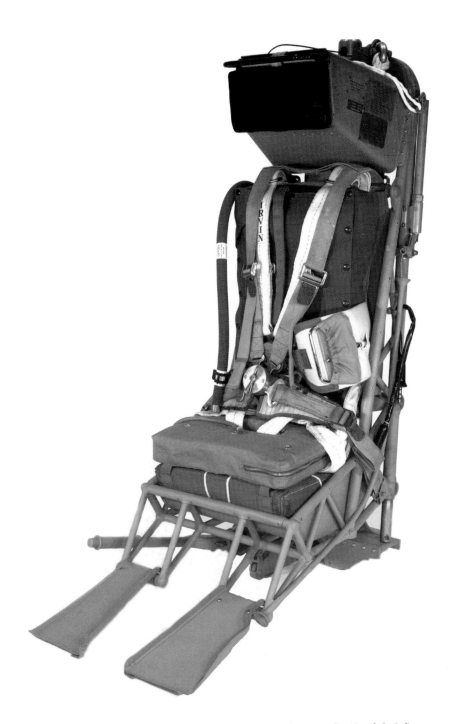

A Martin-Baker Mk 1 ejection seat. *(Photograph courtesy of Martin-Baker Aircraft Co. Ltd)*

Jo Lancaster at the unveiling of the International Bomber Command Centre spire, overlooking Lincoln cathedral, on 2 October 2015. *(Fighting High)*

of-sight device, the signals not able to be bent round the curvature of the earth. Using Mosquitoes, however, with a service ceiling of 30,000 feet, far in excess of any other Bomber Command type, the entire Ruhr industrial area could be covered.

The first of a series of three Oboe-guided attacks on Essen had taken place on the night of 3 January, three out of nineteen Lancasters from 5 Group being lost. The next night, when 12 Squadron participated, another small force of four Mosquitoes and twenty-nine Lancasters was deployed, two Lancasters going down. Reports from Essen indicated that the bombing on the Pathfinders' sky markers was concentrated, but the part the four 12 Squadron crews played was small, since two of the four had to turn back. One was W4791, 'W', captained by Flight Lieutenant Lancaster, which the ORB reports 'Abandoned due to W/OP's sickness and fractured pipe line in rear turret.' Jo elaborates: 'We ourselves turned back because Bill Crimmins's turret went unserviceable and worse Paddy McKenna, who sat on his oxygen pipe, passed out cold. We'd climbed to 22,000 feet as briefed and Ram thought that Paddy was on the point of death, which he might well have been, since the problem was certainly a shortage of oxygen.' Curiously, the other Lancaster crew that turned back, captained by Jo's good friend, 'Kay' Stammers, did so, the ORB tells us, because of 'mental confusion caused by suspected lack of oxygen'. Stammers's crew dropped its cookie on a searchlight concentration, while Jo's jettisoned its bomb load over the North Sea.

The squadron's next operation, and Jo's, was on 8 January, when eight crews were despatched to carry out some gardening off the Norwegian coast. The results were mixed. One crew, captained by Canadian Sergeant D.C. Marshall, failed to return – the first Lancaster loss – while of the remaining seven one abandoned the operation when a generator failed while still in circuit before setting course, and two others brought their mines back, foiled by low cloud and severe icing. Jo and his crew, however, reported 'No low cloud, visibility good', with the mines dropped as detailed. He remembers the minelaying well, and also what happened later, after landing:

It was mine laying again and we went way up to Haugesund Fiord, north of Stavanger, in Norway. I should explain perhaps that these

mines were on parachute drogues and you aimed to release them
from 400 feet and at 160 miles per hour. So we flew up the fiord,
which ran parallel with the coast and was open at each end, and
search lights and light flak came up. All three gunners were very quick
off the mark, however, and firing back at the search lights, which were
quickly doused. We were supposed to divert on return to Dyce, just
north of Aberdeen, but in the event I elected to land at Lossiemouth,
where I could approach from the sea. We duly arrived there safe and
sound and of course they had to find accommodation for us all. I
was put up in the padre's room, he apparently being on leave, and the
sleeping accommodation was in long wooden huts with felted roofs,
and with little cubicles on each side of a central passage-way. Each
cubicle had a little cast iron stove with a chimney going up through
the roof. In my room I found paper, firewood and coal, so I decided
to light the stove, it being a pretty cold night with no other form of
heating. I got into bed and went to sleep but was woken up shortly
thereafter by a roaring noise. The stove and flue pipe were glowing
red hot and I had to vacate the room until it had cooled down.

For some reason, Jo and his crew were not detailed to operate again for a
fortnight. Why is unclear, since despite bad weather – which led to operations being scheduled and then cancelled – the squadron participated
in five small-scale raids on Essen, as experiments with Oboe-carrying
Mosquitoes continued, losing two crews in the process. They also raided
Berlin twice. To the first of these raids, on the night of 16 January, 12
Squadron contributed 16 of the 190 Lancasters participating, all returning
safely even though four had to turn back with a variety of aircraft defects.
The raid was the first on Berlin for 14 months, and represented something of an experiment, in that it saw the first use by the Pathfinder Force
of specialist target indicators. Nonetheless, it was a failure, for reasons
that Middlebrook and Everitt neatly summarise: 'Berlin was well beyond
the range of Gee and Oboe, and H2S radar was not yet ready. Thick cloud
which was encountered on the way to target hindered navigation and
Berlin was found to be covered by haze.'[1] As a consequence bombing
was scattered, most of the 12 Squadron crews that bombed doing so on
ETA, and although there was one spectacular, if accidental, success in the

destruction by fire of the 10,000-seat Deutschlandhalle arena, little else was achieved.

The next night, when Berlin was revisited, the outcome was again disappointing, with the weather better, but the Pathfinders once more unable to mark the city centre accurately, the bombing as a consequence being dispersed and the damage inflicted minor. Whereas on the 16th Bomber Command had lost only one Lancaster on the second raid, however, 22 aircraft were lost, 19 of them Lancasters, representing 11.8% of the 187-strong force. Of those 4 were from 12 Squadron, the ORB noting that it was 'a most unlucky operation for the Squadron, and four good crews . . . were all reported missing'. All were captained by dominion pilots, two RCAF, one RAAF and one RNZAF, and of the 28 aircrew only 7, all from one crew, survived to become prisoners of war. From Middlebrook and Everitt's *The Bomber Command War Diaries* it is clear that the reason for the heavy loss was that to and from Berlin the bombers followed the same routes as the previous night. The German night fighters were thus able to find the bomber stream early and exact a heavy toll.

On 23 January Flight Lieutenant Lancaster and crew, including the recently commissioned 'Ram' Marshall, were detailed, along with six others, to join an attack on Düsseldorf. The target was bombed through ten-tenths cloud, three Pathfinder Mosquitoes having employed the 'Wanganui' target marking system, where parachute flares illuminated the Oboe-determined target over the cloud, obscuring it. The results were disappointing as little damage was done by the eighty-strong force of Lancasters and a 12 Squadron aircrew was one of the two lost. All Jo and his crew could report on return was '10/10 cloud. Bombed on P.F.F. flares. Bursts not seen. Location uncertain. Moderate to heavy intense flak. Very haphazard.' Four nights later, Düsseldorf was again raided but this time the 'Newhaven' system of target marking was employed, with flares set to burst and cascade just above the ground. The result was far more accurate target marking, and well-concentrated bombing causing major damage. Jo and his airmen were not among the seven detailed for this raid, of which four abandoned the operation through a variety of instrument or engine failures.

On 30 January the target was Hamburg, and 12 Squadron contributed six crews to the 148-strong force, predominantly of Lancasters, which were

guided on to the target for the first time by Pathfinder Stirlings and Halifaxes using the new navigational and target-finding aid, the ground-scanning
radar H2S. Even so, bombing was scattered, and only moderate damage
was caused. Once again, 12 Squadron crews were plagued by instrument
failure, Jo's being one of two forced to turn back with unserviceable air
speed indicators. He comments:

> In our very early Lanc ops, starting in January '43, the idea was to
> climb to 20,000 feet or so, but when reaching very low temperature
> levels there were quite a few instances of the ASI gradually dropping
> off to zero. I had one case myself. This was due to ice forming in the
> pitot tube system, and fairly quickly it was cured by re-routing the
> pipe-work. It was deemed advisable to abort if this happened, to
> minimize the chance of still having no ASI for the landing back.

Three nights later, on 2 February, in an attack on Cologne, a further experiment was made, with Pathfinder target marking both by Oboe-equipped
Mosquitoes and by Stirlings and Halifaxes using H2S. On a cloudy night
results were again discouraging, with bombing scattered. No. 12 Squadron contributed seven crews, Jo's among them, but two had to abort, one
when a starboard engine cut, and the other when the navigator was found
unconscious because of oxygen failure. The debriefing comments of the
crew of W4791 were akin to those of the other 12 Squadron crews who
had bombed: 'Load 1 x 4000, 6 SBCs Ex Incd. 9/10 thin cloud much haze.
Bombed marker bombs and flares. No results observed. S/Ls active and
accurate. Heavy flak.' Unremarkable in terms of its outcome, the sortie was
significant, however, in that it was the last of Bill Crimmins's tour. On
4 February the ORB notes that 'P/O W D Crimmins was posted to No. 1656
Conversion Unit on completion of operational tour.' From there in October, he would be posted as gunnery leader to 625 Squadron at Kelstern on
its formation, only to be killed, as Flight Lieutenant Crimmins, DFC, on
16 December, when his Lancaster was shot down during a raid on Berlin,
only one member of the crew surviving. His replacement in Jo's team was
another officer gunner, Pilot Officer W.J. 'Bill' Hill, who was posted in the
day Bill Crimmins departed, and would be Jo's regular rear gunner until
the latter was tour-expired.

Jo's crew was not one of the six who took part in a heavy and highly successful raid on Turin on 4 February, all returning safely, but was one of eight detailed for a raid on Lorient on the 7th. There had been many raids on the port in Brittany, Admiral Karl Dönitz's U-boat base, but attempts to smash the massive concrete U-boat pens that had been constructed having proved fruitless, the decision was made to lay waste to the town that provided the infrastructure for U-boat operations. An all-incendiary attack on the port had been made on the night of 4 February by a 128-strong force, and huge fires started. On the 7th a force more that twice the size, and with Pathfinder marking, took to the skies. No. 12 Squadron contributed 7 aircraft to the 323-strong force, 80 of which were Lancasters. It was a clear night and the mission was a textbook success, resulting in the devastation of the town that the compiler of the 12 Squadron ORB inventively named 'L'Orient'. Jo's crew reported laconically, 'No cloud, slight haze. Bombed P.F.F. Marker bombs. Bursts seen. No results observed. Flak fairly light. S/Ls ineffective', but other crews documented 'extensive large fires' and described the town as 'well ablaze'. Seven bombers were lost, none of them from 12 Squadron.

Lorient was the last operation of Ram Marshall's tour. Posted early in March to No. 28 Operational Training Unit at Wymeswold, to instruct, he later flew a second tour of operations with 51 Squadron, ending the war as Flight Lieutenant R.A. Marshall, DFC. Many years later Jo caught up with him in Exmouth, to find that Ram's life post-war had been in many ways a sad one. The young woman he had hoped to wed had changed her mind, and although he married happily not long after, his wife died of cancer a year later. He never remarried. He also had a leg amputated after suffering a severe embolism later in life, and became something of a recluse.

Ram's replacement was an Australian, Flight Sergeant F.J. 'Sammy' Samuel, whom Jo describes as 'a rare type – a very quiet and reserved Aussie'. He navigated flawlessly on eleven ops, latterly as Pilot Officer Samuel after his commissioning on 4 March.

The Lorient raid was also the first on which Jo and his crew were accompanied by a second pilot, in this case Sergeant L.W. Overton. Comparing his first tour, where newcomers flew an average of seven ops before captaining their own crew, Jo comments:

On 12, I carried eight different pilots, and only one of these twice. It
was only when the 'Battle Order' was promulgated, usually just before
briefing, that you would learn that a supernumerary pilot had been
allocated to your crew, for this particular op. They were really just
onlookers during the flight, usually placed in the astrodome out of
the way, but I did talk to them and try to prepare them as much as
I could. I don't know how many 2nd pilot ops they would normally
do. Certainly not very many, and at one stage a decree was issued
that they would be thrown in straight away, into the deep end. This
made it imperative that they were first briefed as much as possible,
and when I suddenly finished my ops, I was given this job, sometimes
getting airborne to demonstrate evasive action, etc. In spite of this,
the morale of new crews hit rock bottom; fortunately this extreme
folly was discontinued.

Sergeant Overton was in fact from 100 Squadron, which had re-formed
in December 1942 at RAF Waltham, just outside Grimsby, after having
been wiped out in Malaya and Java, flying antiquated Vildebeest torpedo
bombers against the invading Japanese. Few of the re-formed squadron
had operational experience and fewer still such experience in the Lancaster,
so during February and early March the most seasoned crews in 12 Squadron were given a succession of 100 Squadron pilots to introduce to ops on
the Lancaster. Jo himself took five on operations, the last, Sergeant R.N.
Peake, on 8 March to Nuremberg. Thereafter, beginning on 12 March, he
had second pilots on three occasions, but all of them from 12 Squadron,
and recent arrivals.

After Lorient, 12 Squadron did not operate until 11 February, when
Flight Lieutenant Lancaster and crew were one of eleven detailed to operate against Wilhelmshaven, the major Kriegsmarine base on the German
North Sea coast. In what Middlebrook and Everitt describe as 'an interesting and important raid',[2] the Pathfinders were to employ the least reliable
of target indicators, 'Wanganui' sky marking, basing this on the new H2S
ground-scanning radar. In the event the marking was accurate, and as
a consequence the main force bombing, through thick cloud cover, was
concentrated and destructive. Only 3 of the 177 aircraft – the majority of
them Lancasters – despatched were lost, none of them from 12 Squadron.

At debriefing, Jo's crew was one of four to report a 'red glow' through the clouds. This was caused by bombs blowing up the naval ammunition depot at Mariensel, to the south of Wilhelmshaven. The explosion devastated nearly 120 acres and caused widespread damage in the naval dockyard and town.

On 13 February 12 Squadron returned to Lorient, with 12 crews part of a force of 466 bombers, the largest to attack the town during the war. The weather was good, the bombing accurate, and losses light at 1.7%. Two Lancasters went down and one of those from 12 Squadron, occurring on its return, when in circuit and preparing to land – at 22.45 Pilot Officer James Martin's Lancaster crashed at Newball outside Lincoln, killing all aboard. The cause of the accident was determined to have been a stall that occurred during the lowering of the undercarriage. It was the crew's second operation.

On 14 February came a very different target: Milan. Ten crews were detailed, all highly experienced, as part of a 142-strong all-Lancaster force. Bomber Command's take on the raid was that the bombing was concentrated in good visibility on the Pathfinder flares, and that on the return flight fires could be seen from 100 miles away. Rome's spin on the raid was somewhat different, the *Wanganui Chronicle* in New Zealand publishing – tongue in cheek – a brief Italian report, issued on the day of the raid, which stated: 'Enemy aircraft bombed Milan, but were subjected to a hot fire from anti-aircraft guns. Squadrons of Italian aeroplanes counterattacked, and the enemy fled. Six civilians were killed and some injured. The other material damage is slight.' Two Lancasters were lost, while another was severely damaged by a night fighter but returned to base. The flak was reported as fairly heavy but the many searchlights as ineffective. No. 12 Squadron had no losses, and returning crews reported large fires in the centre of the city. One crew, having reached the target, found the bomb doors would not open, and had to bring back its load of a 2,000lb GP bomb and incendiaries. For Jo and his crew, however, frustration came sooner, for while preparing to take off he realised that the artificial horizon was very sluggish to erect. He therefore called for a check, which meant that W4366, 'R' was 25 minutes late taking off. Still not confident about the instrument, and uneasy about a long flight relying only on the bank and turn indicator, he was easily persuaded to abandon the mission when 'Sammy' Samuel expressed his concern about their being so late. They therefore turned back, landing after some 90 minutes in the air.

Two nights later 12 Squadron returned to 'L'Orient', ten crews operating. Two turned back, one with equipment malfunction and the other when a navigation error put them so far off course that it was not feasible to continue. The other aircrews reported accurate bombing in good conditions, and the raid, the last major one on Lorient, by 377 aircraft, left the town an almost deserted ruin. Pathfinder flare marking was provided, but in W4366 again, Flight Lieutenant Lancaster and his aircrew bombed the aiming point visually, comfirming the accuracy of this with a Gee fix at bombing. Other crews reported the flak heavy and accurate, but Jo and his team made no mention of this, simply recording: 'Explosion observed when leaving target area. Fires seemed scattered.'

On the 18th it was back to Wilhelmshaven, with seven crews part of a force of 338 aircraft, with Wellingtons and Halifaxes predominating. The raid was carried out in good conditions, with Pathfinder marking, but the latter was inaccurate, and as a consequence most of the main force bombing fell in open country west of the town. The 12 Squadron crews claimed on return to have identified the docks and Bauhafen, and most bombed visually rather than relying on the Pathfinder marking. Jo and his men could only report that the target was identified visually, and that the bomb bursts were seen and 'believed W of Bauhafen'. They reported, accurately enough, only 'Scattered fires in towns', and rated the light flak as 'intense', but the heavy flak as 'light'. The primary reason for the failure of the raid, which a local report stated caused only slight injuries to three people, was found to be the out-of-date maps that the Pathfinders had been issued, maps which did not show recent town developments. A general updating followed.

Up until now, Jo and his crew had operated predominantly on a mix of German and French targets, with the deepest penetration of Germany being to Hamburg and Essen. In the latter half of his tour the emphasis was to be very much on German targets, with one to Saint-Nazaire and another, the last, to La Spezia the only exceptions. Moreover, three of them were to be deep penetrations, to Nuremberg, Munich and Berlin. Jo comments:

A lot of these targets involved a long haul across Germany and frequently we'd see a good burst of fire. More often than not the target bomber would just burst into flames and go down, which was a bit upsetting. However, we were never intercepted at all. We rarely saw a fighter although over Hamburg once we had a very near collision with what appeared to be a Junkers Ju.88. He passed over the top of us only literally feet above and we heard him clearly. What I used to do was never maintain a steady course and height for more than about 30 or 40 seconds, turn to the left to 15 degrees and then resume the heading, or right 15, resume the heading, go up 500 feet. Then level off, down 500 feet, level off down another 500 feet. I kept that up all the time, trying to maintain the correct course. Of course, maintaining a steady mean height was no problem, or maintaining a steady average course, and I believe this was why we were never intercepted. 'Kay' Stammers used to do the same and he was never intercepted either. The firepower of the fighters at that time was such that if you were intercepted and they got a shot in at you there was very little chance of surviving it.

On 21 February the target was Bremen, 12 Squadron contributing 11 of the 143 Lancasters operating, all of which returned safely. Two 12 Squadron crews turned back when engines failed, the others bombing on Pathfinder sky markers. Jo's crew reported, much as others did: '10/10ths cloud. Visibility good above tops at 4,000ft. Bombed on P.F.F. flares. Burst seen and glows from fires seen through the clouds. Flak fairly heavy.' Because of the cloud no bombing photos were brought back, and nothing is known of the damage inflicted. On return the weather had deteriorated to the point when it was felt advisable to divert crews to other bases, five (including Lancaster's crew in W4366) landing at Linton-on-Ouse.

No. 12 Squadron crews participated, without loss, in heavy raids on Nuremberg and Cologne in the last week of February, and on Berlin on 1 March, but Jo's crew did not operate again until the attack on Hamburg (or 'Chopburg' as it was labelled by 12 Squadron crews) on the 3rd. It was a large strike, with 417 aircraft operating, 10 of these from Wickenby, one of them among 10 that failed to return. Crews variously reported 'good visibility' and 'slight haze' and bombed accurately on Pathfinder Force markers in the face of 'slight heavy flak'. Nonetheless, the raid was not the success it should have been, for reasons which Middlebrook and Everitt spell out:

> Visibility was clear over the target, but the Pathfinders made a mistake, possibly thinking that the H2S indications of mudbanks in the Elbe which had been uncovered by the low tides were sections of the Hamburg docks. Most of the Main Force bombing thus fell 13 miles downstream from the centre of Hamburg, around the small town of Wedel.[3]

The destruction wrought on Wedel was severe, but Middlebrook and Everitt note that 'a proportion of the bombing force did hit Hamburg', where the fire brigade had to deal with 100 fires before going to the assistance of Wedel, where nearly 70% of the houses were either damaged or destroyed. Whether Flight Lieutenant Lancaster's crew, flying as usual in W4366, R-Robert, hit Wedel or Hamburg is uncertain; what is clear from a pencilled note in Jo's logbook is: 'cookie. Photograph nearest in Gp.'

The next operation Jo and his crew flew, on 5/6 March, marked the opening of what Air Chief Marshal Sir Arthur Harris called the 'Battle of the Ruhr'. A four-month campaign that did not end until 24 July, its aim was to devastate Germany's greatest industrial complex by persistent heavy blows, using the new, and now well-tested, target-marking methods. Within range of Oboe, the whole of the Ruhr could be precisely target-marked by 109 Squadron Mosquitoes, with accurate follow-up by the heavy Pathfinder squadrons, either sky or ground marking. During this period there would, of course, be raids on other targets, since to concentrate solely on the Ruhr would invite like concentration of the Luftwaffe's night-fighter force to repel the attacks. Hence during the 'battle' 12 Squadron crews would find themselves bombing a range of German targets.

On the first night of the battle, the target Essen, 12 Squadron put up 10 of the 442 crews participating, 157 of them in Lancasters. It was a highly successful raid, with accurate Oboe marking followed up by equally precise sky marking, which rendered the haze so consistently encountered over the Ruhr no hindrance. Some 14 bombers, 3.2% of the force, were lost, but none by 12 Squadron. One crew had to turn back with a turret unserviceable, but the other nine reported accurate bombing on PFF markers although unable to observe results through the ground haze. Flight Lieutenant Hagerman's crew recounted that 'on leaving target whole area appeared to be on fire', and Jo's a 'large concentration of large red fires'. The usual combination of 4,000lb cookies and masses of incendiaries had wrought massive destruction over 160 acres, with 53 buildings within the Krupp steelworks damaged or destroyed. What the ORB did not record was, as Jo's pencilled note in his logbook tells us, that over the Dutch coast on return to base he had to shut down one engine with a glycol leak. Following this is the laconic comment, 'Good blitz'.

From Essen Bomber Command turned to Nuremberg on 8 March, despatching 355 aircraft to attack the city, which was in many respects the symbolic heart of Nazi Germany. No. 12 Squadron put up twelve crews, one of which aborted; the other eleven reported bombing on the Pathfinder flares, but also on how scattered the resultant fires were. Middlebrook and Everitt explain:

> This distant raid had to be marked by a combination of H2S and
> visual means. The Pathfinders had no moon to help them and,
> although there was no cloud, they found that haze prevented accurate
> visual identification of the target area. The result was that both
> marking and bombing spread over more than 16 miles along the
> line of the attack, with more than half of the bombs falling outside
> the city boundaries. This result would be typical of raids carried out
> beyond the range of Oboe at this period.[4]

Even so, major damage was inflicted, with both the MAN and Siemens factories hit, more than 600 buildings destroyed and 1,400 damaged. On arrival back, Squadron Leader Bell's crew reported that the searchlights 'were operating in small cones' and W4366, 'R' was in fact coned, although this is not recorded in the ORB. Jo does not recall the details of the coning, even if it is noted in his logbook, but on coning generally comments:

> As I witnessed several times, if an aircraft was coned and did nothing
> about it, within a very few seconds it would receive a very bad time,
> either from flak or a fighter. The important thing was to get out of

the lights as quickly as possible by taking the best direction for this, in a dive with as much speed and evasive action as possible. If, as was usually the case, you were over the target, you would just let the bombs go and get out. Alternatively, if circumstances allowed, you could keep them and try to sneak in again.

Since the ORB notes that the crew bombed on the Pathfinder flares, the coning presumably occurred after bombing. It and the evasive action Jo took would have been a salutary experience for Sergeant Peake, the 100 Squadron second pilot on 'R-Robert' that night.

The sortie to Nuremberg was a long one, of some 7½ hours, and Jo's (and the squadron's) next operation, on 9/10 March, was equally long, and the squadron's deepest penetration into southern Germany yet, to Munich. Jo remembers it for a long leg of more than 400 miles, starting on the French coast at Le Tréport, in the midst of which the meticulous 'Sammy' Samuel, newly commissioned as Pilot Officer J.F. Samuel, asked for a course alteration of about 3 degrees! No. 12 Squadron contributed 10 crews to the force of 264; 8 were lost, 3% of the force, but none from 12 Squadron. Returning crews reported a clear sky, accurate bombing on Pathfinder flares and big fires, including what Jo remembers as 'a sudden huge conflagration which lit up the whole sky, comparable to when the torpedo store at Wilhelmshaven was hit'. Much damage was indeed caused, not least to the BMW factory, where the aero-engine assembly shop was put out of action for six weeks. The headquarters of the local flak brigade was burned out and many military buildings destroyed. But there was damage, too, to the cathedral, churches and hospitals.

After contributing to an unsuccessful raid on Stuttgart on 11/12 March, for which the Lancaster crew was not detailed, 12 Squadron next operated against Essen the following night. As Middlebrook and Everitt note, this was 'another very successful Oboe-marked raid. The centre of the bombing area was right across the giant Krupps factory, just west of the city centre, with later bombing drifting back to the north-western outskirts. Photographic interpretation assessed that Krupps received 30 per cent more damage on this night than on the earlier successful raid of 5/6 March.'[5]

The 11 crews that were Wickenby's contribution to the 457-strong force all reported bombing successfully on Pathfinder flares, but several also noted what Warrant Officer Busby's crew described as 'Moderate to intense heavy flak predicted and co-operating with several large searchlight cones. Light flak hosepiped to approximately 15,000 ft.' Jo Lancaster and his crew, which included Sergeant N.F. Hill as second pilot, had a close encounter with the searchlights, being coned on the run-up to the aiming point. For the only time on either tour, Jo ordered the bomb load to be jettisoned, remarking: 'It was not a very pleasant experience at all. It was a gin clear night, no cloud cover at all, I just dived and dived and weaved and eventually outflew the searchlights.'

Jo and his crew were not flying their usual R-Robert that night, nor, for some reason, were they being guided to the target by the excellent 'Sammy' Samuel. In his place was an RCAF navigator, Flying Officer M.L. Abramson, who had been posted to 12 Squadron from No. 1656 Conversion Unit just four days earlier. Jo comments:

> Abramson made a complete cobblers of the op to Essen on 12th March, but fortunately, without a cloud in the night sky and PFF markers leading to the target, I was able to just quietly dispense with his services and navigate visually. Abramson just disappeared the next day. I felt a bit sorry for him because he must have had some serious problem. I learned that much later he re-appeared on 576 Squadron at Fiskerton (just south of Wickenby), but did not survive.

Flying Officer Abramson was indeed killed, along with all his crew, when their Lancaster was shot down over Denmark by a night fighter while on a minelaying operation in Kiel Bay in May 1944.

On the afternoon of 16 March 12 Squadron's last remaining Wellington, a Mark II that had been painstakingly made serviceable, was collected by the Air Transport Auxiliary for ferrying to No. 33 Maintenance Unit. Sadly the effort made to make it airworthy went for naught when, on take-off at 5pm the port engine cut and Z8501 crashed, two of the ATA crew being injured. It was an ignominious end to 12 Squadron's association with the Wellington.

After Essen, persistent bad weather prevented Bomber Command from carrying out any major raids until 22 March, when 12 Squadron contributed 8 of the 357 aircraft sent to bomb Saint-Nazaire, like Lorient one of the

Kriegsmarine's bases on the Atlantic coast of occupied France. The ORB notes that '14 aircraft were detailed but this was cut down to 8 experienced crews only due to doubtful weather conditions'. The attack on the docks was successful, with accurate marking and concentrated bombing, but on return the crews were diverted to airfields in the south Midlands on account of fog. One, captained by Bob Noden, did not hear the diversion signal and landed safely at Wickenby, but the others touched down at a range of airfields in Oxfordshire and Gloucestershire, Jo's at Little Rissington, near Bourton-on-the-Water.

One of the other crews operating that night was captained by Wing Commander R.S.C. Woods, DFC, who had been posted in on 16 February from No. 1656 Conversion Unit to command 12 Squadron upon the appointment of Wing Commander Dabinett to head No. 1662 Conversion Unit. 'Dabs' was a hard act to follow, but Wing Commander Woods proved to be a popular leader, fair-minded and accessible, and the high level of morale attained under his predecessor was maintained. A by-product of this high level of morale was an unwillingness of crews to be posted out to the Pathfinder squadrons, which were constantly in need of airmen to make up for operational losses. Jo remarks:

> During this period every so often a request would come through for volunteers for pathfinder duties in 8 Group. The squadron was a pretty tight unit, having been together since conversion and nobody particularly wanted to leave. The requirement was that those transferring to a pathfinder unit must have done three operations, that's all, and if there were no volunteers and there were usually very few, crews that had done three or more operations would be press-ganged into it. They were usually new crews and it's rather amusing to contemplate this when we're always told the pathfinders were the elite, hand-picked. Well they weren't hand-picked from 12 Squadron that's for sure.

The Operational Record Books show three aircrews transferred to 156 Squadron at Warboys during March and April 1943: Sergeant J.F. Thomson and crew on 22 March, Flight Sergeant R.J. Hudson RAAF and crew three days later, and Warrant Officer D.C.C. Busby and crew on 8 April. Only Thomson would survive the war, both Hudson and Busby failing to return during June, Busby on his fifty-third sortie and recommended for the Conspicuous Gallantry Medal, which was gazetted after his death.

Saint-Nazaire was a comparatively 'easy' target, given the right weather, as witness another raid on the port on 28 March, when all eight crews detailed were relatively recent arrivals. The next operation in which Jo's airmen participated, was, however, far from easy. Eight crews were detailed to take part in a heavy raid on Berlin on 27 March by almost 400 aircraft. On return all the crews reported bombing on the Pathfinder flares and several on the 'large number of big fires all over the town'. Yet the raid was, as Middlebrook and Everitt put it, 'basically a failure'. They explain:

> The bombing force approached the target from the south-west and the Pathfinders established two separate marking areas, but both well short of the city. No bombing photographs were plotted within 5 miles of the aiming point at the centre of Berlin and most of the bombing fell from 7 to 17 miles short of the aiming point.[6]

To add to this German authorities estimated that approximately a quarter of the bombs dropped that night failed to explode. Even so, the scattered bombing did achieve some local successes, as with two bombs that hit a military train bringing soldiers on leave from the Russian Front, killing eighty and injuring sixty-three. An even more adventitious success was achieved south-west of the city, where, as Middlebrook and Everitt relate, a secret Luftwaffe store, hidden in woods at Teltow, was hit:

> By chance this was in the middle of the main concentration of bombs and a large quantity of valuable radio, radar and other technical stores was destroyed. The Luftwaffe decided that the depot was the true target for the R.A.F. raid on this night and were full of admiration for the special unit which had found and bombed it so accurately.[7]

The Berlin raid was the last of 'Paddy' McKenna's tour. Jo does not recall where he was posted, which the missing April ORB would have recorded, but he survived the war. His successor was newly commissioned Pilot Officer Gordon Fisher, a Canadian.

Jo's crew did not operate again until 4 April, although in the interim 12 Squadron participated in raids on Berlin (29 March) and Essen (3 April). From the Berlin raid one aircrew, captained by newcomer Sergeant F.W. Pinkerton, failed to return, and Jo was not surprised, as he comments:

> I couldn't help looking at new crews if they came in and privately weighing up their possibilities and one such was captained by a Sergeant Pinkerton. I didn't really fancy his chances very much at all and sure enough I was right. After two or three ops he was missing. But blow me down, six weeks later he turned up again. Apparently they'd been shot up by flak and bailed out over Holland. He must have been very lucky, for he was the only one in the crew picked up by the Resistance in Holland, was whipped out of Europe and was back again on ops in six weeks.

Sergeant Pinkerton went on to survive the war. In this case, Jo's intuition as to a green pilot's chances of survival could not have gone further astray.

On 4 April Jo's was one of the 12 Squadron crews assigned to participate in a raid by 577 aircraft on Kiel. With both the Form 540s and Form 541s for April missing, it is not possible to detail the activities of the other 12 Squadron crews, save to report that all returned safely from what was, for Bomber Command, a disappointing strike. For Jo, however, the operation ended prematurely when,

> out over the North Sea, heading for Kiel, I felt very, very ill and vomited into my oxygen mask. I felt cold and weak and decided to pack it in and turn back. The Wing Co. was fine about it and suggested I go and see the Medical Officer. I accordingly went to see the Doc., who diagnosed a tummy upset and put me on a restricted diet.
> I thought that it was almost certainly a nervous reaction, and in reality I suspect that the MO did too. But he told me not to eat rich things and probably also not to drink and I was grounded for about a week.

That Jo's nerves might be on edge was hardly surprising, since Kiel would have been his fifty-fourth operation, but he quickly recovered, and on 13 April was one of the 12 Squadron crews detailed to attack the docks at La Spezia, in Italy. For this raid he had a new navigator, the Kiel raid marking the completion of 'Sammy' Samuel's tour. His replacement was a new arrival on squadron, the 'very Welsh' Pilot Officer D.I. Griffiths, known inevitably as 'Griff'. Heavy damage was caused by the 211-strong force, almost all Lancasters, and only 4 aircraft were lost. One was that of 12 Squadron recent arrival, Sergeant F.E.W. Clark, in one of two Lancasters shot down near Le Mans, but for Jo and his crew the sortie was uneventful, at least until they returned to England. He writes:

This was my 54th operation and everything was fine. It involved a long stooge across France as far as Annecy. I remember as we passed over the Alps I could see a Lanc on either side of me and then it was on down to La Spezia, which is something like 50 or 60 miles down the coast south of Genoa and back again. I remember the trip back vividly with a long leg from Grenoble to Le Treport. The sky was dotted with isolated cumulo-nimbus clouds, each of which would from time to time be lit up from within by lightning like pearl light bulbs. It was quite spectacular. I was, as usual, keeping up regular evasive action and Gordon Fisher, our Canadian wireless operator, was operating Mandrel, listening out on German night fighter frequencies. Gordon said there was a lot of German night-fighter RT traffic going on and he was doing his best to jam it all, which was very pleasing.

Anyway we came back and were steaming up England, the gauge happily showing zero after nine hours, and not at all certain what fuel we had left, I requested permission to land at Cranwell. It was only about 30 miles or so short of Wickenby but I wanted to be safe. When we landed the Station Commander turned up in his dressing gown. He was a dear old boy, Air Commodore Probyn, well known in the RAF, and he reminisced about how he once flew over the Alps without oxygen in a Westland Widgeon. Anyway we put some more fuel on and flew back to Wickenby.

The next day, Jo was ordered to report to Wing Commander Woods. Wondering why, he went to the CO's office, knocked and entered, to be given the news that he was tour-expired. A new directive had come through, the CO said, making a second tour twenty ops, rather than thirty, like a first. It was, as Jo says, 'a very, very nice way of finishing', without any of the tension that might arise when an operation was known to be the last of a tour.

Although Jo had completed his tour, his crew had not, and he was relieved when, early in May, Flight Lieutenant A.J. Heyworth was posted in from No. 15 Operational Training Unit, Harwell, to take over the crew. Jim Heyworth had flown his first tour with 12 Squadron and would successfully complete his second as B Flight commander, he and all of Jo's former crew surviving the war.

Viewed in perspective, it can be seen that Jo's second tour differed radically from the first. For one thing, operating had become a very much more highly regulated and, it might be said, professional exercise. At Alconbury in 1941, a bombing operation was carried out more or less individually, with crews selecting their own take-off time and their own route to and from the target. With the introduction of the so-called 'bomber stream', however – originally employed in the first 'Thousand Bomber' raid, on Cologne on 31 May 1942 – crews operated within strict parameters in terms of times and routes, while the formation of the Pathfinder Force, and target marking, meant that precisely where, as well as when, the bombs should be dropped was predetermined.

But there were also considerable differences between the first and second tours so far as the crew and Jo's relationship with them were concerned. The 40 Squadron crew, all sergeants, assembled themselves at Lossiemouth and operated together throughout the entire first tour, save when Bill Harris had to be replaced because of illness. They also spent most of their off-duty time together. On 12 Squadron Jo, now an officer, inherited an initially all-NCO crew partway through its tour, had three additional members allocated to it when conversion to the Lancaster took place, and was also assigned a replacement navigator, wireless operator and rear gunner as each reached the end of his first tour. It is hardly surprising, therefore, that the crew, while a highly efficient team, was less closely knit than the 40 Squadron crew had been, or that they did not much socialise with their skipper. The contrast between the two crews can, perhaps, be summed up in how the two crews addressed each other in the air and on the ground. Jo writes:

On 40 I was 'Ollie' at all times by all the crew, and I always used first names for my crew, in the air and on the ground – never 'navigator', 'rear gunner', etc. The same went for 12, except that I was 'Jo' to most of the crew on the ground, and generally 'Skip' or 'Skipper' by all the crew members when in the air.

That the crew was less given to socialising together does not mean that this never occurred. Jo recalls:

> On stand down nights we regularly went en masse into Lincoln in Liberty buses, which were peculiar American-built Dodges with double doors at the back and steps – pretty uncomfortable things. But of course on stand down nights 12 Squadron wasn't the only squadron stood down, all the 1 and 5 Group squadrons around Lincoln were usually stood down as well and they all did the same thing, all had the same sort of buses and all drove into Lincoln and parked in the station yard. They all went out on the town and at the appointed hour of return, which I think was 11 o'clock, in the pitch dark we found our way back to the station yard where there was a line of identical buses. The problem then was to find out which was your own, and as everybody was pretty merry there was a lot of leg-pulling going on, and my mid-upper gunner, 'Jimmy' Wild, would roll out his party piece. Having found the Wickenby bus he would sit at the back and shout, 'Ingham, Bingham, Basham and Bottesford', just to add confusion. 'Ingham and Bottesford' were in fact real places but of course we weren't going there. 'Bingham and Basham' were his own ideas.

During his second tour, Jo and his crew were never intercepted, and his gunners had to open fire only once, to suppress searchlights during the minelaying sortie to Haugesund Fiord in early January. On two occasions, however, they had had close calls, both involving near-collisions. One, already mentioned, was the occasion over Hamburg when a Ju.88 night fighter passed only a few feet overhead. The other was in circuit at Wickenby, preparatory to landing. Jo recollects:

> During operations it was always a bit of a melee around the airfield and I had a very near miss with Douggie Hagerman, RCAF. We

passed so close in the darkness we could hear the other aircraft and you've got to be jolly close for that. Twelve Squadron organised a rather good little dodge. We got the local defence people to put up what we called a canopy of three searchlights, intersecting over the airfield. When we came back we could see this and provided there was no enemy intruders around, which there usually weren't in 1943, we could make a beeline for the airfield. Unfortunately everybody else caught onto this, and we soon had Lincolnshire full of little triangles of search lights, which rather defeated the object. So we changed ours to a single vertical one.

One last difference between the first and second tours that Jo vividly remembers is the communication with the base on return from an operation. He writes:

In 1941 R/T was via a contraption called TR9, which was virtually useless, and for control at night we simply used Aldis lamps and the downward identification light on the aircraft for communication. Later, however, we were given improved equipment that actually worked. Returning from an op and nearly home, it was just wonderful to call up and announce your arrival, to be answered by the gentle, cheerful and welcoming voice of a WAAF R/T operator. Sanity had returned to the world!

Where would Jo now be posted? He did not want to return to an OTU, training sprog crews on clapped-out Wellington ICs, but that was precisely what loomed when a few days later a transfer came through to No. 15 OTU, Harwell. 'What I wanted', he says, 'was to be a test pilot at a Mainten-ance Unit, flying newly assembled or repaired aircraft and I more or less refused to go.' Fortunately, Wing Commander Woods was sympathetic and arranged to retain Jo at Wickenby. Equally fortuitous, another of the second-tour pilots, Ray Kitney, completed his tour at much the same time and was eager to accept the posting, since he had recently married, and his wife lived near Harwell. Jo flew him to Harwell on 2 May. What was advantageous for Jo, however, was fatally unlucky for Kitney, since on 15 July he was accompanying a crew on a cross-country exercise when the

port engine caught fire and the Wellington IC broke up in mid-air. All
aboard, including four Australians, were killed.

The other second-tour pilots who arrived at much the same time as Jo
all survived the war. David Villiers entered the film industry but died at
forty of natural causes. 'Kay' Stammers, who had in March been posted to
100 Squadron as a flight commander, also died young. He had stayed on
in the RAF and was killed in May 1946 when his Halifax caught fire in the
air and crashed at Whixley, in the West Riding of Yorkshire, shortly after
he had remarried, his first wife having died earlier in the war. Bob Noden,
though, he of the three tours, went on to enjoy a long and distinguished
career with British European Airways and British Airways, and a lengthy
retirement, dying in 1996 at the age of eighty-two.

Thanks to Wing Commander Woods' forbearance, Jo remained, in a
supernumerary capacity, at Wickenby for six weeks, undertaking a range
of odd jobs, including ferrying personel to other RAF stations, local joy
riding in the CO's Tiger Moth, and, more seriously, giving guidance to
new crews on survival:

> During the six weeks or so, thanks to Wing Co. Woods, I was
> supernumerary at Wickenby I fulfilled a number of roles, one of
> which was as a training officer. Stupidly, someone higher up Bomber
> Command had decreed that new crews would go on ops without the
> pilot having done any second dickey trips and of course, to people
> who knew something about it at squadron level, this was absolutely
> ridiculous. The poor crews were demolished before they started and it
> proved catastrophic. I was given the job of talking to these poor chaps
> and demonstrating and in every way trying to convey to them what
> it was like on operations, and describing defensive tactics such as
> weaving and taking evasive action generally. Fortunately top brass saw
> the folly of that policy fairly quickly and it was discontinued.

On 13 May Jo took up three newly arrived pilots for 45 minutes of demonstrating evasion tactics. One of the three was RAAF Flight Sergeant F.W.
Morgan. That night his crew, and another newly arrived, failed to return
from Bochum. The other aircrew ditched in the North Sea and were rescued. Flight Sergeant Morgan was not so fortunate, he and two other

crew members being killed and the other four taken prisoner when their Lancaster crashed near Gelsenkirchen, probably brought down by flak.

Under Wing Commander Woods the social life of the squadron, and particularly the officers' mess, continued to be lively. Jo recalls:

> A few words about the tricks and games that used to crop up in the mess on stand down nights. There was one well known one in the RAF called Hicockalorum where two teams of about six chaps would compete. One team formed a sort of single line rugby scrum and the other team then took a runner and leap-frogged over it, the idea being to try and collapse the ones underneath. This quite often led to minor injuries but it was good fun. There were two other tricks that always amused me. Both could only be pulled on people who hadn't seen them before. One was to put a pint of beer on a billiard cue while stood on a chair, hold the pint of beer up against the ceiling and keep it there with the billiard cue whilst you stood down off the chair. You then got someone to hold the billiard cue whilst you removed the chair and then just left them there, standing there with a pint of beer over their head that would come down on them if they moved the billiard cue, as eventually they had to. Obviously they'd only get caught once at that. The other trick was to persuade someone to put a funnel down the front of their trousers, lean their head back and put a sixpence on their forehead. The idea was that they had to bring their head forward and drop the sixpence in the funnel, but as soon as they got their head back with the sixpence on their forehead everybody poured their beer into the funnel.

For a week early in May Wing Commander Woods was on leave, and David Villiers, CO of A Flight, assumed temporary command. On 7 May the weather was poor, an operation was cancelled, and a mess party was organised. Jo writes:

> About five o'clock on a dull evening, the Tannoy went out all over the station saying 'Officers attending tonight's party please do so in PT kit.' I thought there was something fishy about this, so pretended

I hadn't heard it and in due course went up to the mess to find everybody there looking puzzled but nobody in PT kit. David Villiers hadn't appeared, but in due course a complete stranger, a young Canadian pilot, walked in, in his PT kit. He'd only been posted in that day, it seems, and he heard this Tannoy message and complied, turning up in his PT kit. Totally spontaneously, everybody rushed and grabbed him and carried him across the road to a pond full of stagnant water and threw him in. We pulled him out quickly and cleaned him up and plied him with drink for the rest of the evening. In the end he thought it was all a jolly good thing.

The 'young Canadian pilot' was in all probability Pilot Officer H.G. Ashburner, posted in with his crew that day, the same pilot officer who was one of the three new arrivals given a demonstration of evasive action on 13 May. Happily, Ashburner not only completed his tour with 12 Squadron but survived the war.

Several individuals at Wickenby stand out in Jo's memory. One is the well-liked adjutant, Flight Lieutenant Cottrell, always known to fellow officers as 'Adj'. Jo particularly remembers him as being highly indignant when a directive came through from higher up instructing adjutants to stock and distribute condoms. 'I don't think', Jo adds, 'that this order was ever actually put into effect.'

On religious matters, Jo says 'that throughout all my RAF career, Anglican padres were generally speaking conspicuous by their absence'. By contrast, the Roman Catholic padre was very much on hand and part of the squadron. Jo comments:

Like most Catholic padres he was Irish and like most of them he was a very good sort and mixed in well. When we had a stand down and went into Lincoln in the Liberty buses he would discard his dog collar and put on an ordinary black tie but retain his padre's lapel badge. Off we'd go into Lincoln and he'd join in all the fun. He'd come back with us and into the mess, but when the rude songs round the piano started he just disappeared. He was constantly, quietly, urging somebody to take him on ops with them. This would not have been possible officially and in any case it would have required the agreement of every member of the crew for it to happen, and I'm quite sure that general consent would not have been given. It would have been tempting providence too much.

Another individual whom Jo remembers with affection was an RCAF navigator, Flying Officer Basil Viera. Hailing from St Kitts in the West Indies, he was crewed with a Welsh sergeant pilot, George Elsworthy. Jo recalls returning from one operation and hearing that Elsworthy's crew was missing. 'I retired to bed', Jo records, 'thinking poor old Basil's bought it. But in the morning I got up and dressed and went up to the mess and bumped into him in the doorway. It really was quite a shock to me because I'd had it firmly in my brain that he was no more.' Sadly, Basil Viera did later fail to return. On 28 April Bomber Command carried out its largest minelaying operation of the war, despatching 207 aircraft to lay mines off Heligoland, in the River Elbe, in the Danish straits known as the Great and Little Belts, and off the German Baltic coast. Middlebrook and Everitt note that 'Low cloud over the German and Danish coast forced the minelayers to fly low in order to establish their position before laying their mines and much German light flak activity was seen.'[8] Twenty-two bombers were lost, seven of them Lancasters, and of those seven four were from 12 Squadron. It was the second time in four months that the squadron had lost four crews in a single night. One was George Elsworthy's, shot down off Swinemünde. All aboard, including a second pilot, died. Basil Viera's DFC was gazetted posthumously.

The officers' Nissen huts at Wickenby accommodated four. There was a large and inefficient cast-iron stove in the middle with a bed in each corner. Jo writes:

> I occupied the same bed in the same hut throughout my time at Wickenby and just across from me was my friend Wilf Hide, who was a second-tour wireless operator in Kay Stammers' crew. The other two beds were occupied successively by chaps who didn't make it. When somebody went missing and it was established that the crew had definitely not arrived back in the British Isles in one piece, the Committee of Adjustment rolled into action and it was kept very busy

too. The Committee comprised the adjutant, the padre and usually an airman as a token. They went through the missing person's kit, packed it all up and discreetly removed anything which they thought might cause distress to the next-of-kin to whom it was sent off. Of course the poor old adjutant had to compose a letter of condolence to the family or next-of-kin and it is little wonder that they all tended to take the same form. When somebody went missing there was never any drama or emotional scenes about it, just 'Poor old so and so has got the chop' or 'gone for a Burton' or other expressions meaning the same thing and no matter what we felt inside that was all there was to it.

On 13 May the Operational Record Book noted 'F/LT J O LANCASTER was posted to 1481 Flight on completion of his second operational tour.' Jo, however, did not depart immediately, as witness entries in his logbook on the 15th, 17th and 19th. On the 17th, accompanied by 'Dinger' Bell, Jo carried out an air test on a Halifax V that had been undergoing repair. He remembers the Halifax as 'very similar to the Lanc in flying characteristics, quite pleasant', but also that 'the cockpit crew stations were not good, and the lop-sided windscreen was a bit off-putting at first'.

This was the second bomber type that Jo had flown at Wickenby. At Lossiemouth, feeling it appropriate that an Armstrong Whitworth apprentice should fly an Armstrong Whitworth bomber, he had applied, unsuccessfully, to transfer to an OTU where he would be flying a Whitley. In March he had at last an opportunity to fly one when a Whitley V landed at Wickenby with a technical problem. The crew left by road and when after a few days the Whitley was repaired, 'Jock' Law, the engineer officer based at Binbrook, decided that it should be flight tested. Jo volunteered to carry out the air test and recalls that the aircraft was 'smooth and sedate, and reasonably quiet and pleasant to fly'. Jo would fly Halifaxes again at Boscombe Down later in the war, but he never flew a Whitley again.

Jo's successor as captain of his former crew, Jim Heyworth, had an older brother, Harvey, who was at this time chief civilian test pilot for Rolls-Royce at Hucknall. From time to time he would drop in at Wickenby while flight testing a Spitfire, and engage in fighter affiliation (i.e. mock fighter attacks on the bomber, enabling the latter's crew to practise evasion tactics). On 15 May Jo had an opportunity to reciprocate when, with Jim

Heyworth and Wilf Hide as his crew, he returned from a flight to Harwell via Hucknall. Jo comments: 'Harvey came up to play in a RR Spitfire, but the only times that we spotted him he was either going vertically upwards or vertically downwards!'

Learning that Jo had applied to be posted to a maintenance unit, test flying as many types of aircraft as possible, Harvey Heyworth gave him the name and address of a contact in the Ministry of Aircraft Production to whom Jo could apply for a job as a test pilot. An excess of modesty prevented Jo writing that letter, however, something he later regretted. It might have provided an earlier start to the career as a test pilot that he later embarked upon.

Looking back, Jo is amazed at how much he was able to get away with during the war, in terms of indiscipline. On several occasions, for instance, he completed an air test by flying over nearby Digby, home to several RCAF fighter units. A few low passes over the airfield, 'beating the place up', usually resulted in a Spitfire taking off and engaging the Lancaster in fighter affiliation play, which would end when the pilot of the Spitfire would formate on the Lancaster's wingtip, the two pilots would wave to each other, and the Lancaster would head for Wickenby.

Jo also enjoyed taking any opportunity, during an air test, of showing off the Lancaster's capability. He writes:

> About this time American aircraft – usually B-17s – were becoming more frequently seen. If I came across one cruising along in daytime I'd formate on it, and it was amazing how faces appeared all over the Fortress. I used to like to sit there in formation, then quietly pull the boost override, trim the aircraft nose down and open the throttles right up to 16 w of boost. The Lanc, which was of course very light, set off like a scalded cat. I used to wonder what the Americans thought about that lot; I was rather pleased.

Two other incidents involving the American allies also stick in Jo's mind:

> On 2 May I took the gunnery leader, Flight Lieutenant Wilkinson, down to Horsham St Faith, which the Americans had moved into.

One of our Lancs lost an aileron in an evasive action dive – that did happen when the ailerons overbalanced – and it landed at Horsham, where one of the gunners was admitted to hospital. Wilkie was going to visit him. In those days when you landed at another base you taxied in and somebody would get out and tell the watch office who you were, where you'd come from and where you were going and that was it. I asked Wilkie to book me in and off I went. He told me afterwards that he went in and the clerk in the watch office insisted that the aircraft was a Halifax. Wilkie said, 'Well I ought to know. I came in it and it's a Lancaster.' To which the American replied, 'Aw gee, I know a Halifax when I see one.' In the interests of Anglo-American harmony Wilkie agreed it was a Halifax.

On another occasion, in August, I went down to Bovingdon, another airfield they'd taken over. I was dropping off somebody there, informally, but they weren't going to have that. I had to stop the engine, get out and go and be debriefed. So I did all that, went in, and was debriefed. I was asked what the weather was like on the way from Binbrook. So I told them, and it was all written down. Then I said 'I'm off now' and they said 'Oh no, you've got to be briefed'. So I turned round and we had the same sort of conversation in reverse before back I went to the aircraft, started it and returned home.

'On the evening of the 16th of May I was out on the airfield', Jo writes.

It was quite late, but it was double summer time and still light. The Squadron was stood down and over the airfield went a gaggle of Lancasters at about 1,000 feet heading roughly south-east. Underneath each one there was the most peculiar thing, which I described at the time as looking like an upturned Anderson shelter. It was not until the next day we discovered what it was all about. It was of course the Dams raid, and security had been such that nobody had the slightest idea about it even though Scampton was only five miles away.

SUMMARY of FLYING and ASSESSMENTS FOR [████] COMMENCING ‡ 31·‡·42 – 28·4·43 [███]

‡ * For Officer, insert "JUNE"; For Airman Pilot, insert "AUGUST."]

	S.E. AIRCRAFT		M.E. AIRCRAFT		TOTAL for ~~year~~ PERIOD	GRAND TOTAL All Service Flying
	Day	Night	Day	Night		
DUAL	—	—.	2·35	·35	3·10	
PILOT	·30	—	79·45	131·20	211·35	1070·25
PASSENGER	—	—	—	—		

ASSESSMENT of ABILITY

(To be assessed as :—Exceptional, Above the Average, Average, or Below the Average)

(i) AS A **H.B** † PILOT   *Above the Average.*

(ii) AS PILOT-NAVIGATOR/NAVIGATOR

(iii) IN BOMBING   N/A

(iv) IN AIR GUNNERY

† insert :—"F.", "L.B.", "G.R.", "F.B.", etc.

ANY POINTS IN FLYING OR AIRMANSHIP WHICH SHOULD BE WATCHED

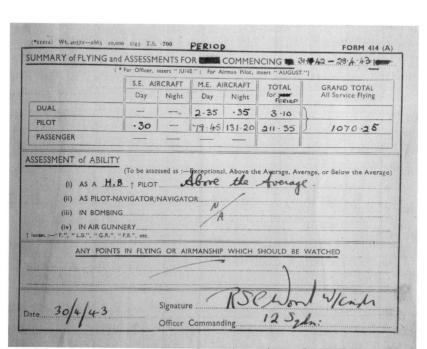

Date 30/4/43

Signature *RSCWood* W/Cmdr

Officer Commanding *12 Sqdn.*

Chapter 7

No. 1481 Flight

As noted in the previous chapter, Binbrook was, until September 1942, home to 12 Squadron. It was also home to No. 1481 (Bomber) Gunnery Flight. Formed in November 1941 as No. 1481 (Target Towing) Flight, equipped with twelve Westland Lysanders for gunnery cooperation with 1 Group squadrons, it was redesignated No. 1481 Target Towing and Gunnery Flight in January 1942 and in December of that year No. 1481 (Bombing) Gunnery Flight. Returning to Binbrook from Lindholme in March 1943, after the new concrete runways had been installed, the flight was equipped with Whitley Vs and Miles Martinet target tugs, but in April, not long before Jo arrived, the Whitleys had been replaced with Wellington IIIs, later supplemented by Wellington Xs. And it was to command the Wellington flight that Jo was posted in. The station commander, to whom he was responsible, was Group Captain Hughie Edwards. Jo had served under him at Wellesbourne Mountford, and had renewed his acquaintance when Edwards, with little to do at Binbrook until it became operational, dropped in from time to time at Wickenby.

Binbrook was also the home of 460 (RAAF) Squadron, the only Australian unit in 1 Group, which arrived from Breighton in mid-May. In the same month, a new structure was put in place, whereby Binbrook became No. 12 Base, its first commanding officer, Air Commodore Wray, responsible not only for Binbrook but also satellite bases at Grimsby and Kelstern. Wounded in the knee while serving with the Royal Flying Corps in the First World War, Wray used a walking stick, but this did not prevent him operating from time to time, Jo recalling that 'he several times volunteered to take an absolutely brand-new crew on operations with him. He was a great fellow.'

The CO of 1481 Gunnery Flight on Jo's arrival was Squadron Leader Browne, who was shortly after replaced by Squadron Leader Denis Murphy. Both, Jo recollects, had been barristers in civilian life, both had completed a tour as rear gunners in 1 Group, both were evidently well-off and both were keen party-goers. 'They knew 1 Group pretty well,' Jo says, 'and were on to all the parties that were going on everywhere and I frequently got the job of flying them there.' Denis Murphy Jo also remembers for another reason: 'He wore a clean shirt every day, whereas the rest of us had to make do with not more than one a week, with detachable collars.' Murphy's adjutant was Flying Officer Max Keddie, DFC, an Australian wireless operator who'd recently completed a tour of operations on 460 Squadron.

There were two aircraft flights, each with six resident pilots, none of whom – in Jo's flight at least – had flown operationally. Jo's was equipped with Wellingtons, and the second, commanded by Flight Lieutenant 'Jonah' Jones, or Gordon-Jones as he preferred to be known, was equipped with Miles Martinet target tugs. The first aircraft to enter service with the RAF designed from the outset as a target tug, the two-seat Martinet was derived from the Master trainer, being powered by the same Bristol Mercury XX engine as the Master II. With either a wind-driven or motorised winch in the rear cockpit, the Martinet could carry six drogue targets. The Wellington turrets were fitted with 12mm cine-camera guns and the gunners, who were on refresher courses from 1 Group squadrons, would be taken up for fighter affiliation. Jo comments:

> We usually used a Martinet as a fighter, the latter making attacks
> from various angles while we demonstrated evasive tactics, though
> very occasionally it was possible to employ a Spitfire. Afterwards the
> results were shown to the gunners on the camera film. But gunners
> also carried out live firing at drogues towed by the Martinets, using
> ammunition marked with paint, which enabled us to determine who
> had hit the drogue, and how often. In addition to towing targets for
> air-to-air gunnery and carrying out fighter affiliation, the Martinets
> also towed targets for an anti-aircraft training unit based at the end of
> Spurn Point.

'My Wellington flight didn't really need much running', Jo says,

> It was pretty self-sustaining, and the administrative duties were
> minimal, so I used to get a lot of other jobs. The station engineer
> officer, Jock Law, used to ask me to do air tests for the 460 Squadron
> Lancasters. It was on one of these I encountered for the first and
> only time an over-speeding propeller, which was, I later discovered,
> a problem very occasionally afflicting Merlin engines at that time.
> For no obvious reason the propeller suddenly went into fully fine
> pitch, the RPM soaring well over 3,000. The prop would not respond
> to the pitch control and would not feather. The best I could do was
> to try to adjust the engine power so that it was neither pulling nor
> windmilling. At a very low airspeed this gave minimum drag and kept
> the RPM as low as possible. It required very careful handling to get it
> down safely.

'The same thing happened at Boscombe Down when the OC Flying,
G/Cpt Bruin Purvis, was flying a Lincoln,' Jo recalls, 'and he had to belly
land it!'

One of Jo's 'other jobs' was ferrying personnel hither and thither. Ferrying Denis Murphy to 1 Group mess parties was one such, since 'anywhere
where there was a mess party on he wanted to go and I took him, usually
in a Wellington but sometimes in a Martinet'. Another task, from time to
time, involved flying the resident Rolls-Royce representative at Binbrook,
a Mr Blount, to Renfrew to visit the Rolls-Royce factory at East Kilbride,
while twice Jo ferried Hughie Edwards to Towyn, a very small airfield in
Wales, to join his wife there on leave. 'It was much too small for Wellingtons really,' Jo comments, 'but with an unladen one it was no problem.'

At Binbrook Jo shared a room with a Flight Lieutenant 'Strach' Stra-
chan. A flying control officer, he had previously been at Wickenby, where
Jo first met him. 'When he was on duty', Jo recalls, 'I quite often used to go
up to flying control. It was very pleasant up there to sit in a chair and have
the WAAFs constantly serving tea and occasionally beans on toast, things
like that. Incidentally the Senior Flying Control Officer's name was Foggo,
which I thought was rather amusing.'

The senior intelligence officer at Binbrook was Squadron Leader de Casalis, the brother of actress Jeanne de Casalis, well known in show-business circles. Through that connection, the station was enlivened by visits from a number of leading West End show-business people, Jo recalling that among them were – in addition to Jeanne de Casalis herself – Laurence Olivier, Vivien Leigh, Beatrice Lillie, Kay Young and John Gielgud. Another was Jo's favourite comic actor, Leslie Henson. 'He had to return early for rehearsals,' Jo remembers, 'and I was given the job of flying him back to Hendon in a Martinet. As he climbed into the rear cockpit he put on my hat, made his funny faces and had the ground crew rolling about on the ground with laughter. When we landed at Hendon he invited me to go along and watch the rehearsals, but of course this was not possible, much to my chagrin!'

Being so close to Wickenby, Jo naturally visited it whenever he could, both to socialise with his former crew, now nearing the end of their tour with Jim Heyworth, and more generally to attend mess parties. Jo recollects one occasion vividly:

> From Binbrook I used frequently to fly to Wickenby to see my old friends and I'd go in a Martinet. I'd land and taxi straight over to B Flight to see my friends. In the flight office I'd pick up the phone to flying control and say 'This is Group Captain Lancaster here, I've just landed in my Martinet' and put the phone down. One day a new station commander, Group Captain B.A.J. 'Basil' Crummy, not known to me, had arrived. He happened to be up in flying control, saw my Martinet land and asked the airman to whom I had apparently spoken, 'Who's that in the Martinet?' To which the airman, not knowing me, said, 'Oh that's Group Captain Lancaster.' The Flight Control Officer had to quickly butt in and explain the situation, because Group Captain Crummy was going to be rather annoyed at another Group Captain landing at his airfield and not coming to pay his respects.

Jo continues:

> The 12 Squadron commander at this time was Wing Commander Craven and whenever they had a mess party on I used to borrow a Martinet, fly over and of course stay the night. On one brilliant

moonlight night when I'd had a lot to drink I announced I was
going to fly back to Binbrook. Fortunately I was persuaded not
to. Whenever I wanted to do any shopping I used to fly over to
Skellingthorpe, a 5 Group station which was right on the outskirts of
Lincoln. I'd land there and catch a bus into Lincoln and home again
the same way.

'In case it should sound as though I wasn't pulling my weight during this
period,' Jo adds, 'I was in fact doing quite a lot of the Wellington flying; in
August I did 37 hours 45 minutes on Wellingtons and 4 hours 50 minutes
on Martinets.'

Another duty on two occasions involved a sea search for an aircraft
reported down in the sea somewhere off the coast. 'We never saw anything,'
Jo comments, 'but we did unfortunately lose a Martinet. The visibility was
bad and for some reason or other he went into the sea. We went looking
for him and what was obviously a Martinet wing was found floating. So
that was the end of them I'm afraid.' This was on 26 October, when RNZAF
pilot, Flight Sergeant R.J. Wright, DFM, took off with an RAAF passenger
to check weather conditions over the firing range at sea. Neither man was
found, and both are commemorated on the Runnymede Memorial.

Periodically, 1 Group stations were visited by an RNZAF pilot in a Spitfire
carrying out fighter affiliation with the squadrons' aircraft. 'Every time he
came to Binbrook,' Jo recalls,

I used to worry him to have a go at his Spitfire and eventually he said
'Alright. I'm going to lunch. I don't know anything about it.' So I got
into his Spitfire and had a jolly nice 15 minute flight in it. There were
absolutely no repercussions, but a couple of days later, in the mess,
Edwards dropped a little remark, the point of which was to let me
know that he knew about my little escapade. As there had been no
suggestion of reproof, I did a repeat six days later, September 9th, this
time for 40 minutes. Now seventy years on, the next little escapade
may be difficult to believe, but nevertheless it is absolutely true.
On November 6th I borrowed Edwards' Tiger Moth, and with Max
Keddie flew to nearby Kirton in Lindsey, which was a fighter training

unit. From there we were directed to their satellite, Hibaldstow, a
Spitfire OTU. As a total stranger I walked into the Flight Office,
introduced myself, said I had flown a Spitfire a couple of times, and
please could I borrow one of theirs to have another go! The answer
was 'Yes', and I enjoyed yet another 45 minutes in a Spitfire. I never
knew who that Flight Commander was, or why he was prepared to
risk a certain court martial by authorising my flight – but he did!

One unusual visiting aircraft that Jo vividly remembers was a USAAF B-24
Liberator. 'One beautiful clear, sunny and cloudless afternoon', he writes,

> a pristine polished aluminium Liberator landed at Binbrook, and
> after refuelling, took off again. My friend in Flying Control, 'Strach'
> Strachan, told me that it was a brand new aircraft which had left a
> US or Canadian east coast airfield on delivery to the UK. It had been
> plotted across Ireland, the Irish Sea, and England and was heading
> for Denmark when an RAF Beaufighter was scrambled and somehow
> managed to persuade it to land at the first airfield it saw, Binbrook.
> The crew must have all been asleep, or engrossed in a game of crap.
> The Germans would have been very grateful to have a brand new
> B-24 delivered to their door.

While Jo was leading what he describes as 'this idyllic life' at Binbrook,
460 Squadron was of course operating, and doing so intensively. Flying
more sorties than any other Australian Bomber Command squadron, and
dropping a greater tonnage of bombs than any other squadron in Bomber Command, 460 Squadron lost 188 aircraft between its formation in
November 1941 and the end of the war. Of those 35 went down during Jo's
six months at Binbrook, and no less than 16 between 23 May and the end
of June. It was a grim period, and in the officers' mess strenuous efforts
were made to sustain morale. Jo recalls plenty of parties, and something
that he never saw actually performed:

> Another thing that happened at various messes, though I never saw it
> actually done, I first saw at Feltwell in the mess anteroom. There were
> black footsteps up one wall, right across the ceiling and down the

other side. This was repeated in various messes including Binbrook. It was done by getting two or even three tables on top of each other and some brave chap going on top of the tables with his shoes and socks off and his feet blacked with soot from the fireplace and beer, then had the tables moved along whilst he placed his footprints across the ceiling. It was quite a performance.

'And of course,' Jo adds, 'there were songs, many of which originated in the peacetime RAF overseas between the wars. Most of them were highly obscene but undeniably very witty.'

While at Binbrook, Jo developed the habit of listening – for his own amusement – to German radio propaganda programmes. 'There was one', he says, 'which they called "The Anzac Half Hour". This consisted of telling rather crude jokes that were fairly funny but made much funnier because they were told in a thick German accent! I am sure this was all angled in the hope of sowing disaffection amongst the Aussies and Kiwis. If they could have had a little peep at 460 in action they would have realised that they were wasting their time!'

Several incidents involving 460 Squadron remain vivid in Jo's memory. One such included an aircraft touching down in murky conditions, the crew uncertain where they were. 'They were extremely lucky,' Jo comments, 'because they were just north of the Humber, at Catfoss, where it is very flat. Fortunately there was nothing in their way and they came to a stop undamaged.' The 460 Squadron ORB records the good fortune of RAAF pilot Flight Sergeant Crosbie and his crew in some detail. Returning in nil visibility, with Gee and other navigational aids unserviceable, they contacted Binbrook, but the response was weak. The crew report continues:

> After circling around for twenty minutes we realised we were lost and Pilot ordered crew to prepare to abandon immediately. Afterwards base was heard instructing us to descend to 400 ft. We estimated we were over base and descended – visibility still nil so Navigator fired yellow cartridge and we saw the ground 10 feet below. Travelling too slowly to attempt to climb – aircraft bellylanded. This was at 03.20 hours and was at Aldborough [sic], Yorkshire.

Jo also recalls an occasion when a Lancaster returned with a severe dent in the top of the starboard outer nacelle and damage to the fin and rudder on that side, yet with the propeller intact. Nobody, he says, could work out what had happened. However, when another Lancaster returned with a hole in its wing, it was very clear it had been caused by a bomb from another aircraft, which fortunately went straight through without exploding. Such incidents, particularly involving incendiaries, were not uncommon, the most serious occuring during an attack on Essen on 25 July. The ORB records the struggle that RAAF Flight Sergeant L.J. Christenson and his crew had to get the damaged aircraft back to Binbrook:

> While over the target . . . incendiaries dropped in and through their aircraft – Starboard engine became u/s and a fire started in Elevator Controls. The return flight was done on trimming tabs which were also not working properly – the aircraft could not be kept on a level course, it was diving and climbing alternately. Height was maintained until the French coast was left behind, they were then attacked by an enemy fighter but it was avoided. After this struggle to Base they attempted to land on trimming which suddenly became even more 'haywire' and the aircraft dived towards the deck. When ten feet from the ground the nose shot up again but suddenly dived and almost immediately burst into flames. The hatches were jettisoned before landing and the crew were in crash position which enabled them to make a quick exit. Fortunately, only minor injuries were sustained.

The most memorable incident, though, took place on 3 July, when a bombed-up Lancaster accidentally shed its load of incendiaries. The 460 Squadron ORB records:

> During the early part of the evening, prior to aircraft going on operations, two aircraft which were bombed up and ready to leave, caught fire and were completely destroyed and three others became unserviceable. For a space of half an hour or so there was much excitement as these aircraft were loaded with 4,000 lb bombs, which fortunately were not fused. After several terrific explosions, which caused not a little damage, obliterating several huts and the vicinity

and smashing the hangar windows the fires were extinguished
and over an area of 500 yards pieces of the aircraft were scattered.
Fortunately no one was injured though several ground staff were in
the aircraft when it caught fire and had to 'run for it'.

In fact at least one of the cookies did explode eventually, Jo recalling that
'I was down by the mess, and I could see all the smoke as the explosion
happened, followed a few seconds later by a huge woosh of very hot air.'

Not being a member of 460 Squadron, although socialising with its officers in the mess, Jo felt its losses less immediately than he had on 12 Squadron. Nonetheless, there was one casualty that did affect him. He writes:

One of my friends from Wymeswold, Flight Lieutenant Jimmy
Drummond, a wireless operator, went back on his second tour to
100 Squadron at Waltham. One night [2 August] I got stranded in
Grimsby for some reason, but found my way out to Waltham. Jimmy
was operating that night, and I think there must have been a difficulty
in finding me a bed because he said I could have his, which I gladly
accepted. Sadly, he was never seen again. He and his crew went
missing and he has no known grave.

Drummond – who had survived the carnage of May 1940, when a wireless operator/air gunner in a Fairey Battle of 218 Squadron, and had been
awarded the DFM – died with all his crew when they were shot down by
a night fighter off the Dutch Frisian Islands.

A happier memory, however, occurred at about the same time: 'I went
to the cinema, it must have been in Grimsby I think, and on the newsreel,
which was probably in July '43, saw the pipe band of the 51st Highland
Division marching proudly into Tripoli eight abreast and I just bloody
well knew we'd won the war when I saw that. It was a marvellous sight.'

It was while he was at Binbrook that Jo took a decision that very probably accounts for his longevity and good health. He writes:

I had started smoking cigarettes when I was about 11 and by 1943 it
was up to probably 40 a day or more. One night I was down in the
Marquess of Granby, which was the pub in Binbrook, with two of

the pilots from 1481 Flight, an Australian called Roberton and an
English chap called Starr. We'd had a few pints, agreed that smoking
was a very silly thing to do and made a pact to stop. I think Roberton
started again the next day, while Starr lasted about three days before
he started again, but I packed it in completely. I've never smoked a
cigarette since that day in August or September '43.

In the inside pocket of my battle dress tunic I used to have a
cigarette case and a lighter and for days and weeks afterwards
I used to find myself with my hand in there and realised that had
the cigarettes been there I'd have taken one out and lit it without
being conscious of the fact. It was pretty dreadful at night in the bar,
everybody was smoking, but it smelt nice. The worst thing was that
people used to take out a packet of cigarettes and hand them round,
so I was always being offered a cigarette. I'd say no and people would
say, 'What's wrong with you?' I didn't give up for health reasons.
There was no question of associating smoking with lung cancer
at that time. I think the reason was that it made us cough in the
morning; anyway I'm jolly glad I did. Some three or four months
later, I took to a pipe and smoked it steadily until about 1971, when
I gave that up purely because the Chancellor of the Exchequer made
tobacco so expensive that I refused to pay him.

As station commander at Binbrook, Hughie Edwards had his own Tiger
Moth, which he rarely used, and was relaxed about Jo borrowing it. He recalls:

On one occasion Max Keddie, our Australian adjutant in 1481, came
with me for some aerobatics. We did a loop and as we were recovering
from it I thought I saw something flash across the front of the
aircraft. I then did a second loop which felt a bit odd and glancing
out to starboard saw there was a wire coming from somewhere
behind us, forward over the upper mainplane, down under the lower
mainplane and aft again. I realised what had happened. After a detail
with a drogue, Martinets would drop the cable on the grassy area of
the airfield and ground crew would go out and detach the drogue.
However, the cable would be left lying there for a little longer and
what had happened was that as we took off on the grass we had

picked up one of these cables on the tail skid. When we did a loop
it had got itself festooned right round the mainplane. We were very
fortunate that it didn't get tangled up in the propeller.

During a very pleasant time with 1481 Flight, Jo remembers only one
unfortunate incident, involving his counterpart in the Martinet flight,
'Jonah' Jones. 'It was being muttered around his flight,' Jo says, 'that he not
only didn't do much flying, if any, but that he was logging flights which
he hadn't carried out. This came to the ears of Max Keddie, who passed it
onto Squadron Leader Murphy. In a matter of hours poor old Jonah was
off the station, posted, if I recall aright, to Eastchurch.'

Happy though he was at Binbrook, Jo nonetheless hankered for a posting to a maintenance unit as a staff pilot, for which he periodically lodged
applications. In November a transfer came through, not to a maintenance
unit but to the Aircraft and Armament Experimental Establishment at
Boscombe Down. 'I was a bit apprehensive about this,' Jo comments, 'I
wondered whether I was up to it. But I took it and it was marvellous. It
was all I could ever have wished for.'

A. & A.E.E.   BOSCOMBE DOWN.

YEAR 1943.		AIRCRAFT		PILOT, OR 1ST PILOT	2ND PILOT, PUPIL OR PASSENGER	DUTY (INCLUDING RESULTS AND REMA
MONTH	DATE	Type	No.			
—	—	—	—	—	—	— TOTALS BROUGHT FORW
NOV.	30.	MITCHELL.	F.V. 906.	S/L. MANN.	SELF.	PHOTOGRAPHY, PORTON.
NOV.	30	MITCHELL.	F.V. 906.	S/L MANN.	SELF.	HANDLING.
DEC.	1.	HAMPDEN.	X.2893.	SELF.	—	HANDLING & LOCAL.
DEC.	2.	DEFIANT. I.	AA. 354.	SELF.	F/L. BARRELL.	TURRET TEST 15,000'.
DEC.	2.	LANC. I.	L.7528.	SELF.	F/L EVANS & CREW.	2 x 4000 lbs. 1,500'. LYME BA
DEC.	4.	ANSON.	DG. 717.	SELF.	CREW.	WEST FREUGH- SQUIRES GATE - EAS
DEC.	5.	BEAUFORT	EK. 997.	SELF.	CPL. VINCENT.	HANDLING & LOCAL.
DEC.	11.	BARRACUDA.	P.9869.	SELF.	F/L. BARRELL.	GUNNERY TEST. POOLE BAY
DEC.	12.	HAMPDEN.	P.4338.	SELF.	F/L. BARRELL.	GUN MOUNTING TEST. LOCAL
DEC.	13.	LANC III.	JA. 870.	SELF.	F/L. THOMPSON.	GUNNERY TEST. LYME BAY.
DEC.	17.	AVENGER TARPON.	FN. 844.	SELF.	—	GUNNERY. WEATHER U/S. D.N.C.O

GRAND TOTAL [Cols. (1) to (10)]

......1280..Hrs....25.........Mins.

TOTALS CARRIED FORWA

Chapter 8

The Aeroplane and Armament
Experimental Establishment

'Ever since I'd finished my second tour', Jo recollects, 'I had been putting up applications for posting to a maintenance unit. I thought that
was a modest way to get into test flying.' He knew from his apprentice
days that new types of aircraft went to Martlesham Heath for evaluation
and acceptance. 'I didn't know the name of the unit that did the testing,'
he adds, 'I just knew it was always referred to as Martlesham Heath.' At
the outbreak of war, however, conscious of the vulnerability of the unit
close to the Suffolk coast, the powers-that-be moved the Aeroplane and
Armament Experimental Establishment, or A&AEE as it was universally
known, to Boscombe Down in Wiltshire. Jo became aware of the unit,
although still ignorant of its name, when he was posted in April 1942 for
a short OTU instructors' course at nearby Upavon. 'I remember flying
over it from Upavon,' he says, 'and it looked like a small grass airfield
with literally hundreds of aircraft of all sorts arranged around it.' When,
to his surprise a posting to the A&AEE came through, he felt somewhat
diffident. 'I didn't know much about what went on there,' he admits, 'or
whether I would be qualified to do it. But I went and I was so pleased at
the way things turned out.'

When Jo arrived in late November 1943, the A&AEE was organised in
two squadrons, one testing aircraft performance and the other armament.
The Armament Testing Squadron, to which Jo was assigned, was, as the
title suggests, responsible for all aspects of bombing and gunnery in the
aircraft types being tested. Jo explains:

This meant that you didn't have much to do with the performance
and handling assessment of aircraft except inasmuch as it was
affected by bombs or guns, which was usually negligibly. What the
pilot needed to be was versatile, competent, safe and confidence-
inspiring, so that he didn't frighten the multitude of technical officers
and boffins who were doing the tests while he flew them around.
To give you some idea of the variety of aircraft this entailed flying,
in April 1944 my monthly summary included the Lancaster I, II and
III, Liberator VI, Halifax III, Buckingham, Boston III, Mosquito IV,
Marauder II, Blenheim IV, Anson, Avenger, Spitfire IX and Hurricane
IIC. That's all in the course of one month, all for some test or other.

The commanding officer of the A&AEE when Jo arrived was Air Commodore D'Arcy Greig, DFC, AFC, a career RAF officer who had flown one of
the British entries in the 1929 Schneider Trophy race, but in July 1944 he
was succeeded by another Schneider Trophy pilot, Air Commodore J.N.
Boothman, DFC, AFC, who had won the 1931 race in a Supermarine S6B,
thus ensuring that the trophy would remain permanently in the United
Kingdom. The Armament Testing Squadron was commanded by Group
Captain H.P. Fraser, AFC, who took over from Boothman as commandant
of the A&AEE in June 1945.

Jo comments:

The armament testing squadron was divided into two flights, A Flight
handled mostly fixed armament, guns and rockets, and B Flight the
bombs and moveable armament, like turrets. I was posted to
B Flight, which was ideal for me. The flight commander was Squadron
Leader Jimmy Mann. He was a rumbustious sort, a short service
commission officer who had served in the Middle East on, I think,
Marylands. Along with him there were two Flight Lieutenants. One
was Dickie Galloway, a regular RAF man who had done a lot of time
in the Middle East and Mesopotamia, and had the medals to prove
it. The other was 'Knocker' Norris. He had flown Vickers Wellesleys
as an NCO pilot in the Eritrea campaign, been taken prisoner by the
Italians, but somehow got himself repatriated on mental grounds.

He was a bit of an eccentric and it's not hard to imagine that. One day he'd had a few in the mess at lunchtime, went off in a Sea Otter amphibian and landed in the sea off Lyme Regis. When he tried to take off again he couldn't get it into the air and eventually had to pump the undercarriage down and taxi up onto the beach. How he explained that I cannot imagine. But it was a happy flight and I felt I fitted in very well.

Jo's first flights were in a North American Mitchell, familiarisation flights in which Jimmy Mann introduced him to American instruments and cockpit layouts. 'From that time on', Jo recalls, 'I was on my own. For the most part the aircraft didn't even have any pilots' notes, so you had to either get somebody to show you or find out for yourself how everything worked.' Clearly Jo measured up well, and evidence of this came when later Group Captain Fraser asked Jo if he knew of anyone with the same background as Jo's who would like a job. Jo says, 'no one I knew was available, though eventually we did have Flight Lieutenant Steve Dawson posted in, ex-Bomber Command.'

When Jo arrived at Boscombe the armament flight was carrying out Tactical Air Force (TAF) trials of rockets and bombs for use in ground sup-port during the coming Normandy invasion, this mostly involving Hawker Typhoons and Mitchells. For the latter complete crews were transferred in from 320 Squadron, which was composed of members of the Royal Netherlands Naval Air Service, individuals whom Jo recalls as 'very lively'. 'It was all very hectic indeed', he adds, 'and the very first job I was given to do did in fact have some bearing on the TAF Trials.' He continues:

They were investigating how low an aircraft could safely fly over explosions from the ground. My first job [on 2 December] was in a Lancaster to drop two 4,000 pound cookies, separately, but on the same sortie, into Lyme Bay, off Lyme Regis. This was to be done from 1,500 feet, which came as a bit of a surprise because in Bomber Command the safety height for jettisoning a 4,000 pounder was always cited as 6,000 feet. We certainly heard the bangs, and the aircraft bounced up a bit, but in the event it was not too frightening! I also had the job of dropping a cookie one summer night on a target on Salisbury Plain. I don't know what that was for, or what the locals thought about it all; I suppose they got used to it with the army blasting off nearby all the time.

Clearly, armament testing required a great deal of space, and Jo comments that where possible it was done over the sea, either in Lyme Bay – where nearby, at Lyme Regis, there was an air-sea research unit with which A&AEE liaised – or in Poole Bay, near Bournemouth. But there were also extensive areas available on land:

> We had the use of a large area of the New Forest, which was called Ashley Walk; this was used for a number of things including the TAF Trials. There various old aircraft and military vehicles of various kinds were installed, so that we could test bombs and rockets on them. There was also Imber, on Salisbury Plain, where they had a rocket range for firing the 75 pound RPs at low level, Crichel Down, where there was another range and Porton Down, which was almost next door to Boscombe, where there was a huge concrete wall you could sling bombs at horizontally.

During his first month at Boscombe, Jo flew eight different types of aircraft, three of them single-engined, four twin-engined and one four-engined. Some flights were simply to give him a sense of how the planes handled, as with the Bristol Beaufort on 5 December. Others involved carrying out a periodic air test, as with the Boulton Paul Defiant on 28 December. But the majority involved either fixed-gun or turret trials. Quite why a 'gun mounting test' was carried out on such an out-dated type as the Handley-Page Hampden is not clear, nor why one was employed to drop five 500lb bombs at Porton Down on New Year's Eve, Tim Mason's *The Secret Years: Flight Testing at Boscombe Down* making no reference to any trials later than 1942. Nor does Mason clarify why a turret test at 15,000 feet was conducted on a Boulton Paul Defiant II. The turret trials performed on a Lockheed Ventura V just before Christmas, however, were clearly to enable the armament specialists to test the low-drag Martin 250 CE7 turret, which replaced the bulbous Boulton Paul turret fitted to earlier marks. The 0.5-inch machine guns plainly provided greatly improved defensive power, the turret was indeed low-drag, and the handling and firing of the turret were praised. On the negative side, however, the searching view was thought too restricted and elevating the guns to the maximum was uncomfortable.

With the Grumman Avenger (briefly known in Fleet Air Arm service as the Tarpon, and initially entered in Jo's logbook as such), likewise, there were trials of the twin 0.5-inch wing-mounted machine guns, which replaced the single fuselage-mounted 0.3 machine gun of earlier models. These trials were carried out over the sea, in Poole and Lyme Bays. An intended trial, on 17 December of Avenger FN844, fitted with the experimental Fraser Nash FN95 remote controlled turret, was called off because of bad weather.

January 1944 saw Jo again carrying out trials in the Hampden, dropping small bomb containers at Ashley Walk, but also piloting a Douglas Boston IIIA, an aircraft he enjoyed operating very much, for the first time, engaging in 'handling and local' flying. He was also reintroduced to the Halifax, although to the much-improved Hercules-engined Mark III, carrying out a 'Periodic Air Test' on 21 January, because, as Jo puts it, 'sometimes an aircraft would not be used for a while, in which case it was always wise to give it a periodic air test, just to dry it out and get rid of the spiders and birds' nests'. Later that day, Jo and a three-man crew flew Lancaster I L7528 to West Freugh, in the Mull of Galloway, to (as Jo describes it) 'drop armour-piercing bombs on a block of concrete they had in the wilds up there'. Between 24 and 30 January eight experimental bomb drops were made over Braid Fell, involving 4,000lb weapons. Mason mentions neither these trials nor their outcome, but Jo recalls that 'the square of very thick concrete was small and difficult to hit'. This may have been why repeated bomb drops were needed.

In early February, Jo's flying was almost entirely restricted to four-engined types, mostly Marks I and III Lancasters, but also the Liberator, which he had not flown before. His logbook describes the duty as 'Exp. Gunnery', and it seems that in BZ945, a Liberator V, the trials were of the 0.5-inch tail turret built by Motor Products. In common with most American turrets it was adjudged to have a poor view to the side and down, although to be otherwise acceptable. The other Liberator, EV828, a Mark VI, was flown the same day, perhaps for assessment of its Consolidated nose turret, which was criticised as being too small and frequently unserviceable. Later trials in February and March involved the replacement Emerson turret, which was considered far superior. Jo recalls the Liberator as pleasant to fly, with wonderful Pratt & Whitney Twin Wasp engines. 'They started up just like electric motors', Jo recalls, 'and didn't leak any oil.'

Some of Jo's most interesting flying in February, however, involved types he had not flown before, including the Martin Marauder, Hawker Hurricane, Hawker Typhoon, Vultee Vigilant and Vultee Vengeance. The Hurricane and Typhoon were both taken up for short spells of 'handling and local flying', Jo's summation of his brief encounter with the latter being 'The Typhoon was OK, but I never enjoyed looking at something like 4,000 RPM on the clock.'

The RAF ordered the Vultee Vengeance dive bomber from the United States manufacturer during 1940, when the Luftwaffe's Ju.87 dive bomber was at its peak of effectiveness, but it did not enter service until 1942, when the limitations of the dive bomber had been demonstrated. As a result, it was considered that the Vengeance could best be used in the Far East, where fighter opposition would be less, and where it could be employed to attack specific jungle targets. The first Vengeance, a Mark I, reached Boscombe Down in August 1942, and attracted a range of criticisms, not least for the ineffective brakes that made for a lengthy landing run, the small calibre of the four 0.3 wing-mounted machine guns, and for the serious carbon monoxide contamination of the rear cockpit caused by the engine exhaust. FD119, the Vengeance IV that Jo flew very shortly after its arrival at Boscombe, had fortunately remedied all these shortcomings, with the landing run reduced from 1,172 to 482 yards, six 0.5-inch machine guns in the wings and (as was found when he and Flying Officer Loader carried out a 'C.O. contamination trial' on 28 February) carbon monoxide seepage into the cockpit described as minimal. When a second Vengeance IV, FD243, was tested on 7 May, however, it was discovered that the American flame dampers with which the aircraft was fitted, once more caused carbon monoxide contamination of the cockpit.

The first Martin Marauder received by Boscombe for testing in September 1942, a Mark I, proved to be fast but very demanding, with a high wing loading and hence a high stalling speed, requiring high take-off and landing speeds also. The Marauder II, which arrived at Boscombe in November 1943, had a 7-foot increase in wingspan, and hence lower stalling and landing speeds, but Jo still felt that it 'had a very high wing-loading and required what to me was an uncomfortably high boost setting to maintain the necessary airspeed'. The Marauder was used only for gunnery trials over Poole Bay, one of which Jo flew on 20 February and another on 5 April. Mason summarises the results of the tests thus:

> There were originally no fewer than twelve 0.5 in guns; ground trials revealed serious shortcomings in the hand held and nose fixed guns which were removed for air tests. The upper Martin 250 CE4 turret was satisfactory with minor changes while the open beam hatches made the gunners excessively cold: heated clothing was recommended. Firing the four guns in the fuselage blisters caused the pilot's sight to vibrate; however, acceptable accuracy was achieved using the auxiliary ring and bead. Firing from the Bell Sunstrand M-6 tail turret was inaccurate due to flimsy mounting of the sight.[1]

In March the main emphasis continued to be gunnery trials involving the Lancaster and Liberator, although on the 8th and 9th Jo flew TAF trials involving a Douglas Boston IIIA at Ashley Walk. One of six IIIAs at Boscombe, BZ384 would eventually be written off while parked, when a Grumman Wildcat crashed into it on take-off.

On 31 March Jo piloted one of the A&AEE's Hampdens to enable one of the resident photographers, a 'Mr Williams', to photograph a Blackburn Firebrand. The Firebrand had had a remarkably long and painful gestation, with trials of the Napier Sabre-engined Firebrand I beginning in April 1942. Disappointing flight characteristics, never fully overcome, led to the decision to turn what had been a fleet fighter into a torpedo strike aircraft, and it may have been this Firebrand TF.II that was being photographed. More likely, though, it was the first of the Bristol Centaurus-engined TF.IIIs, which arrived in February, the Air Ministry having forced an engine change on manufacturers Blackburn when it decided to allocate the entire Napier Sabre production to the Hawker Typhoon.

April was a particularly busy month for Jo, during which he flew twelve different types, including, for the first time, the Bristol Hercules-engined

Lancaster II, a Mosquito IV and the Bristol Buckingham. The prototype of the latter, intended as a fast, well-defended day bomber, had arrived at Boscombe in October 1943 but had been found unpleasant to fly, with poor longitudinal and directional stability, as well as problems with the Bristol upper turret. Four more Buckinghams were assigned to the A&AEE, these incorporating enlargements to the tail unit, but it is not clear whether these modifications had been made to DX249, which Jo flew first on 2 April. His recollection of flying the Buckingham relates solely to how impressive he found the power of the two 2,400hp Bristol Centaurus engines!

On 23 April Jo had his first flight in a Mosquito, his logbook giving the duty as 'R.P. firing: Enford'. He recalls the occasion vividly:

One of my evening drinking friends was Flight Lieutenant Sheppard, an armament officer connected with the 75 pound rocket projectiles, the ones which did so much damage in the Falaise Gap later on. He was involved in their development; in fact he claimed to have invented them. He said one night, 'Would you like to fly a Mosquito?' I hadn't flown one at that time but it was arranged without any fuss. I went down and we got into this Mosquito VI. He was a schoolmaster and he showed me the taps for the fuel system and off we went. Not only that but we fired off four pairs of rockets at low level at a target, and I found there was quite an art in this because there was a considerable drop in their trajectory.

A week later he was to fly a Mosquito again, this time the Mark IV bomber version, engaged in a rather hazardous enterprise. His logbook states 'Exp. 2700 lb inc. 120 ft Critchel'. He explains:

Another test connected with ground support I did in six sorties in a Mosquito, dropping 4,000 pound cookie shells filled with Napalm, although it wasn't to my knowledge called Napalm at that time. This had to be done from low level and I'd drop the cookie from something like 60 feet and then go back and reload. Then those running the test would come on the telephone and say I wasn't low enough. Eventually I was dropping it as low as I possibly could. Afterwards I saw film of it,

with the Mosquito scuttling along just a few feet off the ground and a
huge burst of flame flaring up into the sky and falling, like a clutching
hand, just missing the tail plane of the Mosquito. It was alarming to
see it on film. I'm glad I couldn't see the real thing.

It had long been recognised that the 0.303-inch Browning machine gun
with which bomber turrets were equipped was inadequate to counter the
firepower of Luftwaffe night fighters, and in 1942 the Air Staff identified a
requirement to fit Lancasters with a turret carrying two 0.5-inch machine
guns 'as soon as possible'. Frustrated at slow progress on the project, the
C-in-C Bomber Command, Air Marshal Sir Arthur Harris, decided to go
outside official channels and personally asked Rose Brothers, a Gainsborough firm specialising in agricultural machinery – which had produced
for him in 1940 an improved gun mounting for the Handley Page Hampden – to develop such a turret for the Lancaster. With technical advice
from Air Vice Marshal E.A.B. Rice, AOC of 1 Group, and Air Ministry
concurrence, work on the Rose (or as it was later called, the Rose-Rice)
turret went ahead. Fraser Nash, which had produced many of the turrets
used by the RAF's heavy bomber force, also went ahead with the design of
a 0.5-inch-equipped turret. Theirs, the FN82, was not placed in production until 1945; Rose Brothers, despite early teething troubles, had theirs in
production in May 1944, when two turrets were fitted to Lancasters of
101 Squadron. The turrets were brought directly into operational use,
without prior evaluation at Boscombe Down, but Jo recalls that 'early
in '44 we did get a couple to evaluate in which I was involved, flying the
aircraft while the armament chaps tested it'. He also had the opportunity
to visit Rose Brothers with Flight Lieutenant Frank Barrell, the technical
officer in charge of the turret evaluation:

> Four of us went up on 2 May, landed at Blyton and visited Rose
> Brothers in Gainsborough. It was a lovely firm, very friendly, and
> Alfred Rose, the remaining brother, showed us round. I was fascinated
> at the ingenious things they were making and by the way he knew
> all his employees and their families. At the end of the day he took
> us down to the well-appointed staff sports and social club where
> he shared a drink with quite a number of his employees and it was

obvious they all admired him greatly. It was a very happy place
indeed. That evening we were invited to dinner with him and his
mother. After the meal Mrs Rose asked us to put our signatures on a
tablecloth. She apparently did this with all her visitors. She later very
cleverly embroidered all the signatures, and after her death, and the
closure in the 1960s of Rose Brothers, the tablecloth came into the
possession of the Gainsborough Heritage Society. I have since visited
and seen it, with all the signatures – Arthur Harris, Roy Chadwick,
designer of the Lancaster, Guy Gibson, Jo Lancaster et al!

Although Mason does not mention this, it seems that Lancaster ME613
was equipped with the Rose-Rice turret, since it engaged in gunnery trials
at Lyme Bay before being flown north to Blyton, and again over Hartland
Point, North Devon, two days after returning from Blyton.

Jo was also involved in Halifax turret trials during May, piloting Halifax
III, HX238, one of three provided with the new Boulton Paul Type D tail
turret armed with two 0.5-inch machine guns, and fitted with the airborne gun-laying turret (AGLT) blind tracking radar system, code named
'Village Inn'. Enabling a target to be tracked and fired on in total darkness,
'Village Inn' accurately computed the target's range and even allowed for
deflection and bullet drop. The two occasions when Jo flew the aircraft
during May both involved fighter affiliation. In July he would fly a Boston
on another fighter affiliation trial of 'Village Inn'.

Perhaps the oddest of all fighter affiliation work that Jo undertook
also occurred in May, and involved a Northrop P-61A Black Widow night
fighter briefly loaned to the A&AEE by the USAAF's 9th Air Force. Quite
why it was tested is not clear, since there is no evidence that the RAF
intended to operate the type. Nonetheless, it flew 30 hours in May, 3 hours
40 minutes of that in Jo's hands. After two flights to test the P-61's fixed
and turret armament, a series of fighter affiliation flights were carried out,
Jo piloting the Black Widow on four of these, and flying the Spitfire for
a fifth. His recollections of the P-61 are not especially positive. He writes:
'The pilot sat a long way back from the windshield and the cockpit was
generally "untidy", with a far from "cosy" feeling. In general it was not
unpleasant to fly, but the performance was not particularly impressive.'

During June trials of 'Village Inn' rear turrets were continued, Jo flying both Halifaxes and Lancasters in a series of tests of the Boulton Paul D turret fitted to the former and the Fraser Nash FN82 (also 0.5-inch with the AGLT) of the latter, some flights involving fighter affiliation. The trials of the Boulton Paul turret ended in October, but those of the FN82 continued almost until he left the A&AEE, the last three logbook entries relating to this being on 28 January 1945 ('AGLT Trials 28,000 ft'), 10 February ('Tracking Trials FN82') and 28 February ('Exper. Gunnery: Lyme Bay').

Jo was also quite heavily involved in testing carried out on the Emerson nose turret fitted to BZ970, a Liberator Mark VI, the Consolidated turret fitted to earlier Liberators tested at Boscombe having proved unsatisfactory. The Emerson was well received, once a disposal problem with empty cartridge cases had been resolved. A trial of a different nature, also involving BZ970, was that on 12 June, when three 500lb mines were dropped from a height of 250 feet at Porton. The other Liberator sortie, at night on 11 July encompassing flame-damping trials, is self-explanatory. Exhaust flames had been a problem since the first Liberators IIs were received in 1941, and various remedies had been tried, none with complete success.

July also saw Jo included for the first time in testing Lancaster JB456, which had been fitted with the new Bristol B.17 mid-upper turret, equipped with two 20mm cannon, and intended for the new 'super Lancaster', the Avro Lincoln. Tests would continue for months, with Jo heavily involved between November and February. No details of the protracted trials are available, and his logbook entries are generally confined to 'B.17 trials Lyme Bay'.

Boscombe was also involved in testing target indicators (TIs), and in May Jo was tasked with the dropping of two types, weighing 250lb and 1,000lb, from a Mitchell 15,000 feet over Crichel Down. In July the testing involved drops of 500lb TIs, again from a Mitchell, and once more over Crichel, at heights as low as 11,000 feet. Mason records no details as to the reasons for the trials or their outcome. Nor is there anything about the dropping of three 8,000lb cookies over Lyme Bay on 27 and 28 July, although this may have been to test blast effects.

The Barracuda was not one of Fairey Aviation's successes. A dive and torpedo bomber, designed to replace the Fairey Albacore, it had a lengthy gestation and in its original form proved underpowered, displaying unpleasant flying characteristics, particularly in the dive. By the time Jo first flew one, in December 1943, Barracudas of various marks had been under test for two years. Many of the original handling faults had been ironed out, while Merlin engines of greater power had improved the Mark II's overall performance. Later trials throughout 1944 thus largely involved evaluating a fantastic variety of weapons and stores that the RAF and Fleet Air Arm seemed to think might usefully be attached to the Barracuda. One assessment Jo was not connected with saw two 'Cuda' floats slung below the wings, each designed to accommodate two parachutists. Trials proved the concept feasible, although it was not proceeded with. Appraisals were also made with an assortment of weapons, the Barracuda proving not very amenable to most of them, and Jo's testing experience of the type involved the carriage of three 500lb mines. Mason does not mention the outcome of the trials, in which during July embraced both the aircraft's handling when thus loaded, and also the release of the mines. Jo's opinion of the Barracuda was not favourable: 'It looked a mess and its flying characteristics seemed to match its gawky appearance. In my opinion it should never have gone into production – but of course it was a Fleet Air Arm aircraft!'

August saw Jo continuing to fly a miscellany of types, nine in all, including a Fairey Swordfish on a taxi run to Gosport, a Hurricane IIC – which he flew to Blyton, returning via Binbrook, where he met old friends, and on to Boscombe – and a Boston that he also flew to Blyton, arriving back via Baginton, again visiting old haunts. He also flew, for the last time, the Bristol Buckingham, carrying out a low-level bombing trial, dropping five 500lb bombs at Crichel Down. Earlier in the year it had been decided that the Buckingham was not required for day operations over northern Europe; instead it was intended to be tropicalised and used to replace Wellingtons in the Far East. Now, ironically, in August the decision had been taken to abandon the Buckingham as a day bomber entirely and convert completed aircraft to fast four-seat transports as the Buckingham C1.

One August flight, in Lancaster JB457, is of considerable interest, involving as it did 'Flare Chute Trials'. Mason notes that there had been a persistent and intractable problem with the flare chute, updraft preventing the flares falling freely. Three attempts had been made to solve the problem, but only when the chute was shifted from the tail of the aircraft to the nose was the problem remedied. It may well have been this new disposition of the chute that was being tested on 10 August.

Small-scale when war broke out, the A&AEE had grown like Topsy in response to the massive increase in the demands made on it. This had resulted in a structure that was, by the time Jo was posted in, complex to say the least. Thus, besides A, B, C and D Flights, the Performance Squadron had a High Altitude Flight, while the Armament Squadron had A and B Flights, as well as Special Duties Flight, an Intensive Flying Development Flight and a Gun Proofing Flight, the latter testing, for some reason, all 40mm cannon for aircraft, most of which were being sent to North Africa for installation in tank-busting Hurricanes. To Air Commodore Boothman, who assumed command in July 1944, there seemed an urgent need for reorganisation and rationalisation in order to eliminate duplication and waste. In August 1944 his proposals were accepted, and in September a new structure came into effect. Under it, a single Flying Wing, reporting directly to the CO, combined both performance and armament functions, and was arranged into four squadrons – A, B, C and D – along with a Communications and Special Duties Flight. Within the four squadrons there was also rationalisation, A Flight testing only single-engined aircraft, B Flight four-engined aircraft, C Flight naval aircraft and D Flight twin-engined aircraft.

Had this reorganisation taken full effect immediately, Jo, in B Flight, would have flown only four-engined types in September, but the restructuring took some time to introduce, and it was not until November that he was so restricted. In September and October, therefore, he continued to fly an eclectic mix of single-, twin- and four-engined types. Many of the September trials were continuations, it seems, of those begun earlier, as with testing of the FN82 turret in a Lancaster on 5 September, but two new developments are worthy of note.

One began on 3 September, when Jo piloted Lancaster HK543 for local 'Azon' trials. Azon was an American smart bomb equivalent of the successful Fritz X employed by the Luftwaffe against naval vessels, achieving its greatest success in sinking the Italian battleship *Roma* in September 1943. Essentially a 1,000lb general purpose bomb equipped with radio-controlled tail fins, Azon was steerable laterally, but not vertically, which meant that it had to be accurately released to ensure that it did not undershoot or overshoot its target. A flare in the tail provided a smoke trail that enabled the bombardier to clearly observe and control the bomb's trajectory from up to 15,000 feet. The Azon bomb was originally designed for attacks on difficult targets in the Far East, such as railway bridges in Burma, but the USAAF made limited operational use of the weapon over Germany, ten crews from the 458th Bombardment Group at Horsham St Faith, operating B-24 Liberators, being trained in its use. With the RAF, Azon never got beyond the trial process at Boscombe, no doubt because it was found to be highly unreliable. Of twenty drops from a Lancaster, Mason reports, ten bombs failed to respond and three flares failed, leaving only seven functioning as intended. Jo's only other flight involving Azon occurred on 9 December, when four bombs were dropped at the Ashley Walk range.

The other significant trials in September involved the use of Mosquito VI HR135 with a variety of ordnance. On 1 September two runs were made over the Porton range, dropping each time two 250lb depth charges at speeds of 350 and then 365mph. Then, after trials of the parachute release system on 17 September, the following day three drops of two 500lb mines were made at Porton.

Despite the type's retirement as a bomber, in the autumn of 1944 Boscombe still had Stirling IIIs on charge, and on 23 September Jo flew one for the first time since his Flying Training School friend, George Bayley, had introduced him to the type in May 1942. Jo's task was experimental bombing from 15,000 feet over the Porton range. An air test of the same aircraft, LJ571, on 24 October would be his last flight in what was both the first and least successful of the wartime RAF's four-engined bombers. He remembers the Stirling as 'very gawky-looking on the ground, and a handful on take-off because of its tendency to swing, but once airborne smooth and generally pleasant on the controls'.

A first for Jo, in September, came with an air test carried out on a Warwick. Big brother of the highly successful Wellington, the Warwick was designed as a complement to it, not as its successor, and intended to take advantage of two high-powered engines then under development, the Rolls-Royce

Vulture and the Napier Sabre. With the former a failure and the latter needed for Typhoon and Tempest fighters, resort was made to the American Pratt & Whitney Double Wasp, but by this time the Warwick was clearly outmoded as a bomber, with the Stirling, Halifax and then Lancaster coming into service, and the type was never employed as originally intended. Some were converted to serve as transports, while other were modified for air-sea rescue work. Later Warwicks were powered by the 2,500hp Bristol Centaurus engine, and it was a Warwick GR V, designed for maritime reconnaissance and anti-submarine work, that Jo tested.

Four Mark Vs had been delivered to the A&AEE in June, and the directional instability that had plagued the aircraft throughout its life was still in evidence. Indeed, in early 1945 Vickers test pilots would be involved in three crashes, one of them fatal, caused by rudder aerodynamic overbalance. The cure involved both reduced rudder travel and the fitting of a dorsal fin. That, however, was for others to explore and diagnose, Jo's piloting of the Warwick being limited to participation in what Mason describes as 'protracted' bombing trials carried out on PN710, which resulted in the listing of no less than forty-four essential modifications. On 8 October, Jo piloted the aircraft twice over the Porton range at 1,000 feet, first ten 500lb bombs and then twenty of 250lb being dropped. His summing up of how the Warwick – which he only flew once more, in January, carrying out tests of the promising Bristol B.12 Mark II mid-upper turret – functioned in the air, was that 'it performed rather as it looked, like a big brother of the Wellington'.

Brief though his acquaintance with type was, however, it was in a Warwick that Jo first encountered the phenomenon known as 'coring'. 'This happened', he writes, 'when the oil cooler became virtually blocked by very viscous cold oil, and the pumped oil circulation was then diverted through the radiator by-pass, resulting in an alarmingly high indicated oil temperature. The cure was to fix a vertical baffle down part of the radiator.'

Another first was the air test that Jo carried out on an Avro York on 21 October. Moreover, it was that rare bird, the solitary York II, fitted with Bristol Hercules radial engines rather than Rolls-Royce Merlins. His recollection is of it sitting unused and only taken up for periodic air tests. He found the pilot's visibility poor and disliked intensely the sliding controls in the cockpit roof. His somewhat negative view was reinforced when, in 1949 at Armstrong Whitworth, during the Berlin Air Lift, a succession of Yorks were brought in for major inspections and refurbishment. 'I never enjoyed flying them much', he observes.

October was the last month in which Jo flew single- and twin-engined aircraft, although he continued with four-engined types. In November his flying was restricted entirely to the latter, and indeed to Lancasters and Halifaxes, carrying out further trials on the B.17 mid-upper turret and the Boulton Paul D and Fraser Nash FN82 tail turrets with the AGLT. The most interesting of these entries in his logbook occurs on 9 November, when the entry reads 'B.17 trials 380 mph! Lyme Bay'. Jo comments:

> I see in my log book that I did a number of flights with Lanc JB 456 between Nov. '44 and Feb. '45. This aircraft was fitted with a Bristol B.17 mid-upper turret, with two 20 mm cannon, destined ultimately for the Lincoln. My memory tells me that it was not a success – the ammunition feed system gave trouble, there was serious vibration and there was a gun cooling problem. During a burst of firing the guns would become very hot indeed. When firing was stopped, the next round was already in the breech, and it could become so hot that it would 'cook off' (i.e. spontaneously combust) giving the gunner a severe fright, particularly as it was a 20 mm cannon shell! The dive would have been to check the turret operation at high airspeeds, and to check for any ill effects on aircraft behaviour.

December's flying was even more restricted, with – apart from 80 minutes' local flying in an Auster V – only Azon and B.17 trials in Lancasters, until on New Year's Eve Jo carried out an air test on one of three Fortress IIIs (equivalent to the B-17G of the USAAF) on charge to the A&AEE at the time. Another air test on the same aircraft on 20 January was followed on the 28th by what the logbook entry describes as a 'Ball turret tracking trial'. Mason makes no mention of specific trials on HB762, but does refer to earlier trials on a Fortress II, which found that 'the Sperry ball turret under the fuselage had a very poor view, was cramped and awkward to use'. Presumably some improvement was being assessed. Jo's recollection of flying the Fortress is primarily of its docility; it was, he said, 'pleasant to fly – just like a big Anson'.

The new year, 1945, saw a further contraction in the number of types flown to just two, the Lancaster and its intended replacement, the Avro Lincoln. The Lancasters were engaged on continuing bombing and gunnery trials, one of the former involving bombing from only 500 feet at Crichel Down, while the latter included tracking trials of the FN82 low-profile mid-upper turret, originally intended for the Bristol Buckingham. On 17 January, however, Jo flew Lancaster LN730 to RAF Hornchurch, from where that day and the next he carried out low-level bombing trials at Shoeburyness, an army gunnery range on the south-east Essex coast. He comments:

> Somebody somewhere had had a good idea, which was to put a long steel spike on the nose of 250 or 500 lb bombs, with the idea that this would make them dig-in, instead of bouncing, when dropped from low level on a railway track, for instance. There was a stretch of track at Shoeburyness, and we tried these out from different heights. I think that the results were mixed, but with the war's end now well in sight they were probably soon forgotten about anyway. During the return to Hornchurch after the last sortie I actually saw a large explosion in a built-up area, and after landing was told that I had witnessed the arrival of a V2.

Rodded bombs had, in fact, been widely used in North Africa, to ensure that they exploded before the bomb could embed itself in the sand. The Shoeburyness tests, it seems, were designed specifically to see if railway embankments could be successfully breached.

The Avro Lancaster was an inspired emergency response to the failure of its twin-engined predecessor, the Manchester. The Avro Lincoln was a considered response to the success of the Lancaster, an enlarged version of the latter intended primarily for the Pacific theatre of operations, with a better performance, heavier armament and, crucially, a very long range. The prototype, PW925, first flew in June 1944, and on 15 July was delivered for testing to Boscombe Down, where it proved to have the same magnificent handling qualities as its progenitor. Two further aircraft were

delivered later that year, and it was one of these, PW929, that Jo first flew on
1 February. The task was 'experimental gunnery: Lyme Bay'. This may have
been a test of the new Boulton Paul Type F turret, specifically designed
for the nose of the Lincoln. It had been found that nose turrets were sel-
dom used on Bomber Command aircraft, but that if an attack developed
during the bombing run, the turret could not easily be operated by the
bomb aimer. The Boulton Paul Type F turret was designed to solve this
problem in that, mounted above the bomb aimer's compartment, it was
remotely aimed and fired from below. Mason records (*The Secret Years*,
p. 109) that the new turret was found acceptable for service use with some
eight modifications.

In February, Jo would pilot the Lincoln on five further turret trials over
Lyme Bay, although whether this was to test further the nose turret, the
B.17 upper turret or the Boulton Paul D in the tail is unclear. Mason notes
that there was excessive carbon monoxide contamination in the nose and
tail turrets, and that opening panels to vent it were recommended. Jo also
flew the Lincoln on 1 March for local flap trials. It had earlier been recommended, after testing one of the other Lincolns, that the flap selector
be modified so as to obviate the need to select flaps up initially when
moving from mid to fully down. Presumably this modification had been
introduced. Mason merely comments that 'Further flap improvements
were approved on PW929.'[2]

While flying the Lincoln, Jo made two non-local flights. The first, on 7
February, was from Boscombe to RAF Kelstern, near Binbrook, returning
on the 9th. Jo recalls why:

Hangars had been tailor-made to accommodate the Lancaster's
102 ft wing-span, so when the Lincoln was coming along with its
120 ft wing-span there was going to be a problem. Why Kelstern
was chosen I have no idea, but they installed there a little system of
trollies on railway tracks which would enable a Lincoln to be pushed
into the hangar sideways! My visit was just to provide the Lincoln
so that they could try it out. It worked, but I don't think that it was
ever adopted anywhere else. This visit had a bonus for me, however,
because it turned out that a very good friend from Wymeswold days,
Jack Stevens, was there, on 625 Squadron, on his second tour, which

happily he was to survive.

About the second non-local flight, on 2 March, following flap trials the previous day, Jo writes:

> On 2 March 1945 I flew Lincoln PW929 on what my logbook
> describes as 'turret endurance'. It was a flight of nearly four hours,
> and we landed at Jurby on the Isle of Man to refuel. I went into the
> Watch Office to sign in and the airman there had noted down the
> aircraft type as 'Lancaster'. As he was about to ask the pilot's name, I
> said, 'Well you can cross Lancaster out and put it in the next column
> and write Lincoln there.' He thought I'd gone mad. He'd never
> heard of a Lincoln and as far as he was concerned the aircraft was a
> Lancaster, so it was very confusing for the poor chap.

Given its crucial importance, it is astonishing how primitive facilities at Boscombe Down were. Until its completion in early 1945, for instance, there was no concrete runway. Mason explains:

> The pre-war airfield sloped down from 420 ft above sea level in
> the NW corner to 360 ft in the SE. It was downland, i.e. short grass
> on chalk with rough and uneven patches. Take-offs and landings
> could be made in any direction, with the longest run of 1,800 yd in
> a NW/SE direction. A light south-easterly wind could prove a bit
> embarrassing on landing if the speed was just a little high, as floating
> down the hill resulted in touch-down about half way along the
> available run.[3]

Not surprisingly, the aerodrome surface became rutted and uneven and caused a number of expensive structural failures, and even when the concrete runway was completed, Mason notes that the single access point to it, via steel mesh, 'became worn, rough and boggy in wet weather – aggravated by the extra water draining off the concrete'.[4]

The accommodation at Boscombe was equally primitive. In 1939 there were less than 700 people employed at the A&AEE. In 1944/45 this had risen to more than 2,000, but there had been hardly any additions to the perma-

nent structures, some dating back to the First World War and the rest to
1929/30. There were three messes (officers', sergeants' and airmen's), some
barrack blocks and married quarters, but these were manifestly inadequate,
hence there sprang up, both on the domestic and airfield sites, what Mason
describes as 'a myriad of wooden and prefabricated huts'.[5] He comments:

> The temporary huts built for offices, workshops and flight huts to
> supplement the permanent buildings were always crowded, muddy
> in wet weather, and alternatively freezing or boiling depending on the
> state of the inevitable coal-burning smoking stove. Living conditions
> were equally unappealing for those not fortunate enough to occupy
> pre-war buildings; huts sprouted up as annexes to all three Service
> messes.[6]

Mason adds:

> If living conditions in the Officers' Mess were cramped, lunch times
> could be extremely cosy: the small bar was totally inadequate and
> the corridor became the de facto watering-hole – known as 'the wind
> tunnel' from the continual opening of doors.[7]

Even so, for Jo the posting to Boscombe Down was a delight, both on and
off duty. He writes:

> I have very happy memories of my time at Boscombe, of Salisbury and
> of Salisbury Plain, which late on a summer's evening could be quite
> magical too. The mess was very overcrowded and the mess itself was of
> '20s vintage. While it had central heating it wasn't very good and there
> were no power points for electricity. Hence many of us used to plug
> our various appliances into the lighting circuit and the single fusebox,
> in the batman's room (or batwoman's room as it was then), was
> constantly going. Eventually we finished up with large pieces of copper
> wire where the fuse wire ought to be. The cable coming out of the
> ground was set in pitch, but got so hot that the pitch started melting.

It was not only the electrical system in the mess that was deficient. So, too, was hygiene, it seems. Jo recollects:

> At night after the dining room had shut down and was left in darkness, we younger ones used to go in there. Somebody would switch the lights on and the floor would be covered with cockroaches. We would then dance round squashing all the cockroaches. It was pretty disgusting but that was the way things were.

Jo also recalls vividly the bar of the officers' mess, which was in the main hall opposite the principal entrance, and the stag's head over the bar itself. He writes:

> It was really a skeleton, not a head, a skeleton with antlers and on one occasion the skeleton disappeared. It reappeared a week or two later with eyes and a microswitch attached to the beer pump, so that when the pump was operated the eyes lit up, one winked and a tongue came down out of its mouth and went back in again. This was the work of Wing Commander Fitton, the Station Engineer Officer.

'It would be quite easy', Jo observes,

> to get the impression that everything going on at Boscombe was slap-happy and casual but in fact everybody, without exception, was very keen. We all had our jobs and whenever we could get on with them we did. In the spring of '44 we were frequently flying till dark just to get tasks completed in the least possible time. As always throughout the airforce during wartime, weekends didn't exist; we just carried on seven days a week. We were entitled, nominally, to one day off a week but most of us didn't bother to take this; we just carried on enjoying doing the job. But when the weather was duff a gang of us would go off into Salisbury. On market days the pubs were open practically all day and there was a lovely little café called the Moonrakers near the cathedral. We used to start off the day with toasted teacakes and tea, sitting there chatting, and then adjourn to the pubs and do our shopping or whatever. There was one lovely pub called the Haunch of Venison that dated back to 1344. It was a great favourite of ours

and it was also a haunt of Squadron Leader Ralph Reader, famous for the pre-war Gang Shows in the Boy Scouts. His RAF post involved organising entertainment I suppose.

In fact, Reader was originally persuaded, pre-war, to join the Royal Air Force Volunteer Reserve as an intelligence officer, this in anticipation of a visit he was to make to Germany at the invitation of Joachim von Ribbentrop, the German ambassador in London. This never took place, but on the outbreak of war, Reader was sent to France for undercover work, in the guise of running a concert party, for which former Gang Show members were recruited into the RAF. So successful was the show itself that on return Reader was ordered to expand the Gang Show, which he did, eventually raising twenty-four Gang Show units, touring every theatre of war. Among those who served in the RAF units, and later achieved fame, were Peter Sellers, Dick Emery, Cardew Robinson and Tony Hancock.

Jo's accommodation was a room shared with another officer. He writes:

I shared my room at different times with three different officers. One was a flying control officer whose name I forget. I used to save the twelve-sided threepenny pieces at that time in a tin. One time he was going on leave and he wanted to buy all my threepenny bits to take home to show his wife how he'd been saving. Another, I forget his name too, used, in the morning, to sit up in bed, sling his feet over the side, reach out, light a cigarette and then put the cigarette down and start coughing; he'd cough and cough and cough. I didn't think much of that. The third officer with whom I shared was Wing Commander Rex Hayter. He was one of the doyens of the service test pilot world and he and his ilk used to go into the bar at six o'clock and have their sherries, scotches and the like. Then they'd go onto the dining room, eat, and go to bed early. The young ones, including me, used to do just the opposite. We'd eat and then go down and start drinking. So I used to go to bed late. Rex had beside his bed a bottle of whisky and I used to hear sounds in the night of him uncorking the bottle and going 'glug glug glug' and I thought what a perverted old B. he is. But one night when he wasn't in the room I uncorked the bottle and found it was just plain water he'd got!

Jo adds:

> Somewhere Rex had a cannon hidden away – a miniature version of
> an HMS Victory type, on a little trolley, and on very special occasions
> he would produce this, mount it on the steps of the mess main
> entrance, ceremoniously load its muzzle with items removed from
> dissected Very cartridges, and fire it, much to the delight of the large
> audience which would have by this time assembled! Unfortunately, on
> one occasion it set fire to the large beech hedge, and the fire brigade
> had to be summoned!
>
> Sadly, in May '44 we got news of the 50 Sagan officer escapees
> murdered by the Gestapo, and Rex's brother Anthony was one of them.

Inevitably, with so much experimental flight testing, there were fatalities,
but of those that occurred in Jo's time at Boscombe he can think of only
two, both involving Typhoons. Officially they were put down to 'Loss of
control at low altitude', but Jo's recollection is that in both cases this was
due to tailplane failure, resulting from a structural weakness in the early
Typhoons. Sadly, one of the pilots killed was Squadron Leader H.N. 'Bill'
Fowler, who had successfully escaped from Colditz in September 1942,
made his way to Switzerland and thence across Vichy France to Spain
and eventually Gibraltar, an exploit for which he had been awarded the
Military Cross.

Jo himself had only one near miss, as he describes:

> The only really 'shakey-do' I recall was when taking off in a Liberator.
> P/O Paddy Eardley, a flight engineer, was in the right-hand seat.
> I was having difficulty in selecting gear up. Paddy stood up in his
> seat trying to sort it out and inadvertently managed to feather both
> starboard engines with his head! I felt the sudden loss of power but
> could not see the engines. I shouted to Paddy to feather both starboard
> engines. He looked out and saw that they were already feathered, and
> promptly unfeathered them again, still with the throttles set at take-
> off boost! It can't have done the Pratt and Whitney Double Wasps
> much good! It was a bit of a tussle, I recall, but we managed to get
> round the circuit with the gear and flaps still down, and land safely.

A few days later Bruin Purvis [Group Captain H.A. Purvis, OC Flight Wing] happened to occupy the next stall in the loo, and he took the opportunity to congratulate me! How did he know? It was a bit like Hughie Edwards getting wind of my Spitfire episode.

Jo's logbook records the name of aircrew and technical armament officers with whom he regularly flew, but he particularly remembers three flight engineers, all from Belfast, Northern Ireland, and all called 'Paddy'. Jo comments:

What their religions were, no one cared, but for many years I had always had the impression that in Northern Ireland it was the RCs who were the bigots. One Paddy met a WAAF on the station who hailed from Sheffield, and they fell in love and became engaged. It emerged that Paddy was a Protestant and the little WAAF from Sheffield was an RC and when Paddy wrote home to tell them the glad tidings of their engagement, his sister replied that she had rather that he had been killed on operations than marry a Catholic. I saw the letter.

By the end of February, Jo's time with the A&AEE was drawing to a close. He had been accepted for the third Empire Test Pilots' School (ETPS) course, which was to begin in mid-March. Before he left, however, he was looking forward to one last flight in a Lancaster, dropping a 22,000lb Grand Slam bomb. Performance trials of the giant weapon had been conducted in the autumn and early winter using two Lancasters modified by the removal of the nose and mid-upper turrets, and the fitting of Merlin 24 engines, giving an extra 330hp at take-off. These, though, had taken place with the weapon filled with sand; the March trial was to be the first using a live Grand Slam. Keen to carry out the test, Jo waited for the weather to improve sufficiently for the trial to be run. Sadly, the weather had not cleared enough by 13 March, when ETPS No. 3 Course began, so it was Steve Dawson who, that day – just a day before the weapon was first used operationally by 617 Squadron – dropped a live Grand Slam from 16,000 feet over Ashley Walk.

YEAR 1944		AIRCRAFT		PILOT, OR 1ST PILOT	2ND PILOT, PUPIL OR PASSENGER	DUTY (INCLUDING RESULTS AND REMARKS)
MONTH	DATE	Type	No.			
—	—	—	—	—	—	TOTALS BROUGHT FORWARD
MAY.	27.	SPITFIRE.	EF.561.	SELF.	—	FIGHTER AFFIL : LOCAL.
MAY.	27.	BLACK·WIDOW.	25496.	SELF	F/L. THOMPSON.	FIGHTER AFFIL : LOCAL
MAY.	27.	BEAUFIGHTER.	NE.352.	SELF.	ARMOURER.	EXP. GUNNERY : STERT FLATS.
MAY.	29.	MITCHELL.	FW.266.	SELF.	F/L. COLE.	EXP. GUNNERY. N.C.O. A/C V/S.
MAY.	29.	LANCASTER.	JA.870.	SELF.	F/L. DOLLEYMORE.	TURRET TRIALS : LOCAL.
MAY.	30.	BLACK WIDOW.	25496.	SELF.	S/L. LOCKIE.	FIGHTER AFFIL. 25,000'
		SUMMARY FOR : MAY 1944.				1. LANCASTER I,II,III.
		UNIT : A.&.A.E.E.				2. HALIFAX III.
		DATE: 1/6/44.				3. MITCHELL. II.
		SIGNATURE : J.B.Lancaster. F/LT				4. BOSTON III.IV.
						5. BLACK WIDOW.
						6. BEAUFIGHTER.
						7. ANSON.
						8. SPITFIRE Vs.
						9. FIREFLY.
						10. AVENGER.
						11. VENGEANCE.

GRAND TOTAL [Cols. (1) to (10)]

1451 Hrs. 35 Mins.

TOTALS CARRIED FORWARD

Nº 3 COURSE. E.T.P.S. BOSCOMBE DOWN.

YEAR 1945		AIRCRAFT		PILOT, OR 1ST PILOT	2ND PILOT, PUPIL OR PASSENGER	DUTY (INCLUDING RESULTS AND REM...)
MONTH	DATE	Type	No.			
—	—	—	—	—	—	→ TOTALS BROUGHT FORW...
MARCH.	13.	LANCASTER.	ME.830.	SELF.	F/O. HARE.	AIR TEST.
MARCH.	14.	HARVARD.	FX.354.	SELF.	—	L.F.P.
MARCH.	15.	SPITFIRE.	ML.174.	SELF.	—	L.F.P.
MARCH.	16.	SPITFIRE.	NH.478.	SELF.	—	L.F.P.
MARCH.	17.	SWORDFISH.	HS.642.	SELF.	S/L. GALE.	HULLAVINGTON & RETURN.
MARCH.	21.	LANCASTER.	R.5842.	S/L McCLURE	SELF.	OBSERVER PARTIALS.
MARCH.	22.	LANCASTER.	R.5842.	SELF.	S/L. McCLURE.	PARTIALS. 20-21,000'.
MARCH.	23.	TEMPEST.	JN.732.	SELF.	—	L.F.P.
MARCH.	24.	MOSQUITO.	RF.648.	SELF.	—	PARTIALS.
MARCH.	27.	TEMPEST.	JN.739.	SELF.	—	PARTIALS. 8-10,000'

SUMMARY FOR MARCH 1945.
UNIT. T.P.S. BOSCOMBE DOWN.
DATE 1·A·45.
SIGNATURE. Lancaster F/LT.

1. LANCASTER I.
2. MOSQUITO
3. TEMPEST V.
4. SPITFIRE IX.
5. SWORDFISH
6. HARVARD.

G/CAPT.
COMMANDANT. E.T.P.S. BOSCOMBE DOWN.

GRAND TOTAL [Cols. (1) to (10)]
1677 Hrs. 30 Mins.

TOTALS CARRIED FORW...

Chapter 9

The Empire Test Pilots' School

In the early years of the war, many service and civilian pilots died testing the plethora of new aircraft types being produced, and in December 1942 Air Marshal Francis Linnell, the comptroller of Research and Development in the Ministry of Aircraft Production, proposed that twelve above-average pilots with academic degrees should be selected and sent in pairs for training to the A&AEE, the Royal Aircraft Establishment (RAE) at Farnborough, and four aircraft firms, after which they would be posted to various developmental organisations. Under his successor, Air Vice Marshal Ralph Sorley, the project came to fruition, but with the requirement for a degree dropped and with training only at Boscombe Down, where Sorley had been commandant of the A&AEE between February 1940 and May 1941. As the Test Pilots' Training Flight (TPTF), established on 21 June 1943 as a unit within the A&AEE, its remit was 'to provide suitably trained pilots for testing duties in aeronautical research and development establishments within the service and the industry'. Initially it had a staff of two: the commandant, Wing Commander S. 'Sammy' Wroath, AFC, and his chief technical instructor, G. Maclaren Humphreys.

Wing Commander Wroath was posted to the United States during the second course, to return in 1945 to Boscombe to command the Performance Testing Squadron. His successor was the hugely experienced Wing Commander J.F.X. McKenna, who had been with the A&AEE since 1939, but he was killed in January 1945 when during a high-speed dive an ammunition panel on the upper side of the wing of his Mustang came away, and structural failure of the wing resulted. Next to take over was the equally experienced Group Captain H.J. 'Willy' Wilson, AFC, from the Royal Aircraft Establishment at Farnborough, where he had been responsible for the testing of captured German aircraft. He would achieve fame in November 1945, setting a new world speed record for aircraft in a Gloster Meteor Mark IV.

At the time of his appointment, working in the Bomber Testing Section at Boscombe, Maclaren Humphreys had both a BSc degree and a teaching diploma, and it may have been the latter that singled him out as the right man to develop a syllabus from scratch. He designed a nine-month course, of which two months were to be spent visiting firms and the Royal Aircraft Establishment. All aspects of the course proved eminently successful, save the setting aside of a two-month block for visits. So welcoming had been the aircraft firms, and so overwhelming their hospitality, that it was decided with subsequent courses to schedule the visits intermittently throughout the course.

Starting with just one Nissen hut, the TPTF soon expanded into three more, as well as two wooden huts and a washhouse, all of them very basic. It also had only the most elementary range of aircraft, a Halifax I and Master III being first acquired, and then, over the duration of the course, a Bristol Beaufort II, Hurricane II, Percival Proctor, Airspeed Oxford and a North American Mitchell. But through Sammy Wroath's close links with the A&AEE, aircraft were also borrowed from the latter location from time to time.

No. 1 Course began in June 1943, but of the eighteen students – drawn from the RAF, Fleet Air Arm and the Bristol Aeroplane Company – five quickly dropped out, finding the required standard of mathematics beyond them. Of the thirteen who completed the course in February 1944, four were appointed to positions in the A&AEE. Five of those who finished the course later died testing aircraft.

This course was by way of an experiment; success would assure its continuance, and as this was proved, it became clear that further staff were needed. One was an assistant commandant, and Wing Commander H.P. Powell, AFC (inevitably nicknamed 'Sandy'), who was commanding C Flight of the A&AEE, was appointed. He immediately sought an adjutant, and convinced Flight Lieutenant F.R. Arnold, of the Armament Squadron at A&AEE to take on the role. In his fifties, and a machine-gunner in the First World War who had flown as a rear gunner in Coastal Command, Fred Arnold proved ideal for the role.

The No. 2 Course, which ran between June 1944 and February 1945, had a much larger and more wide-ranging intake of twenty-eight, including three civilians and two Chinese pilots. One of those was Eric Franklin, who took up an appointment with Armstrong Whitworth, and with whom Jo would later work. Handicapped by language problems, as well as by their limited flying experience, the two Chinese pilots, Captains Chen and Loh, were obliged to repeat the course. Of the other twenty-six, three were killed in accidents during the course and five others died later during flight testing.

As No. 2 Course drew to a conclusion, applications for No. 3 Course were invited, and both Jo and his flight commander at A&AEE, Jimmy Mann, applied and were accepted. No. 3 Course started on 13 March with an enrolment of thirty-one students. Besides the aforementioned two Chinese Air Force officers the intake included several from the RAF, five from the Fleet Air Arm, two each from the RAAF, RCAF, US Navy and US Army Air Force, two also from the aircraft industry, and one each from the RNZAF, Free French Air Force, Royal Netherlands Navy and the Belgian Air Force. Additional staff had been recruited both to assist with flying training and with theoretical instruction. Jo recalls:

Our chief technical instructor was a civilian, G Maclaren Humphreys, who had been a senior technician in the performance department at Boscombe Down. He had technical and teaching qualifications, so he was pushed into the job and made a magnificent job of it. He had unlimited patience and understanding and it must have been very hard work for him. We had to start off with mathematical refreshers, the theory of logarithms and calculus and all that sort of thing before we could really get into the technical side of things. 'Humph', as he was always called, had an assistant, a young technical chap [F.D. Hilson] who helped as much as he could to keep us pointing in the right direction and answer all our numerous questions. It became evident that we needed a flying instructor as well because a number of the pilots who were posted in on the course had only flown two or three types of aircraft before and were horrified at the suggestion that they climb into a type they hadn't flown before and just fly it. I never suffered from that problem at all. I think they had two flying instructors on later courses. The Commandant of the School was Group Captain 'Willy' Wilson, but we didn't see very much of him. The Chief Flying Instructor was Wing Commander 'Sandy' Powell; he'd been at Boscombe Down for years. He was one of the doyens of the test-flying world.

Typically, mornings were given over to classroom work, succinctly described by Squadron Leader R.E. Havercroft, a member of No. 2 Course, in John Rawlings' and Hilary Sedgwick's history of the Empire Test Pilots' School, *Learn to Test, Test to Learn*: 'The technical side was always dealt with by M.H. (Maclaren Humphreys) and he would lay down a programme of 'Why you did it, How you did it' on the Blackboard in the classroom. Then Sandy Powell would tell you the technique of doing it in the aircraft itself.'[1]

Afternoons were typically spent in the air, as Squadron Leader Havercroft recalls:

We would do partial climbs, stability, roll performance, yaw performance, handling in dives, handling in the stall, spinning, cockpit assessment. You had to take the aircraft through these exercises, bring back your results on your knee pad and then get down and work out quantitatively the results and then plot them on graphs, working out all the results, which would be kept in a folder as part of your course. The reports were given to M.H. and he would check them and write an assessment – 'This is good, not good enough, what about this, did you do that?' SP would do the same thing from a flying standpoint.[2]

Jo's recollection of this part of the course, four months' classroom work in the morning and flying in the afternoon, is that 'going through the actual practical part of performance measurements and then reducing data to get the results corrected for all the varying factors was quite tricky, quite hard work'.

Along with the usual lectures by ETPS staff there were occasional lectures by high-profile visitors, among those whom Jo remembers speaking to No. 3 Course being Peter Masefield, the journalist who at the time was secretary of the War Cabinet committee on post-war civil air transport and later became chief executive of British European Airways, and Major Alexander Seversky, founder of what became Republic Aviation and a great advocate of air power. Leading technical experts from the Royal Aircraft Establishment at Farnborough also gave lectures.

No. 3 Course was cosmopolitan and friendly, but Jo remembers with particular vividness Lieutenant Commander M.W. 'Butch' Davenport of the United States Navy. 'He was a lovely chap and very friendly,' Jo says.

> Although I'd been at Boscombe for quite a time and seen Stonehenge from the air many times I'd never actually been to see it on the ground until Butch said, 'Come on Jo, show me your Stonehenge.' The four Americans on the course had a jeep each and on two or three occasions Butch said, 'Come on up to London with me', and we'd jump in his jeep, drive up to London and go to what they called Rainbow Corner. There was one in Tottenham Court Road and we'd sit at the bar there and have pancakes, maple syrup and real coffee; it was quite a treat.

Sadly one of the four Americans on the course was its only fatality, Major E.W. Leach being killed in July when the Airspeed Oxford he was piloting crashed on the Isle of Wight. The cause of the accident was never established.

There is, however, one other fatal accident that Jo recalls, since it occurred on the airfield at Boscombe. On 1 April Air Commodore David Waghorn – younger brother of H.R.D. Waghorn, who won the Schneider Trophy race in 1929, and who was himself a member of the RAAF High Speed Flight Team in 1931 – flew in to lunch with Air Commodore D'Arcy Greig. Jo writes:

> After lunch this eminent visitor climbed back into his Spitfire XIX to return to wherever he came from. The weather was clear, but there was a very strong, gusty wind. After take-off he turned back to beat-up the airfield, but unfortunately crashed on the field, and in the parlance of the times, he was 'strawberry jam'.

Some of the members of No. 3 Course had flown only a few different aircraft. Jo came to it with test-flying experience of a wide range of types. Hence of the eighteen separate models or marks he flew during the course, he was already familiar with all but five. Among those he encountered for the first time were the Armstrong Whitworth Albemarle, the Spitfire XXI, Tempest II and the RAF's first jet fighter, the Meteor Marks 1 and 3.

About the Albemarle, which Jo flew on 11 July for a photography shoot over the Larkhill Range, he comments: 'Boscombe had its own Albemarle, whose use seemed to be confined to air-to-air photography. I only flew it once, and as an ex-AWA man, I was rather disappointed. The performance was unimpressive, and it felt slightly unstable – nothing there to be proud of.'

The Albemarle was indeed a disappointment, but for reasons not of Armstrong Whitworth's making. The aircraft began life as the Bristol 155, a response to an Air Ministry requirement – issued in anticipation of a shortage of alloys and a possible devastation of British aircraft factories – for a reconnaissance bomber largely of wood and steel, and capable of being built by subcontractors used to working in those materials. Handed on to Armstrong Whitworth for development, by the time it was ready for flight testing, the Albemarle was redundant as a bomber. Hence the decision was taken to convert it into a glider tug and special duties transport, roles it performed creditably during 'Operation Husky', the invasion of Sicily, and 'Operation Overlord', the invasion of Normandy. Yet less than stellar it certainly was, and for a former Armstrong Whitworth apprentice, undoubtedly disappointing.

The Spitfire XXI, the latest mark of the iconic aircraft that Jo flew, he was not overly impressed with, either. The Rolls-Royce Griffon engine was one with which, as he confesses, 'probably for no valid practical reason', he was 'never completely happy'. 'The Mark VIII and IX Spitfires were, I think,' he says, 'the ultimate; the later marks became rougher to fly because they were over-powered.'

Jo's logbook shows that while on the course he flew on average 10 to 15 hours a month, carrying out a variety of tests. His first, on 21 and 22 March involved 'partials' in a Lancaster. He explains:

Partial climbs were to establish the optimum climbing speed. With a specified power setting, the aircraft would be set into a stable climb condition and timed through, say, 2,000 feet. This would be repeated at several different IAS (indicated air speeds), and from these results the optimum climbing speed for those conditions could be established.

Later in the month he carried out partials also on a Mosquito VI and Tempest V, following these in April with climbs to heights varying from 15,000 feet, in a Swordfish, Hudson, Harvard and Oxford, to 30,000 feet in the Tempest. After that came two flights in the Lancaster testing 'cooling levels' and in an Oxford, Boston and Harvard involving 'level speeds'. More of these took place in May, in a Tempest and Mosquito, succeeded by more sophisticated tests, requiring a 'flowmeter check' and 'fuel consumptions' in a Lancaster, 'position error trials' in a Hudson and 'measured take-offs' in a Harvard.

In April, the ETPS had acquired an example of the RAF's first jet fighter, the Gloster Meteor Mark 1, and on 25 May Jo was given the opportunity of flying it for the first time, even if only for 15 minutes' local flying. He remembers the occasion vividly:

The Meteor that was lent to ETPS, EE213, was a Mk.1, with Rolls-Royce Welland W2B/23C engines. I think that they gave about 1600 lbs thrust. Gas turbine power settings are normally by indicated RPM, but in the case of these early engines it was by indicated fuel pressure, and we were warned that under 300 psi there was risk of the lights going out. With 300 lbs fuel pressure there was still some appreciable residual thrust, which of course affected the landing technique. One of our Chinese students, 'Charlie' Chen, floated gently up the runway three times before he had the courage to throttle back enough for the Meteor to actually sit down! Compared with any prop aircraft, the Meteor slid through the air so easily. When I decided to try a loop I set a speed of probably about 300 mph at about 2,000ft before pulling quite gently upwards, and when the horizon re-appeared, upside down, I gently half-rolled out to find that I was at 10,000ft. I'd gone up 8,000ft! Even with less than half the thrust of the Derwent-powered Meteors that were to follow, it was really a joy to fly.

In June, a month during which Jo did less than 5 hours' flying, he took the Meteor up again, this time for half an hour local flying. Only two test flights were carried out that month, 'generator tests' on the prototype Lincoln, with which Jo was well acquainted, and 'measured take-offs' in an Oxford, of which he writes: 'I first encountered the Airspeed Oxford on the CFS OTU Instructors' course at Upavon in '42, and again at intervals from then until I was with Boulton-Paul in '46. The poor old Oxbox was, I suppose, a perfectly innocuous aircraft, but I never, ever, felt friendly towards it.' In July, however, more flying was involved, and more advanced handling tests with the Tempest V and Lancaster.

As part of the evolving curriculum, students of No. 2 Course were, towards the end of it, required to carry out a complete handling assess-ment of an aircraft, usually one that they had hitherto flown only rarely or not at all. The innovation was highly successful, and became a staple of the course. Far from being confronted with an aircraft whose perfor-mance they knew nothing about, however, Jo and his bosom friend, Cana-dian 'Frankie' Phripp, were teamed for the assessment of a Lancaster, on which both had flown a tour of operations. Accordingly, they decided to dispense with a good deal of the handling assessment, writing it up out of their considerable experience of the type. Jo recalls:

By this time [July 1945] the war in Europe was over and lots of people were flying over to Germany to see what was what. However, work on the ETPS was pretty intensive and we couldn't take time off to go. So Frankie and I, having decided that we could write our report without doing all the test flights, dashed off, just the two of us aboard this Lanc, to Germany. We had no maps of course, though we roughly knew the way by then, but we were beaten by the weather the first time, finishing somewhere over Belgium before we turned back. The second time, however, we reached Cologne, which was where we were aiming for and we flew quite low, at about 500 feet, over the city, which was a terrible sight; a scene of total devastation. Frankie was flying, I was standing beside him and suddenly there was an almighty bang; a bird had hit the windscreen and cracked it. It frightened us to death, though we had a jolly good laugh about it afterwards. In recounting this episode, Frankie always maintained that the bird must have been a turkey.

The Lancaster appraisal was completed on 14 August with a 'trim change' trial, but Jo flew a variety of tests on other aircraft, involving 'stick force' on a Swordfish, 'stability' on a Tempest V, and lateral and directional stability on a Spitfire IX, Harvard and Tempest II. The latter, powered by the Bristol Centaurus radial that Jo had already encountered in the Bristol Buckingham, was, he says, one of his favourite aircraft: 'A very nice aircraft for aerobatics.' In August, also, Jo carried out a 'phugoids' test on a Mosquito. He explains:

> The purpose of Phugoids was to investigate and evaluate the longitudinal 'stick-free' stability of an aircraft, and to determine its Centre of Gravity limits. The aircraft would be set into a stable condition of level flight, trimmed to fly 'hands-off'. Once this was achieved, momentary pressure would be applied to the stick, nose up or nose down, and the resultant behaviour observed. In the case of a positively stable aircraft, the result would be undulating flight about the original height, gradually damping out to resume level flight. This undulating flight path is known as a phugoid.

No. 3 Course ended with what Jo describes as 'the ordeal of several very challenging technical exams', out of which he emerged eighth out of thirty-two, a placing he regarded as 'not too bad'. Then members of the course were moved to Farnborough, where they observed the test work being undertaken by the Royal Aircraft Establishment, had the opportunity to look over the collection of captured German aircraft, and carried out what Jo describes as 'odd jobs'. For him, the most interesting of these involved flying, with three others, to Schleswig, close to the Danish frontier, to bring back three German aircraft. He writes:

> We went in a German aircraft, a Siebel 204, which was about the same size as the Anson, but much smarter generally, and with much sweeter engines. We flew via Brussels to Schleswig and I brought back the Messerschmitt Me.410 and the other two chaps brought

back a Focke-Wulf Fw.190 apiece. I landed at Schiphol, Amsterdam, and overnighted there, which was quite interesting and so back to Farnborough. In both the Siebel and the Messerschmitt 410, the main problems were sorting out the fuel systems, and doing mental arithmetic converting airspeeds and altitudes, etc.

Interspersed with these 'odd jobs' were visits to major firms in the aircraft industry, Jo particularly recalling Avro, Rolls-Royce, de Havilland, Rotol and Power Jets, as well as to the Marine Aircraft Experimental Establishment (MAEE) at Felixstowe. Having set up the programme of visits, 'Sandy' Powell later came to see it as a mistake, for reasons he gives in *Learn to Test, Test to Learn*:

> I thought we would do the work first and would reserve two months for going around the aircraft industry. . . . But every firm we went to, and of course there were about twenty-eight in the country then, laid on a directors' lunch and a test pilots' evening and it was only a few days and we were a bunch of wrecks. The firms all pushed the boat out because they wanted to find new test pilots.[3]

Jo says of these visits only that 'we were right royally entertained by all of them', but Maclaren Humphreys goes into details about one such series of visits:

> It was very heavy going. We went to Rolls-Royce and we visited Derby first. We had dinner in the evening at Derby and lunch the following day at Hucknall. They had done us so well we thought the least we could do was to do something about reciprocating. We invited quite a lot of the Rolls people to come back to the hotel with us, which turned into a dreadful orgy. The following day we were due to visit A.V. Roe at Manchester and arrived at the Grand Hotel at about six o'clock – most of us feeling terrible and thinking thank goodness we have a night's rest ready for A.V. Roe tomorrow. About 6.30 pm I had a phone call from the then Chief Test Pilot to welcome us and to say they would be over at eight o'clock for a dinner which they had arranged. So we were there until about two o'clock the following morning.[4]

In October 1945, the members of the No. 3 Course received their various postings. Jo's was back to the A&AEE at Boscombe, where he joined 'B per T' (B Flight performance testing), his last flights there being on 5 December when he flew a Miles M.57 Aerovan to the Miles aerodrome at Woodley, near Reading. Intended for the post-war civil market, the Aerovan was aptly named, being a twin-engined high-wing monoplane with a pod and boom fuselage, and a fixed tricycle undercarriage. Clamshell doors at the rear allowed the easy loading of bulky cargo, up to the size, it was claimed, of a family car. The Aerovan had been thoroughly tested at Boscombe, and while found easy and pleasant to fly, had been severely criticised for – among other things – an inability to maintain height on one engine and a cabin that leaked in rain. Its plastic-bonded plywood construction was also denounced as flimsy. While at Woodley, Jo also had the opportunity to fly one of the most recent of Miles's products, the M.28 Mercury, which he remembers as 'a neat little single-engined four-seater with retractable undercarriage'. His other memory of the visit to Woodley, made in the company of Squadron Leader Handaside, RAAF, from No. 3 Course, was being told that Miles 'were involved in marketing the very first ball-point pens under the name Biro – the price 55s, rather expensive at that time!'

At Boscombe, with the war over, Jo had a decision to make. Off the record, he had been informed by the adjutant, Fred Arnold, that he would shortly get his 'scraper ring' (i.e. promotion to squadron leader), the implication being, perhaps, that this might influence Jo to remain in the RAF. He and several others provisionally applied for permanent commissions, and attended interviews at Group Headquarters at South Cerney. He comments:

> Permanent commissions were not being given at this time. Instead we were offered four-year extended service commissions, assured that non-acceptance of this would in no way influence the eventual award of a permanent commission. As we suspected at the time, this proved to be totally untrue. In the event, permanent commissions were only awarded to those who had previously accepted the extended service commission. But none of this affected me, because I had already

decided to accept the offer of a job as test pilot with Boulton-Paul Aircraft at Wolverhampton, to whom I was seconded in January '46, pending de-mob shortly after.

There was, however, another reason why Jo decided against an RAF career. For in December 1945 Jo had married Grace Elizabeth Freeman. He and Betty, as she was always known, had met in January of that year when she was posted to Boscombe Down as WAAF Assistant Section Officer Freeman, on code and cypher duties. They became friends, and when the basic petrol ration was restored, and Jo recommissioned his 1933 Morris Ten, he was able to visit her at her parents' home at Cheriton, about 8 miles east of Winchester. Looking back on his marriage, Jo sees it as one of many that occurred 'amid all the euphoria of the end of the war', a strong desire to put down roots and lead a settled domestic life. 'After five years of living in digs, followed immediately by six years in RAF messes,' he says, 'I was keen to set up my own little home.'

MISCELLANEOUS FLYING WITH E.T.P.S.

YEAR 1945		AIRCRAFT		PILOT, OR 1ST PILOT	2ND PILOT, PUPIL OR PASSENGER	DUTY (INCLUDING RESULTS AND REMARKS)
MONTH	DATE	Type	No.			
—	—	—	—	—	—	TOTALS BROUGHT FORWARD
OCT.	31	LIBERATOR	BZ.959	SELF	MR. T. LUCK.	LOCAL, FARNBOROUGH.
NOV.	8	SIEBEL	"AM 4".	SELF.	LT/CDR. BURGERHOOT.	FARNBOROUGH — BRUSSELS EVÈRE
NOV.	9	SIEBEL	"AM 4".	SELF.	LT/CDR. BURGERHOOT.	BRUSSELS EVÈRE · SCHLESWIG.
NOV.	10	ME.410	"V₂"	SELF.	—	AIR TEST — SCHLESWIG.
NOV.	10	ME.410	"V₂"	SELF.	—	SCHLESWIG — SCHIPOL.
NOV.	11	ME.410	"V₂"	SELF.	—	SCHIPOL — MANSTON.
NOV.	11	ME.410	"V₂"	SELF.	—	MANSTON — FARNBOROUGH.
DEC.	4	SUNDERLAND	?	F/LT. ?	SELF.	LOCAL, FELIXTOWE.
DEC.	5	AEROVAN.	G·AGOZ	SELF.	S/LDR. HANDASYDE	LOCAL, READING.
DEC.	5	MERCURY.	G·AGVX.	SELF.	S/LDR. HANDASYDE	LOCAL, READING.

SUMMARY FOR OCTOBER 6ᵀᴴ
TO DECEMBER 31ˢᵀ 1945.
DATE :- 1.1.46.
SIGNATURE :- _[signature]_ F/LT.

1. LIBERATOR.
2. SUNDERLAND.
3. ME. 410.A.
4. SIEBEL 204.
5. AEROVAN.
6. MERCURY.

GRAND TOTAL [Cols. (1) to (10)]
1759 Hrs. 10 Mins.

TOTALS CARRIED FORWARD

YEAR 1946		AIRCRAFT		PILOT, OR 1ST PILOT	2ND PILOT, PUPIL OR PASSENGER	DUTY (INCLUDING RESULTS AND
MONTH	DATE	Type	No.			
—	—	—	—	—		— TOTALS BROUGHT
JAN.	9.	OXFORD.	V.3772.	SELF.	MR. LINDSAY. NEALE	DESFORD . BAGINTON & EE
JAN.	14.	MOSQUITO	TA.501	SELF.	—	AIR TEST AT BOSCOMB
JAN.	14.	DAKOTA.		SELF.	F/LT. FARREE.	HANDWING, BOSCOMBE.
JAN.	15.	AUSTER.	513.	SELF.	F/LT. ASHWORTH.	COWES & RETURN, BOS
JAN.	18.	LINCOLN.		SELF.	F/LT. RILEY..	LOCAL FLYING. BOSCO
JAN.	21.	LANCASTER.	HK.543.	SELF.	S/LDR. EASBY.	LOCAL FLYING. BOSCO
			SUMMARY FOR JANUARY.			LINCOLN.
			B-P AIRCRAFT, WOLVERHAMPTON			LANCASTER.
			& A.&A.E.E. BOSCOMBE DOWN.			DAKOTA.
			JLancaster F/LT.			MOSQUITO.
						OXFORD.
						AUSTER.
FEB.	11.	OXFORD.	V.3772	SELF.	MR. STEVENS.	TO DONCASTER & RETU
FEB.	19.	PROCTOR.	LZ.621.	SELF.	—	TO WALSALL & RETURN
FEB.	21.	OXFORD.	V.3772	SELF.	MR. NEALE.	TO HENDON & RETURN
FEB.	27.	PROCTOR.	LZ.621	SELF.	—	TO WALSALL & RETURN
			SUMMARY FOR FEBRUARY.			PROCTOR.
			B-P AIRCRAFT, WOLVERHAMPTON.			OXFORD.
			JLancaster F/LT.			

GRAND TOTAL [Cols. (1) to (10)]

.....1768.....Hrs.....25.....Mins.

TOTALS CARRIED F

Chapter 10

Boulton Paul and Saunders-Roe

It was customary, and with obvious advantages, for most aircraft manufacturers to have a resident technical representative at Boscombe. It was
also usual for the chief test pilots from these firms to visit the A&AEE
regularly, by way of liaison. It was on one such occasion, while Jo was a
member of the ETPS No. 3 Course that the chief test pilot of Boulton Paul
Aircraft, Cyril Feather, approached him. He recalls:

> Cyril Feather asked me if I wanted a job when I'd finished the course
> because he was retiring and he said the other pilot, Robin Lindsay-
> Neale, was leaving. So I went up to Wolverhampton and had a brief
> interview with Ralph Beasley, who was the General Manager, and
> then he took me to meet J.D. North, who was a famous name in
> aviation at that time, and it was arranged that I would be seconded to
> them awaiting my demob. So sometime in January 1946 I presented
> myself at Boulton Paul's factory at Wolverhampton, only to find
> that Robin Lindsay-Neale was still there and was unaware that I was
> coming. It was a peculiar situation, and there was no explanation
> forthcoming. Neither of us was very pleased, and understandably
> Robin was indignant and a bit hostile to start with, but eventually we
> made friends and got along reasonably well.

Boulton Paul Aircraft had its origins in an ironmongery and stove grate
manufacturing business set up in Norwich in 1797. During the nineteenth century, in the hands of Dawson Paul and William Boulton, it had

expanded greatly, manufacturing for a burgeoning country estates market everything from greenhouses to dog kennels and aviaries to wire netting. Further diversification into the structural steel business was followed by the design and construction of marine engines and then the building of motorboats. During the First World War the company manufactured prefabricated buildings and prodigious quantities of wire netting, invaluable for holding up the sides of trenches, but in 1915 approached the War Office with an offer to diversify into any branch of war production that seemed appropriate. With a workforce highly skilled in both metal and woodworking, they were asked to manufacture aircraft under licence. This they did with conspicuous success, setting up a highly sophisticated production-line system.

Encouraged, the firm's directors decided to move into aircraft design, and in 1917 appointed John North as chief designer; he would remain with the company until his death in 1968, after Boulton Paul's merger with the Dowty Group, recognised as a doyen among aircraft designers. But the company had only limited success after the First World War in winning either civilian or military contracts, and in 1934 Boulton & Paul Ltd sold off its Aircraft Department to a London financial group, General Industries Trust Ltd, which formed a new company, Boulton Paul Aircraft Ltd. The fledgling business also had little success with its original designs – only its Defiant turret fighter entered RAF service in appreciable numbers – but burgeoned with contracts to build Hawker Demons, Blackburn Rocs, and Fairey Barracudas under licence. The company also developed a highly successful specialisation in power turret design, some of its products being fitted to the Lancasters and Halifaxes that Jo had tested at Boscombe Down.

The end of the war brought the cancellation of contracts, however, and when Jo joined Boulton Paul in January 1946, the firm had only just secured its future with a crucial contract to convert Wellington X bombers to Wellington T.10 configuration for Flying Training Command. Some 270 Wellingtons would be converted between 1946 and 1950, and undoubtedly Jo would have been heavily involved in testing the refurbished aircraft had he continued with the company. As it was, his stay was brief. He explains:

While I was seconded to Boulton Paul in January, for administrative purposes I'd been put in the care of the Air Ministry Unit, which had managed to lose my documents, so my demob was delayed until the end of March '46. I stayed on at Boulton Paul as a civilian for the time being, although there was practically nothing to do. One of the duties that did fall to me was, almost every Friday evening, to fly two of the directors down to Hendon in the firm's Oxford. They used to drive down to the airfield in a large car and sit in it until I'd got both engines started. Then they'd get in and sit down and at Hendon get out without so much as a 'How's your father', which I didn't take to very much at all. From that point of view I didn't like Boulton Paul very much. Anyway in about May '46 the ETPS had their annual end of term dinner, to which former graduates were invited. This time it was at Cranfield, where they'd recently moved, and the Commandant, by that time Group Captain Ubee, asked me how I was getting on, and whether I was happy at Wolverhampton. I said I wasn't, and he said, 'Well, Saunders-Roe are looking for someone. How about that?' I thought it was a good idea and I went down to Cowes, was interviewed and got the job. Ralph Beasley was far from pleased when I gave him my notice but so be it. In the event less than three years later [February 1949] Robin Lindsay-Neale and his assistant, Peter Tisshaw, were killed in an accident in the Boulton Paul Balliol trainer. In a high speed dive the windscreen disintegrated, perhaps because of a bird strike, and the aircraft crashed.

For Jo the move to Saunders-Roe was a relief. 'I'd really done no useful work in the almost six months I was with Boulton Paul,' he says, 'and was just a glorified chauffeur. Except for the delivery of a Mustang to Llandow, over the next three months my flying was limited to communication flights in the company's Oxford, with, in May and June, eight air tests on converted Wellingtons. That was my lot at Wolverhampton.' Domestically, the shift south was a relief also. For Betty, demobbed in April, had moved north to join Jo in his Wolverhampton bedsit. With him working on the Isle of Wight, she would be able, as an interim arrangement, to return to her parents' home at Cheriton while he found family accommodation in Cowes.

Saunders-Roe, the company that Jo joined in July 1946, had its origins in a small family boat-building company established in the 1830s at

Streatley, on the Thames, by Moses Saunders. It was, however, Moses's grandson, Sam Saunders, who set the firm on the path that eventually led it into aircraft production, first developing and patenting a new method of wooden hull construction – Consuta, involving mahogany plywood sheeting sewn together with copper or bronze wire – and then moving into the development and construction of fast waterborne craft. The technique proved highly successful, as did Saunders-designed and built speedboats, and it was a logical progression that, in 1909, took S.E. Saunders Ltd – now located on the Isle of Wight – into aeronautics, advising on the use of Consuta in aircraft hull designs and constructing hulls for several aircraft manufacturers. On the outbreak of war in 1914, Saunders was ordered by the Admiralty to concentrate its efforts on aircraft production. At first this meant simply the construction of floats and hulls for other companies, but alongside this Saunders won contracts to build complete aircraft under licence, and by the end of the war was constructing Porte/Felixstowe flying boats.

The war's end brought an inevitable contraction in the aero industry, but Sam Saunders persisted, concentrating – although not exclusively – on flying boats, building a series of prototypes designed by Henry Knowler, who had joined the firm in 1923. Failure to win Royal Air Force contracts, along with the superseding of Consuta by metal hull construction, meant that the aircraft division was operating at a loss. Restructuring was inevitable, but came about unusually, through the entrepreneurial activities of John Siddeley, who had acquired a controlling interest in A.V. Roe and Company. This led to the founders of A.V. Roe, Sir Alliott Verdon Roe and John Lord, selling their shares in the company and in 1928 acquiring a controlling interest in Saunders. Saunders-Roe, as the company became the following year, adopted metal hull design and in the 1930s produced several modestly successful flying-boat types for civil and military use. However, its only new design introduced to service during the Second World War, the Lerwick, proved a disaster, and production was early terminated, while Saro (as it was commonly called) spent most of the war building Supermarine Walruses and Sea Otters under licence.

By 1939 there were only two companies in Britain specialising in flying-boat construction; Saunders-Roe and the much bigger Short Brothers and Harland at Rochester. In 1943, after a lengthy but unsuccessful attempt by the Ministry of Aircraft Production to improve production rates at Rochester, Shorts was nationalised, whereupon Sir Arthur Gouge, the general manager and chief designer, resigned, joining Saro as chairman of the board. Jo recalls the situation at Cowes when he arrived:

> When I joined the company in July 1946, I was taken to meet Sir Arthur Gouge just once, but thereafter I hardly ever saw him. The Managing Director was Captain E.D. Clarke, and at that time the company was thick on the ground with retired Royal Navy captains. I thought Clarke was one of these, but it turned out he was a captain in the Royal Flying Corps during World War I, which was a somewhat lowlier rank. I never really worked out how or why he became Managing Director, because he wasn't particularly well-informed technically.
>
> The man who first interviewed me was the General Manager, Robert Perfect. He was, I believe, a nephew of Humphrey Verdon Roe, Alliott's brother, and Marie Stopes, Humphrey's wife, who was famous in her own right as a scientist and proponent of birth control. Rob Perfect was a very pleasant chap, easy to get on with. He later became Sales and Publicity Director.
>
> Henry Knowler was Chief Designer and a director and he was a cheerful, bright and breezy individual. He had one of the first Triumph Roadsters, a little open two-seater, a pretty car, and he used to drive round in this with the hood down. Apparently he was quite a one for the ladies too. That was his reputation. He had a son, Peter, a nice chap, who had been a Fleet Air Arm pilot and had a job in the drawing office I think, but he seemed to be a bit of a free agent, and occasionally flew a Sea Otter.

In his first months with Saro, Jo's main task was testing newly completed Supermarine Sea Otters, built under licence from Vickers Supermarine, the last of them, RD894, being flown on 3 November. Developed from the highly successful Walrus, which Saro had also built in numbers, the Sea Otter was, like the Walrus, a biplane amphibian, but fitted with a tractor engine, the 965hp Bristol Mercury, rather than a pusher, the 750hp Bristol Pegasus. The Sea Otter was of course faster, and had a slightly longer

range, but Jo, who had previously flown a Walrus, was not entirely enthusiastic about the latter's successor. He comments:

> When the Sea Otter was developed from the Walrus, they altered the
> planing bottom and step in order to give extra clearance when passing
> over the crest of a standard slipway. This caused some deterioration
> in its water performance, making it much more prone to 'porpoising'.
> Also the Walrus seemed much smoother and quieter because one was
> not sitting immediately beneath the engine and propeller.

In his first months with Saunders-Roe, the only aircraft Jo flew, apart from
the Sea Otters, was the company communication aircraft, an Avro Club
Cadet, 'similar', Jo remarks, 'to the Cadets that I flew at Anstey, but with a
De Havilland Gypsy Major engine. Peter Knowler on occasion came with
me and we'd go over to Eastleigh and sundry places. Peter was eventually
transferred to Beaumaris, in North Wales, where Saro had a factory and a
research and development unit, and had spent the war in the specialized
business of converting American flying boats like the Catalina to RAF
requirements.'

While the construction of Sea Otters was bread and butter work for
Saunders-Roe, attention in the Design Department was focused on what
was to be a truly revolutionary aircraft, the world's first jet-powered
flying- boat fighter, the SR.A/1. Proposed jointly by Saro and Metropolitan-
Vickers' Gas Turbine Department, the fighter would be capable of
operating from sheltered coastal waters, and might, Saro considered, prove
useful in a Pacific island-hopping campaign. The Ministry of Aircraft
Production was impressed, issued a specification, E.6/44, covering the
submission, and ordered three prototypes. Although the Ministry of
Supply suggested in January 1946 that as an economy measure one should
be cancelled, in the event all three were completed and flight tested.

Crucial to the success of the 'Squirt', as the SR.A/1 was colloquially
known, was the Metropolitan-Vickers Beryl axial-flow engine, initially
developing 3,230lb of static thrust, but small in diameter compared to the
centrifugal-type compressors then in production, this making it possible
to install two Beryls side by side without creating a fuselage excessively
broad in the beam. Armament was four 20mm Hispano cannon, and an

ejection seat was fitted, the first to be delivered to a manufacturer by the
Martin-Baker Aircraft Company Ltd.

The first prototype, TG263, first flew on 16 July 1947, with chief test pilot
Geoffrey Tyson at the controls. Jo recalls the circumstances in which he
learned of Tyson's appointment:

> In September 1946 I was able to go on a Sunderland conversion course,
> an RAF conversion course at RAF Pembroke Dock, home of No. 4 (C)
> OTU. This was a wonderful experience for me flying Sunderland 5s.
> I was down there for about two and a half months and took the full
> RAF course, something over 60 hours flying, which included night
> flying and manoeuvring on the water. This was quite complicated,
> because with the flying boat you can't go astern or stop; it's got a
> large beam area that makes it susceptible to wind effect and the large
> fin constantly wants to turn into the wind like a weathercock. So
> manoeuvring, mooring or anchoring can be quite exciting at times.
> The full syllabus included night flying, which was interesting in that
> you are able to land completely blind in a flying boat. The system for
> night landings in a Sunderland, even though you had a flare path,
> involved maintaining a fixed air speed, which I think was 90 mph,
> and, using the elevator and the throttle, adjusting the rate of descent
> to 400 feet a minute, gritting your teeth and holding this until you hit
> the water. Hitting the water was rather critical because sometimes it
> was difficult to tell that you'd arrived. There had been accidents where
> pilots had thought they'd arrived, throttled back and stalled. The nose
> dropped and if they hit the water at too sharp an angle the aircraft
> went over on its back. So you had to be absolutely certain that you
> were down on the water before you throttled back.
>
> While I was at Pembroke Dock I received a letter from the
> Managing Director, Captain Clarke, to say that Geoffrey Tyson would
> be joining the company as chief test pilot and I would be his assistant.
> This didn't faze me at all. At the end of the war Short Brothers,
> being nationalized, were ordered to move lock stock and barrel
> from Rochester to Belfast and this was not a popular move at all. It
> probably had something to do with Geoffrey moving to Saunders-
> Roe. When I got back from Pembroke Dock, Geoffrey was of course

already installed but also I found other changes made there. Robert Perfect was now Sales Director and his place as General Manager had been taken by Walter Browning, another refugee from Belfast. He turned out to be very unpopular. The Works Manager was replaced by another refugee, Harry Winkworth, and there were several newcomers, a number of them also refugees from Belfast.

Geoffrey was established in the same office as me at Seaholme, a lovely waterside house, part of the company precinct alongside the main slipway and the main factory buildings at East Cowes. He soon moved his office to the Osborne House Estate, where the drawing house and most of the administration were. The centre of attention at that time of course was the SR.A/1. I felt equipped to undertake its testing, but as this was a Ministry of Aircraft Production contract, it was only reasonable that they should want the early flying done by the most experienced flying boat pilot available, and that was Geoffrey. I was quite happy about his arrival, and though I had never met him, was looking forward to working with him and under his direction. I don't remember him ever coming to Cowes before I went to Pembroke Dock, and he was firmly installed when I came back towards the end of November 1946. I found him from the outset to be aloof, cool and unwilling to talk. We shared the same birthday, although he was 12 years older than I was, and I firmly believe that it was probably he who gave me my first-ever flight in Cumberland in August 1935. Of course I told him this, but he appeared to be quite uninterested and never checked his logbook or even bothered to discuss it.

I had absolutely no social association with Geoffrey; he lived in a flat in Ryde. The only time he drank was at formal dinners, when he was known to have an occasional cigar as well; otherwise he didn't smoke. He was a very keen golfer and squash player, and every weekend went to Rochester to see his mother. He never showed the slightest interest in my background, either flying or anything else, and he was always reluctant to talk about his own to me, although he probably talked to lots of other people. It always seemed to me that he was held in great reverence by the directors, who used to hang on his every word and so it must have been a particularly big shock when I publicly disagreed with him. The directors and senior staff lunched together in the Promenade Building at East Cowes, which had a fine view over the harbour. The Managing Director, 'Captain' Clarke, always sat at the head of his table, and pompously would detail people to sit on either side of him, and one day it was Geoffrey and me. With the Princess in the offing the topic of discussion was wing strength in very large aircraft, and there were ideas for 'gust-alleviation' being thought up. To my utter astonishment, Geoffrey said, rather grandly, 'I believe that a good pilot can anticipate turbulence, don't you think so, Jo?' Very undiplomatically, I spoke my mind and said 'No'. After a pause, the topic of conversation was changed. I guess it was not a very good career move on my part – or perhaps in the long run it was!

Jo returned from Pembroke Dock not only to a new colleague, but also, within days, to a new state: parenthood. For on 13 November 1946, his son Graham was born. At this time, with a critical housing shortage, Betty was still living with her parents at Cheriton, whither Jo, who had a bedsit in Cowes, went every weekend. In March 1947, however, Osborne Court, a large block of flats on the seafront in West Cowes, was de-requisitioned from the Navy and Jo, married with a baby, had priority, with No. 17 becoming their first home. Overlooking the Solent, Osborne Court provided wonderful vistas, none better than one fine summer morning when, Jo recalls, 'we witnessed the two great Cunard liners, Queen Mary and Queen Elizabeth passing each other, greeting each other with their foghorns'. Until warmer weather came, however, Osborne Court was not particularly comfortable, as Jo remembers only too well:

These flats had communal central heating and built-in electric fires. At that time the east wind blew hard for six weeks, the central heating was forever breaking down, no doubt due to years of navy neglect, and we had frequent power cuts: all this with a 5 month old infant, fed on National Dried Milk, and in nappies that had to be laundered. I had to resort to a Primus stove and a paraffin heater, and even then I had to get a doctor's note to confirm that we had an infant before I could get any paraffin.

For most of 1947 Jo was kept busy testing Sea Otters as they came off the production line, the last on 3 November. But during this period he was also given two special assignments. One was to accompany one of the marine crew to find an ex-service launch to convert into a seaplane tender. 'We checked out marine craft, covering Plymouth, Portsmouth and Chichester Harbour,' he says, and 'eventually found a suitable ex-Navy launch at Chichester, which was quite handy because it wasn't far to bring it.'

The other assignment was Jo's alone. He explains:

> I was delegated to find a communications aircraft, a Proctor, to
> replace the Avro Club Cadet that we had, and on 16 April I went off
> in the Club Cadet, visiting all eight RAF Maintenance Units where
> there were Air Ministry surplus Proctors offered for tender. The most
> northerly MU was Edzell, north of the Forth, but I finally selected
> a Proctor at High Ercall, in Shropshire, for which we successfully
> tendered, and which I collected on 18 June. It flew beautifully – sweet
> as a nut – but for its Certificate of Airworthiness the engine had to
> undergo a complete strip, and it was never as good again!

In connection with the departure from Cowes on 16 April Jo recalls that 'as I crossed the Solent, either the Queen Mary or Queen Elizabeth (I forget which) had run aground just south of Calshot. A no doubt very red-faced pilot had taken a chance with the tide – and lost! It was three days before she could be moved.'

Besides the Proctor, Saunders-Roe also had, for a time, an Auster float-plane. Jo explains:

> This was a standard military Auster Mark 6 with a Gypsy Major
> engine, fitted with floats designed and made by Saunders Roe. The
> only other modification to the aircraft was a small ventral fin to boost
> directional stability with the floats fitted. Geoffrey and I shared the
> flying, but there wasn't very much to do, related more to handling
> than performance. I think we shared about 50/50. I recall one Sunday
> morning when I took it out to carry some test. The Solent was glassy
> calm. I tried to take off but the Auster went for about four miles,

right across to Calshot, and wouldn't unstick. I'd heard about this phenomenon before. You need disturbed water to get an aircraft planing. On another occasion Geoffrey was flying it and brought it back with one wing leading edge damaged; I never heard a proper explanation of how that happened. Of course the wing was of wood and fabric construction and very vulnerable to being hit by seawater.

Geoffrey Tyson made the initial flight in TG263, the first prototype of the SR.A/1, on 16 July 1947 and he reported generally positively on how the aircraft handled both on the water and in the air. After being exhibited at the 1947 SBAC show at Radlett, TG263 was passed to the Marine Aircraft Experimental Establishment (MAEE) for type trials. Jo recalls that 'it was about 10 flights and 5 months before I was allowed to get my mitts on it'. That was on 12 December, 'after which', he adds, 'I did get a fair whack of the SR.A/1 flying, though I don't remember ever being able to discuss things generally with Geoffrey on a one to one. He would go away and write his report, I would do the same, and we'd read each other's reports. But there wasn't very much discussion about it.'

Jo recalls the SR.A/1 vividly. It was, he says,

a very pleasant aircraft to fly although in the early days it suffered from snaking or 'Dutch roll', as it was popularly described. This meant it picked up an oscillation both directionally and laterally. This was remedied by the addition of a fin/tailplane acorn fairing, reducing the rudder horn balance, and fitting small 'spoilers' to the rudder trailing edge and round the jet-pipe fairings. The SR.A/1 was probably the first aircraft, apart from Martin-Baker's, to have an ejection seat from the start. We used to view it with some suspicion and would go aboard armed with a large box spanner and a cartridge in our pocket and load it up as we got into the cockpit. That system was probably more dangerous than the later system, where it was loaded up on the ground with a safety pin through the firing pin sear to stop it being inadvertently fired. One of the aircraft was also fitted with anti-G suit equipment and we went to Farnborough to have anti-G suits fitted. I remember pulling something like 5G without too much problem.

The SR.A/1 had integral wing fuel tanks, which meant there were no bags, just part of the wing structure internally sealed and used as a tank. It was planned to pressurize these integral fuel tanks in place of booster pumps, but this proved unsatisfactory. The engines were Metropolitan Vickers Beryls giving about 3,200 pounds of thrust apiece. Metropolitan Vickers were the only British firm producing jet engines with axial flow compressors. Eventually the Ministry of Supply forced them to sell their jet engine division to Armstrong Siddeley, so its up-and-coming engine, the Sapphire, became Armstrong Siddeley's, who continued its development. Metropolitan Vickers were also at this time developing a gas turbine marine engine for the Navy. I was able to go over to Portsmouth one day, where they had one of these engines, I think based on the Sapphire, on test. The boat, about 90 feet long, originally had three large Packard engines, but the Metrovic now replaced the centre one. It was intended to motor out on the two Packards, but in the event neither would start, so we motored out on the Metrovic! The boat proved to have a very lively performance on just the one engine.

With TG263 passed to the MAEE at Felixstowe in June 1948, attention at Cowes focused on the second and third prototypes. Geoffrey Tyson carried out the first flight test of TG267 on 30 April of that year, and of TG271 on 17 August. Jo only flew the second prototype four times, the last of which was delivering it to Felixstowe on 29 December. Along with Geoffrey Tyson, however, he was scheduled to fly the third prototype at the 1948 SBAC air show at Farnborough, as he recollects:

We both had a couple of flights to practise our display routines, and by chance finished up with much the same plan. The flying control authorities needed to know in advance what was planned. Geoffrey flew the aircraft at Farnborough on Wednesday and Thursday, 7 & 8 September, and I was due to fly the remaining three days, the Friday, Saturday and Sunday. Saturday's flight was in fact cancelled because of appalling weather, so I flew it on the 9th and 11th. I was there as a spectator on the Wednesday when Geoffrey flew it and he attracted a great deal of attention by doing an inverted flight down

the runway at what I would estimate at 150 feet. In later years he
would have been grounded for that but at the time it was hailed as a
great performance. I did much the same thing but I don't know what
height I was; you don't measure this by the altimeter when flying
inverted at a few hundred feet but by visual reference to the ground.
On the Sunday after the display I drove up to Farnborough where the
ETPS had returned, and had their own mess, which was the honeypot
for the test pilots on the last night of the show. The party was in full
swing when I got there, but several people congratulated me on my
performance, John Derry and Eric Franklin among them. So I think it
was fairly well received.

   After the Farnborough display I did three displays elsewhere,
so-called Battle of Britain displays, one of them at Beaulieu. There
was only a bit of communication flying done in October '48 but in
November I did several test flights on the third prototype. These
included some of maximum weight of 19,000 pounds I think, in
which under wing slipper tanks, overload tanks, were fitted. I have
some very good photographs taken during that exercise.

It was during one of Jo's last flights in the SR.A/1 that for the only time he
experienced a problem. He writes:

   On one of my last flights on the SR.A/1 in December 1948 the
   starboard float would not lower; it was stuck in the retracted
   position. In my efforts to get it down by repeated re-selections, and
   the application of 'G', at one stage the port float stuck up as well.
   Having managed to get that one down again, I decided to settle for
   that. I had considered the option of running the aircraft into the salt-
   marshes north of Calshot, but decided on a normal landing. I landed
   cross-wind, with the wind from starboard, with the canopy open
   and Sutton and parachute harnesses undone. As soon as the aircraft
   dropped off the step, I leapt out and sat on the port wing, and the
   recovery crew took me in tow and all was well.

Two of the SR.A/1s came to grief during 1949. In August the highly
experienced service test pilot, Lieutenant Commander Eric 'Winkle' Brown

from the RAE was flying TG271, the third prototype, when on alighting at Cowes he struck a submerged object, the aircraft cartwheeled, and sank. Brown was rescued by Geoffrey Tyson, who dived from a safety launch and pulled him aboard. Then, the following month, 17 September 1949, a good friend of Jo's at Felixstowe, Squadron Leader 'Pete' Major, was practising aerobatics in poor weather for a Battle of Britain air display and crashed into the sea. The wreckage was recovered and examined but provided no evidence as to why the crash occurred, and it was suggested that the pilot had lost control in a roll.

Happily, the first prototype survives. Last flown publicly in June 1951, for a display on the Thames as part of the Festival of Britain, it went to the College of Aeronautics at Cranfield, and later passed to the Imperial War Museum collection at Duxford, where it was fully restored, although lacking one of its Beryl engines, which was removed at Cranfield for use by Donald Campbell in his ill-fated attempt, in Bluebird K7, on the world water speed record in January 1967. TG263 is now with the Solent Sky Museum in Southampton.

The SR.A/1 was striking evidence of Saunders-Roe's belief in the flying boat. Even more striking was the other project on which the company was working during Jo's time there, the SR.45 Princess. Design of a large six-engined civil flying boat was proposed in 1944, and in 1945 it crystallised as the even larger SR.45, three prototypes of which were authorised by the Ministry of Supply in May 1946. By any measure the Saunders-Roe Princess, as it was named, was ambitious. Powered by ten of the new, and not yet fully developed, Bristol Proteus turbo-prop engines, eight of them coupled, it was to be pressurised, have a range of 3,000 miles, and carry 105 passengers in tourist and first-class cabins.

Completed in 1952 and flown for the first time on 22 August, the first prototype Princess, the only one completed, proved remarkably successful in all ways but one. It failed to find a buyer. The Ministry of Supply had been keen, but the British Overseas Airways Corporation (BOAC), forerunner of British Airways, had always been coy, never actually committing to buy it, and inclining to the view that landplanes were the future of civil aviation. This was of course right, and Saunders-Roe wrong in their views of the future of long-distance air travel. As a result the other two of the three Princesses ordered by the Ministry of Supply were never completed, while the first Princess, G-ALUN, languished on the slipway at Cowes, latterly cocooned, until finally broken up in 1967.

Had Jo remained with Saunders-Roe, no doubt he would have participated in the lengthy flight-testing programme, but as it was he played only a very small part in the massive venture. 'Because I hadn't flown a Sunderland for quite some time,' Jo says, 'with Ernie Taylor, a fitter in the flight shed who was my regular crewman when testing Sea Otters, I popped across to Calshot and borrowed one from the RAF for a quick refresher. Then, on 26 July, with Ernie and two others, Welford and Rann, I travelled by night train to Stranraer. There, from RAF Wig Bay, we collected Sunderland Mk.5, RN 297 and flew it down to Calshot – there because we did not yet have a suitable mooring buoy at Cowes. The Sunderland had been allocated to Saunders-Roe as a test aircraft for the development of the power controls intended for the Princess.'

Jo had never got on well with Geoffrey Tyson, try though he had, and something happened shortly after the Farnborough display which for Jo was a nail in the coffin so far as their relationship was concerned. He explains:

A spy in the system showed me a memo that I was not supposed to know about. It was from Captain Clarke, the Managing Director, to Geoffrey, saying roughly this: 'It was a good idea of yours to allow Lancaster to participate in the show; it demonstrated that the aircraft was not a one pilot aircraft.' What the hell is 'a one pilot aircraft,' I wondered. This incensed me very much indeed and made me wonder what on earth Geoffrey had been saying to evoke such a memo. He had never had cause to criticize me, but somehow we clashed. Even so I wasn't fully prepared for what happened at the beginning of January 1949. Geoffrey came down to Seaholme, Samuel Saunders's one-time house on the waterfront at East Cowes, where my office then was, to tell me that as from the end of January John Booth would be joining the company, as his assistant. John had been on the same ETPS course as me, and had joined Shorts at Rochester, later to move with all the rest to Belfast. So he was just another in the procession of people deserting Shorts in Belfast to join Saunders-Roe in the much more attractive Isle of Wight. I took my cue immediately, got on the phone to Eric Franklin at Armstrong Whitworths and he said there was a job for me. I borrowed the Proctor, flew up to Baginton on 11 January and arranged to join the company as from the 24th. I was away before John Booth actually arrived. It was not a very nice incident, but in many ways I was much better off. I was sorry, though, to be leaving the Isle of Wight and sorry to leave behind some very good friends I had made within Saunders Roe and elsewhere.

Geoffrey Tyson retired from flying in 1956 and joined the Aviation Division of Dunlop for two years, finally retiring in 1958. Jo knew a number of Tyson's colleagues at Dunlop and was told that the latter 'had acquired a reputation for being cantankerous and a grumbler'. 'He later married', Jo adds, 'and I gather from somebody who knew his wife that she was a bit of a dragon and used to bully him.'

John Booth remained with Saunders-Roe, succeeding Geoffrey Tyson as chief test pilot, only to be killed when the promising SR.53, an interceptor fighter with both jet and rocket engines, crashed on take-off in June 1958. The cause was never satisfactorily explained.

Jo's departure from Cowes was not made in the happiest of circumstances personally as well as professionally, for it coincided with a tragedy that struck within weeks of his move to Armstrong Whitworth. Betty was pregnant with a second child and elected to remain at Osborne Court, and in the care of their excellent GP, until after the baby was born, while, as the due date approached, son Graham went to Cheriton in the care of a local woman who had looked after Betty from birth. When Betty went into labour, Jo was notified and hurried down, arriving within 6 hours. By then their second son had been born but was just clinging to life. The doctors informed Jo and Betty that their son was a 'blue baby' with a serious and inoperable heart defect. Within 24 hours Michael Charles, as they named him, died. When she was fit to travel, Jo took Betty to Cheriton, since he had to return to Coventry. In due course Betty and Graham returned to Cowes, where they remained until Jo, who was living in bed and breakfast accommodation, was able to find a flat.

YEAR 1948		AIRCRAFT		PILOT, OR 1ST PILOT	2ND PILOT, PUPIL OR PASSENGER	DUTY (INCLUDING RESULTS AND REMARKS)
MONTH	DATE	Type	No.			
—	—	—	—	—	—	— Totals Brought Forward
SEPT.	1.	SR/A.1.	TG.271.	SELF.	—	TEST.
SEPT.	5.	SR/A.1.	TG.271.	SELF.	—	TEST.
SEPT.	6.	SR/A.1.	TG.271.	SELF.	—	TEST.
SEPT.	9.	SR/A.1.	TG.271.	SELF.	—	S.B.A.C. DISPLAY.
SEPT.	11.	SR/A.1.	TG.271.	SELF.	—	S.B.A.C. DISPLAY.
SEPT.	16.	SR/A.1.	TG.271.	SELF.	—	TEST.
SEPT.	18.	SR/A.1.	TG.271.	SELF.	—	"BATTLE OF BRITAIN" DISPLAYS.
SEPT.	21.	SR/A.1.	TG.271.	SELF.	—	TEST.
SEPT.	22	PROCTOR	G.AJVJ.	SELF.	P.D. IRONS.	GATWICK - WO'TON - COWES.
				SUMMARY FOR SEPT 1948		SRVI
				SAUNDERS-ROE LTD COWES		PROCTOR
OCT	6	PROCTOR.	G.AJVJ	SELF.	TAYLOR	OIL CONS TEST.
OCT	11	PROCTOR.	G.AJVJ	SELF.	P.D. IRONS	EASTLEIGH & RETURN.
OCT	14	PROCTOR.	G.AJVJ	SELF.	WELBSTEAD	MARTLESHAM & RETURN.
OCT	20	PROCTOR.	G.AJVJ	SELF	RV PERFECT	EASTLEIGH & RETURN.
OCT	25	PROCTOR.	G.AJVJ	SELF	P.D. IRONS	EASTLEIGH & RETURN.
OCT	26	PROCTOR.	G.AJVJ	SELF	P.D. IRONS	EASTLEIGH & RETURN.
OCT	30	PROCTOR.	G.AJVJ	SELF.	P.D. IRONS	WO'TON - VALLEY - COWES.
				SUMMARY FOR OCT 1948		PROCTOR
				SAUNDERS-ROE LTD COWES		

GRAND TOTAL [Cols. (1) to (10)]

....2095....Hrs.......30......Mins.

TOTALS CARRIED FORWARD

YEAR 1949.		AIRCRAFT		PILOT, OR 1ST PILOT	2ND PILOT, PUPIL OR PASSENGER	DUTY (INCLUDING RESULTS AND REMA
MONTH	DATE	Type	No.			
—	—	—	—	—	—	— TOTALS BROUGHT FORW
MAY	30	AW 52	TS 363	SELF	—	HANDLING (BALED OUT BY M.B. S
				SUMMARY FOR MAY 1949		LINCOLN
				SIR W.G. ARMSTRONG-WHITWORTH		LANCASTER
				AIRCRAFT LTD COVENTRY.		YORK
						A.W. 52
						A.W. 52 G
						METEOR
						DOMINIE PROCTOR AUSTER
AUG.	9	DOMINIE	G.AEML	SELF.	—	LOCAL.
AUG.	9	DOMINIE	G.AEML	SELF.	MR HALL & LOCKWOOD	FROM BITTESWELL
AUG.	10	DOMINIE	G.AEML	SELF.	WATSON & 5 OTHERS	FARNBORO' & RETURN
AUG.	11	DOMINIE	G.AEML	SELF.	FAIRLIE & 3 OTHERS	FARNBORO' & RETURN
AUG.	15	LANCASTER	PA.366	SELF	EGF, WHE, PAYNE	TO BITTESWELL
AUG.	15	LANCASTER	PA.366	SELF	PAYNE, EARDLEY	TOWING AW 52 G
AUG.	15	LANCASTER	PA.366	SELF	EGF, WHE, PAYNE	FROM BITTESWELL
AUG.	16	YORK	MW.309	SELF	BIGGS, AUSTIN	TEST
AUG.	17	DOMINIE	G.AEML	SELF	HALL	BITTESWELL & RETURN
AUG.	17	DOMINIE	G.AEML	SELF	KEENE	FARNBORO' & RETURN
AUG.	18	LANCASTER	PA.366	SELF	EGF, WOODCOCK	LOCAL.
AUG.	18	METEOR IV	VZ.389	SELF	—	TEST
AUG.	18	METEOR IV	VZ.389	SELF	—	TEST

GRAND TOTAL [Cols. (1) to (10)]

2172 Hrs. 05 Mins.

TOTALS CARRIED FORWAR

Chapter 11

Armstrong Whitworth:
the Apollo, AW.52 and Meteors

'So it came about', Jo writes, 'that in January 1949 I was back at Armstrong Whitworth almost exactly nine years after I'd left them at the beginning of the War. I was delighted to find there were still quite a few old friends working there who dated back to the time when I was an apprentice.' The Armstrong Whitworth of 1949 was not, however, what it had been in 1939, but rather one of five major aircraft companies within the Hawker Siddeley Group, the others being Avro, Hawker, Gloster and Armstrong Siddeley Motors. The small airfield at Whitley had long been closed and the factory there was devoted to guided-missile development, while aircraft production was at Baginton, where Armstrong Whitworth had built a modern factory in the late 1930s. Baginton, however, had no hard runway, and when post-war it became obvious that one was required, Hawker Siddeley approached the city council, which owned the aerodrome, offering to pay half the cost. The council declined the offer, so Hawker Siddeley bought an ex-RAF airfield at Bitteswell, 12 miles east of Coventry, and from 1949 conducted all its experimental work there. Amazingly, as it now seems, all Armstrong Whitworth's new and refurbished aircraft – Lancasters, Lincolns, Yorks and the F.4, F.8 and early NF.11 Meteors – were flown and tested out of a grass airfield where, as Jo comments, 'there were areas where, after rain, it became exceedingly boggy, which restricted the areas which we could use. It was also a bit dodgy using brakes, because aircraft skidded very easily on the wet muddy ground.' Ironically, a few years later the Coventry city council recognised that a hard runway was required at Baginton, and had to bear the entire cost of construction.

When Jo left Armstrong Whitworth in 1940, Baginton was busy turning out the firm's own product, the Whitley. But no home-grown successor followed it. The two prototypes of the undistinguished Albemarle, in origin a Bristol design, were constructed at Armstrong Whitworth's subsidiary, Air Service Training Ltd, at Hamble, and the 600 production aircraft by A.W. Hawksley Ltd, at Brockworth, a subsidiary company of the Hawker Siddeley Group. Thus, when the 1,814th and last Whitley came off the production line in July 1943, it was followed by the Lancaster, of which 1,328 were built before production was terminated in favour of the Lincoln. But from the first, Armstrong Whitworth had a fine reputation for both the speed and quality of production, as was evident when in January 1943 Sir Stafford Cripps, Minister of Aircraft Production, asked the company to take charge of the Short Brothers' factory at Swindon, where Stirlings were built, and later to be responsible for the production of Fairey Barracudas by Boulton Paul at Wolverhampton.

Central to the efficiency of the Baginton factory were two men, Herbert Woodhams and Walter Lockwood, both of whom Jo remembers with respect and affection. Lockwood, always known as 'Lockie', had joined the design department of the firm in 1919, but in 1921 left the design team to become assistant works manager, and in 1940 works manager. Jo recalls that Lockwood had been gassed during the First World War and invalided out of the army, but adds, 'the gassing obviously did not affect him in later life because he died aged 96'. Jo had no contact with him during his apprenticeship but came to know him quite well subsequently. 'He was a very affable and approachable chap,' Jo says. 'He circulated around the factory frequently and we knew him as "Lockie". We were always invited to a party at his house at Christmas.'

The second key figure, Herbert Woodhams, was always referred to as 'Woody', but not to his face. He had joined the company in 1923 as chief inspector, having in 1919 become the first possessor of an Air Ministry ground engineer's licence for aero engines. Later works manager, he was promoted to general manager in 1937 and afterwards managing director. Jo remembers Woody as 'a fairly dour, reserved sort of chap', but one with 'his better points'. He recalls:

When I rejoined the company in 1949 Woody called me into his office to give me a quiet welcome. Later, after my ejection, he invited me to lunch; he normally lunched in solitary state apparently. We had lunch just the two of us, and I don't think he said anything very much about the AW.52, but he told me a very filthy joke. And several times when I'd done a demonstration he would ring me up afterwards and say 'Hello Jo, I'm going to make a very long speech. Thank you', and ring off, which was rewarding anyway.

Jo also recollects that Woody had a parsimonious streak: 'We built some Meteor NF.11s for the Danish Air Force. Pilots used to come over to collect them and every time they came they invited us to visit Denmark with them but for some reason Woody would never let us go.'

When Jo was an apprentice at Armstrong Whitworth, the chief test pilot had been Charles Turner-Hughes, generally referred to as 'Toc-H', who had joined the company in 1923. He retired in 1946, after sustaining severe head injuries when a large bird shattered the windscreen of the Lancaster he was testing, and been succeeded by his deputy, F.R. Midgley. He stayed only two years, however, his replacement being Eric Franklin. Jo comments:

> Eric Franklin, the chief test pilot when I went back to Armstrong
> Whitworths, had been an apprentice before the war. He was a year
> younger than me but joined as an apprentice two years later so
> although I had heard his name our paths never actually crossed until
> we met at Boscombe Down. We had had similar careers in the RAF;
> he'd done a tour on Whitleys in 4 Group, and got a DFC for his tour
> there. He'd then done some work on Halifaxes and gone back for
> a second tour on 35 Squadron, a Pathfinder squadron. He did the
> Number 2 ETPS Course and then went to Armstrong Whitworths,
> carrying out the first test flights in the A.W.52G at the end of the war.
> He was joined soon after by Bill Else, who had been on Number 4
> Course. He had gone to Boscombe Down to participate in TAF trials,
> flying Typhoons, and firing rockets at a selection of targets as part of
> the research prior to the D-Day invasion. He must have joined about
> the end of 1948.

When Jo arrived the test pilots' offices were still at Baginton and they commuted to Bitteswell mostly by air, their communication aircraft first a de Havilland Dragon Rapide, later a Proctor and later still an Anson. Most of Jo's early flying involved testing the last Avro Lincolns that were coming off the production line, but there were also some Lancasters being refurbished for sale overseas, and some Yorks, about which he comments:

> At that time the Berlin airlift was in full swing and Yorks were coming in for major servicing. They were notoriously full of coal dust and other junk in the bilges; it was quite a job making them fit for flight again, but we aimed to clean, overhaul and flight test them with a three day turnaround. I never enjoyed flying the Yorks very much. They seemed to wallow about a bit in flight and the cockpit felt somewhat claustrophobic, with the visibility nothing like it was in a Lancaster. Also a lot of the engine controls – throttles etc. – were up in the roof, which were pretty awkward to operate. But I suppose as a stopgap transport it served its purpose pretty well.

Along with this bread and butter work, Armstrong Whitworth was working on a number of advanced projects. One of these was the AW.55 Apollo, a four-engined airliner, rival to the Vickers Viscount, then also under development. Both were successful tenders in response to the Brabazon Committee's Category II recommendation for a turboprop airliner carrying twenty-four passengers, and suitable for short- and medium-haul routes in Europe. The Apollo first flew on 10 April 1949, and demonstrated good flying characteristics. Its Achilles heel, however, was its engines. True to form, Armstrong Whitworth had opted to employ the Mamba, an engine by its sister company Armstrong Siddeley, but this, with an axial flow compressor, was still under development, whereas the Viscount's Rolls-Royce Dart, with a centrifugal compressor, was already proven. Jo comments:

> On 10 April 1949 the Apollo made its first flight, but, afflicted by Armstrong Siddeley engines, over about three years did only about 300 hours flying, most of which seemed to involve engine development. The Mambas were under-developed, down on power and suffered from compressor stall. A second Apollo flew but neither

came to anything and they both finished up at Farnborough. One at least was with the ETPS, where it was not very popular because of the engines. It was a pretty uninspired design really, for a modern turboprop airliner, and I had very little to do with it. I only flew it half a dozen times during the whole time it was under development.

Meanwhile, at Bitteswell Armstrong Whitworth were working concurrently on a much more radical aircraft, the AW.52 jet-powered flying wing research aircraft. In response to a government-initiated plan for the development of a huge flying wing airliner, Armstrong Whitworth proposed early in 1942 the construction of a glider as a test vehicle for a jet-powered aircraft, the AW.52, the latter approximately two-thirds the size of the projected airliner. Construction started in March 1943 and the glider, built of wood and designated the AW.52G, first flew on 2 March 1945. Testing continued for about two years and had long ended by the time Jo arrived, but he nonetheless had to fly the glider in order to prepare for testing the AW.52, and so he was sent down to Airspeed at Christchurch, Hampshire, to take a quick course in flying a Horsa glider under the tutelage of Ron Clare, a friend and fellow member of No. 3 Course at the ETPS. Jo comments:

The Horsa glider was no problem; it had enormous air brakes and when you wanted to land it you just pointed it at the runway at about 45 degrees, put the air brakes out and down you went. All you needed was to have a little bit of spare speed to enable you to round out and you were there. I carried out 14 test flights on the 52G, something like seven hours in toto. When I joined Armstrong Whitworths they used a Whitley to tow the 52G. It was the last one off the production line and was in prime condition, but they decided to replace it with a Lancaster as a tug because it could get the glider up to the required altitude much more quickly. In 1949 they took that almost brand-new Whitley away and broke it up and now there isn't a Whitley anywhere in the world. On 1 June 1950 I delivered the 52G to Beaulieu, which was then the home of the Airborne Forces Experimental Establishment. There I did a couple of flights with it as demonstrations, being towed by a Vickers Valetta, which was the aircraft the RAF were going to tow it with. Eventually, the 52G was taken back to Baginton and rather unwisely it was placed outside the main entrance to the offices, where very quickly the weather got to it, as it was made of plywood, and it fell apart.

Powered by two 5,000lb Rolls-Royce Nene engines, the first prototype AW.52, TS363, had flown on 13 November 1947 and the second prototype on 1 September 1948, powered by 3,500lb Rolls-Royce Derwent engines. In that month the first prototype had put on an impressive display at the SBAC show at Farnborough, but testing had already left the designer of the AW.52, John Lloyd, disappointed by several aspects of the aircraft's performance and, accordingly, in 1949 the flying wing programme was terminated. No doubt the decision to end it was influenced by what happened to Jo on his third flight in the Nene-engined prototype on 30 May 1949. Jo's account runs as follows:

During the first months of 1949 the first prototype . . . was undergoing modifications to increase structural stiffness. Meanwhile, Bill Else made a few flights in the second prototype, TS368. During one of these flights, on pulling out from a shallow dive at about 280 mph, he encountered an oscillation in pitch of about two cycles a second, which then damped out again. Strangely, I do not remember any great consternation in high places at the time about what he had experienced.

In due course TS363 re-emerged to resume flights tests from Bitteswell with an increased limiting speed. I forget the exact figure, but it was close to 350 mph. I was detailed for familiarisation flights, and to investigate behaviour up to the revised limiting speed.

There were lofty cumulus clouds about, and quite a lot of turbulence. At about 5,000 ft, and in a shallow dive, I had reached, to the best of my recollection, about 320 mph when the oscillation in pitch set in. My estimate was that it was again about two cycles/sec, but the amplitude built up almost instantaneously to become of such extreme violence as almost to incapacitate me both physically and mentally. I recall, too, that it was accompanied by a very loud noise, which at the time seemed to suggest that structural failure was imminent.

In my very confused mental state I decided to eject. In doing this I was fortunate to escape with both my legs intact, because the control column was of the 'spectacles' type and, had I carried out the correct ejection drill and withdrawn my feet to the seat's footrests, my knees would have been severely mangled. This situation had, in fact, been catered for in the design. In the cockpit, alongside the canopy jettison toggle, was a similar one that, in addition to jettisoning the canopy, also cut the control cables and operated a spring that pushed the control column forward. Perhaps not surprisingly, this little gadget was generally regarded with considerable diffidence, and the normal practice was to not withdraw the small safety pin before flight. In my own circumstances I stood no chance of being able to withdraw this pin; I consider that I was indeed very lucky to have been able to grab the hood jettison toggle.

Although Martin-Baker was a pioneer in the field, the company's Mk I ejection seat was still in the early stages of development. Unlike the sophisticated automatic seats of today, it was necessary for the pilot to release his seat harness after ejection and fall clear of the seat before pulling his parachute ripcord. When I ejected it was the first time a British seat had been used in a genuine emergency, although a handful of very brave chaps had made a number of live ejections 'in cold blood' in the course of its development.

The AW.52 had an observer's position directly behind the pilot, but it was not fitted with an ejection seat. This introduced the possibility of a dreadful dilemma for the pilot. I am so grateful that I was alone.

There are several published accounts of the loss of TS363, and most of them contain errors of fact. Not least of these is the assertion, which first appears in Oliver Tapper's *Armstrong Whitworth Aircraft since 1913*, that after Jo ejected, the aircraft 'left to its own devices, stopped fluttering and glided down to land itself in open country with relatively little damage'.[1] In fact the aircraft was far from intact, as this summary of the accident report makes clear: 'Subsequent to the ejection the aircraft stabilized and made a slow descent into a field where it struck the only large tree in the vicinity with the leading edge of the starboard wing, outboard of the engine intake. The aircraft then slid along the ground, disintegrating, for half a mile.'[2]

The AW.52 crashed near Broadwell, south-west of Rugby, while Jo landed in a field at the rear of the Cuttle Inn at Long Itchington, narrowly
avoiding splashing down in the adjacent Grand Union Canal. His knees
had come through bruised but otherwise unscathed but his back had not,
and X-rays revealed that he had a compression fracture of his first and
second lumbar vertebrae, as well as a broken bone in his shoulder. The
lumbar fractures were the second he had suffered, it emerged, the first time
being without his knowledge, when he ejected on the test rig at Martin-
Baker's works at High Denham in January 1947.

Two months later Jo was cleared to fly again, although the certificate
of fitness paradoxically declared him to be a 'fit civilian test pilot but not
to be exposed to the hazards of the Martin-Baker ejection seat'. 'We had
a laugh about this,' Jo says, 'because it is rather like somebody who is
shipwrecked being told they could go back to sea again but they mustn't
use a lifeboat.' In any case, Jo elected not to fly the second AW.52 again.
With a much reduced limiting air speed, it subsequently carried out a programme with sophisticated vibration measuring equipment, then went
to Farnborough. There they attempted some laminar flow tests, but these
proved unsuccessful. Thereafter it was rarely flown and was regarded as
something of a curiosity before being scrapped in June 1954.

Following his two months' recuperation, Jo returned to flying just in
time to flight test a long subcontract production run of Gloster Meteors.
The first British jet fighter, the Meteor had initially flown in January 1944,
and the first of a limited run of twenty F.1s reached No. 616 Squadron in
July. The more powerful F.3 followed in December and the Rolls-Royce
Derwent-powered F.4 in mid-1945, Armstrong Whitworth originally
building components and then, under licence, constructing 46 of the 535
aircraft built in toto. Directional stability had plagued the Meteor from
the outset, with a range of measures undertaken to try to effect improvements including, as on the Saro SR.A/1, the fitting of a small acorn fairing
at the junction of the intersection of the fin and tailplane. Despite this, a
measure of instability remained, and Jo was unenthusiastic about the F.4:

> In August 1949 we embarked on a subcontract building Meteor 4s for
> Glosters. I didn't particularly enjoy flying the Meteor 4. The controls
> were not good, and it was often a lot of trouble getting them 'off test',

primarily because of the ailerons. None of the Meteors had pilot-controlled aileron trimmers, and the aim was to get it to fly literally hands off throughout the speed range up to about 400 miles an hour, which was not catered for in the means of adjustment available. This often resulted in a lot of extra flights. On average, I suppose, a Meteor production test would involve three flights, but I remember one particular aircraft did 40 flights before it was actually disposed of, and even then the ailerons were not as they should have been.

None of these aircraft had any on-board navigation aids except a compass. The only help we had was from the manual homer at Bitteswell. We could get a bearing on that but it was not always certain whether it was a QDM or a reciprocal QDR; you just had to use your commonsense over that. But we had to be very discreet about what sort of weather we were likely to encounter. With the production line churning out aircraft regardless of the weather, we used to get quite a lot of bottlenecks, particularly with the Mark 4 Meteors. The only mishap occurred when Jim McCowan got very low on fuel for some reason, and landed the Meteor safely, wheels down, in a field at Hatfield Broad Oak in Hertfordshire. Eric Franklin went down, rolled up his sleeves and decided to fly it out, but hit a fence on take off and didn't do the Meteor any good at all.

The Meteor's directional instability was improved, somewhat fortuitously, when in the Mark 7 trainer a 30-inch-longer forward fuselage was fitted to accommodate the second pilot. In the F.8, Gloster brought together this longer fuselage and also a larger rectangular tailplane, which had been successfully tested on a T.7. Fitted also with a more streamlined cockpit canopy and an ejector seat, Armstrong Whitworth began building the single-seat F.8 in late 1950, producing 430 before production ceased in 1953. About the F.8 Jo felt more positive; it was, he thought, 'a much nicer aircraft', since it had 'spring tab ailerons that were much easier to adjust and to fly hands off throughout the speed range'.

In late 1953 Armstrong Whitworth was commissioned to convert the last Meteor F.8 off the production line to test the practicability of a prone pilot position, the RAF Institute of Aviation Medicine wishing to test the theory that a pilot flying thus would be less likely to black out in tight turns. The converted aircraft, which first flew in February 1954, had an extended nose containing a prone pilot position, but retained the standard cockpit in which, for safety, a second pilot always flew. Jo never flew the aircraft, either as second pilot or in the prone position, although he did have one opportunity to fly prone, as he relates:

> Not long before the prone Meteor flew I had been down at Farnborough, where I was talking to a Squadron Leader Bezarnick, a Polish pilot attached to the RAF Institute of Aviation Medicine, and he invited me to have a go in a converted Reid and Sigrist Desford, a little twin-engined trainer that never went into series production. Of course I accepted with alacrity and had a flight. When I went back to Bitteswell I told Eric Franklin I'd done that and for some reason he threw a terrific fit of pique. The sensible thing to do would have been to have said, 'Jolly good, let me have a report on it', but he didn't and I never got a chance to fly the prone Meteor. In fact the aircraft did very little flying at Armstrong Whitworths before it went down to Farnborough for full assessment of the theory of prone pilot use.

The adverse response by Eric Franklin was not an isolated incident. 'For years', Jo says, 'we had been very good friends, socialising together quite a lot and getting on very well', but the two fell out, irrevocably, when Eric tried to lecture Jo on his failing marriage. This is a subject Jo is naturally reticent about, but he explains that over several years he tried unavailingly to sustain the relationship with his wife:

> For about two and a half years we lived in a second floor flat in St Paul's Vicarage in Warwick. It was quite comfortable, but in the summer became very claustrophobic. At this time my marriage was becoming increasingly difficult, and in the hope of rescuing it I thought we might be happier in a house, which I found very difficult to find. In desperation I went to Woody and explained the situation. He said, 'Okay, find a house and let me know.' I found a semi-detached house in a leafy suburb of Kenilworth, the company bought it and I paid rent out of my wages for it. It was redecorated to our own specification.

With a garden came a boxer dog, chosen by Graham and named Fritz. 'Fritz had a Kennel Club pedigree,' Jo says, 'but I suspect that, had the Kennel Club actually seen him, he would have been expelled on the spot, because he was white, and instead of a nice smooth shiny and slightly moist nose, his was rough and dry, but it seemed to work just as well.' Sadly, however, neither the house nor the dog brought any improvement to Jo's marriage, which deteriorated to a point where Betty accused him of having a girlfriend, which, he states, 'was certainly never the case'. 'Then one day in 1952 when I arrived home', he writes,

> I found the remains of a box of chocolates very much in evidence. It emerged that my wife had phoned Eric Franklin's wife, Marjorie, no doubt sounding very distressed, resulting in Marjory visiting my wife complete with the box of chocolates. I don't know what she told Marjory but the next morning Eric called me into his office and started to lecture me. I don't recall exactly what I said but I told him in no uncertain terms that I discussed my matrimonial affairs with no one and that it was none of his business. I was certainly not diplomatic. He clearly couldn't take being told that it was not his business and that was when the rift opened. The animosity and veiled hostility, sometimes not very veiled, never abated, and coloured our working relationship ever after.

Subsequently, Jo made several attempts to try to sort matters out with Franklin, only to be told that he (Eric) did not hold a grudge, that he was not like that at all, and that Jo had a persecution complex. 'All my other colleagues were quite bemused about this', Jo adds, 'and couldn't understand why things were as they were. Nor could I for that matter.' But an animus towards Jo there definitely was, as two later incidents testify.

'At one stage in the mid 50's,' Jo says, 'when I thought I deserved more salary than I was getting, I went to Eric Franklin and he declined to do anything about it. So I said, "Well, you won't mind if I go to see Woody myself, will you?" He couldn't object, so I went to see Woody and he just said, "Leave it with me, Jo", and a little while later a chit came through from the wages department saying I had quite a handsome rise. Eric was absolutely livid about that.'

The other incident arose when in 1954 Jo was experiencing repeated sore throats and eventually tingling in the legs. Jo saw Armstrong Whitworth's Dr Cartwright at Bitteswell's medical centre, who referred him to a specialist who promptly removed Jo's tonsils at company expense in a private health clinic. 'During the week I was in there,' Jo comments, 'Eric Franklin turned up to visit me. For two years he'd hardly been able to exchange a civil word, and we'd had no sort of general conversation, so it was a pretty frosty encounter. Clearly, the only reason he'd come was so that he could report to Woody and Lockie that he'd been the sympathetic Chief Test Pilot in visiting one of his team. But when Dr Cartwright finally signed me off to resume flying he did so with the proviso that my flying be as low and slow as possible to start with. So I went out to Bitteswell and reported to Eric, who thumped the desk and said, "Are you bloody fit or not?" I just said "I'm fit" and walked out.'

In 1952 Jo and his wife separated, and when in 1957 Betty wished to remarry, they divorced. Fritz, however, remained with Jo, becoming his faithful companion for another ten years. 'Fritz had a built-in sat-nav and clock', Jo says, 'and I'm sure that, so far as I was concerned, he was telepathic. My car had a bench front seat, and he would always lie with his head on my lap, covering my trousers with slobber and white hairs, but whenever we approached a place he knew he would stand up, and at home he always knew when I was intending to go out, because I would find him sitting by the front door. When my mother first saw him, she said that she had never seen such an ugly dog! She was probably right! Finally he developed a series of abdominal lumps, and very sadly had to be put to sleep.'

While building Meteor F.4s and F.8s, Armstrong Whitworth was also delegated full design and production responsibility for developing nightfighter versions of the aircraft. The first of these was the NF.11, developed out of the Mark 7 two-seat trainer. Something of a hybrid, the NF.11 had the Mark 7's cockpit and lengthened nose, the F.8's tail unit, and reinforced long-span wings similar to those of the photo-reconnaissance version of the Meteor, the PR.10. The first true prototype flew on 31 May 1950, and Jo remembers vividly flying it and the two others that followed:

In due course we had three flying mockup prototypes of the NF.11

night fighter, all based at Bitteswell. One of the problems we had
was that we were using just the internal tank, which held 325 gallons,
which very much limited the time available to carry out testing, a lot
of which was done at 30,000 feet. When you came down quickly, the
windows and windscreen would frost up, just as you were hoping to
land. We managed to get over this to some extent by carrying with
us a rag soaked in anti-freeze. Wiping the windows beforehand with
Glycol tended to delay the formation of ice and frost. Eventually
we had a DV [direct vision] panel, so part of the port side of the
windscreen could open and you could get a direct view through that,
but that didn't come along for two or three years.

The first production NF.11 was delivered to the RAF early in 1951 and the
last left Baginton in May 1954. It was succeeded by the NF.12, which differed
only in having a longer nose to accommodate an American radar system,
100 being delivered in 1953–54, and by the NF.13, which actually ante-
dated the NF.12, and was essentially a tropicalised NF.11 with, Jo recalls, air
conditioning through an expansion turbine so powerful that 'you could
have your own private snow storm in the cockpit if you liked'. The NF.13
equipped just two RAF squadrons, both in the Middle East. Finally, in
October 1953, came the first flight of the ultimate night-fighter variant,
and the last production version of the Meteor, the NF.14. Equipped with
a two-piece blown cockpit canopy instead of the old heavy-framed hood,
a revised windscreen and a further lengthened nose, the NF.14 was much
the most elegant of the two-seat Meteors and in Jo's opinion, 'by far the
nicest of all Meteors ever'. He adds: 'One of our bright young designers,
Jim Calder, designed some new ailerons with spring tab balancing and they
were very much better, quite transforming the aircraft.' Total production
of all the night fighters was 592, all built at Baginton.

The Meteor production test schedule, much the same for the F.4, F.8
and the night fighters, was, Jo comments, 'pretty wearing'. He writes:

We would climb up to 30,000 feet to check the engine performance
all the way up, check the pressurization at the top and dive to the
limiting Mach number, which was usually about .81, establish level
speed performance at 10,000 ft, and then work on the controls to

make sure that they were all as they should be. The F.8 and N.11
series all had spring tab ailerons, which made a tremendous
difference, reducing the number of retests a great deal. An average
aircraft would be off testing after perhaps three or four flights and in
those days it was not uncommon for each pilot to do eight, nine or
ten flights a day. We once worked out that the average duration of a
test production flight was 17 minutes. So there were an awful lot of
take-offs and landings involved, and climbs to 30,000 feet.

One unusual series of test flights that Jo had to make remains vivid:

> About 1954/55, at the height of the Cold War, it was feared in official
> circles that we might be deprived of sources of kerosene. To minimize
> the risk, there was the possibility of operating the aircraft on what
> they called wide-cut gasoline or HB4. All service aircraft had to be
> checked out using this. The fuel system was adjusted on the ground,
> after which the aircraft was loaded up with fuel heated in a tank on
> the ground to something like 60 degrees centigrade. I then had to
> climb as quickly as possible to 30,000 feet and fly inverted for
> 45 seconds or so, and you feel very foolish flying inverted at 30,000
> feet. What they were checking for, of course, was fuel vaporization.
> If that happened in the fuel supply line it would very rapidly put
> the light out and you'd have to relight the engine, which can be very
> awkward. Anyway all went well; there was no fuel vaporization.

By 1950, with Meteors coming off the production line thick and fast, additional test pilots were required, so two new ones were taken on: Jack
Akers and Jim McCowan. Both were recent graduates from the RAF's jet
training school at Bentwaters. 'Jim took to the job pretty well', Jo says.

> Jack, however, ex-Transport Command, just didn't seem cut out for
> test flying somehow; he preferred flying big aircraft. Moreover, his
> relationship with Eric Franklin was not too good and following a
> robust exchange of opinions one day he decided to leave. In his place
> we got Martin Walton, who was the CO of the local Royal Auxiliary
> Air Force squadron, No. 605 (County of Warwick). He had a BSc and

he took to test flying like the proverbial duck to water.

While testing production Meteors, Jo had two mishaps, one of which
could have been much more serious. The lesser episode came about when
– following his only engine failure in a Meteor, 'just for the fun of it' – he
was practising dead stick landings. 'On one occasion I stretched it just a
little bit too far', he comments, 'and one of the main landing wheels hit a
fence post and was knocked off.' The second incident occurred 'when the
oxygen filler cover just ahead of the windscreen came off in flight'.

> I was doing 400 and something knots, it shattered the cockpit canopy
> and a shard of Perspex cut my forehead. I was only wearing a fabric
> helmet, the wind blew into the wound and blood was spattering all
> over the place; I thought I was going to die from loss of blood. In
> fact it was quite a minor cut. I landed, they took me off to the sick
> quarters where it was sewn up and all was well. But after that we
> quickly got ourselves equipped with 'bone dome' crash helmets.

One of the highlights for any test pilot is to carry out demonstration
flights. So it was for Jo, who 'was always a bit surprised that, for some
reason, I got 99% of the demonstration flying, which I didn't mind in the
least!'. He suspects that it was the sales director, ex-pilot Claude Emery,
who for some reason plumped for Jo when demonstrations were required.
His first demonstration was at an RAF display on 7 and 8 July 1950.

> On the 7th the King and Queen were there, and the next day the Prime
> Minister, Clement Attlee. The RAF put on a grand show, re-enacting
> the 1944 low-level attack on the Amiens Prison and showing off mass
> formations of different aircraft, with some 250 aircraft involved.
> Presumably as a taste of things to come, five up-and-coming aircraft
> were displayed. They were the Meteor NF.11, which I flew, the English
> Electric Canberra, flown by Roly Beamont, the De Havilland Venom,
> flown by John Derry, the Hawker P.1081, which was the forerunner
> of the Hunter, flown by 'Wimpy' Wade, and the early version of the
> Supermarine Swift, flown by Mike Lithgow. We each had the usual eight-
> minute turn to do and I had at my disposal a large Ford shooting brake,

which was the biggest vehicle we had between the five of us, so each day
we climbed into it and went to the Bush Hotel in Farnham for lunch.

A few weeks later Jo flew the NF.11 at the SBAC show at Farnborough. 'It
really was a dangerous aircraft to try and do a show in,' he says, 'because
with the heavy Gloster-designed ailerons you had to be very careful when
flying inverted at low altitude. Also during that SBAC show the weather
on some of the days was not at all nice and not having a DV panel made
it very dodgy, because if we'd had heavy rain it would have been very difficult to land the thing back at Farnborough.'

In 1952 Jo demonstrated the NF.11 again at Farnborough, this time fitted with a DV window and spring tab ailerons, which made it 'a different
proposition altogether'. But what Jo remembers particularly about the
SBAC show was that

> it was the year that John Derry was killed. It was Saturday, and I was
> being strapped in by our faithful parachute-wallah and flight-line
> attendant, Billy Armstrong, when he suddenly said 'Bloody hell. Look
> at that.' I looked up, he pointed, I looked up and saw the DH.110 in
> three large pieces falling onto the airfield, while two black objects
> carried on and hit the hill, amongst the spectators, in a big cloud of
> dust. John and his observer, Teddy Richards, were killed, of course,
> but because the engines carried on, so were about 30 people on the
> hill beyond the airfield. Legend has it that Neville Duke was lined up
> on the runway and in due course took off, because the show must go
> on. But according to my recollection it wasn't Neville Duke but Bob
> Penderleith, a De Havilland engines test pilot, who was flying the
> Venom night fighter. Of course when the press got hold of these stories,
> everybody had heard of Neville Duke, whereas nobody had heard of
> Bob Penderleith, so it probably suited their purpose to say it was Neville.

Besides the demonstration flights, the other pleasurable break from flight
testing production Meteors was their occasional delivery to overseas pur-
chasers. The first of these in which Jo was involved was the delivery, in
December 1952, of four F.8s to Syria. This was part of an order for twelve,
originally intended for delivery in 1951, but embargoed. He writes:

In late November 1952 I was called upon with Jim Cooksley and Brian Smith of Glosters and Andrew McDowell, a Rolls-Royce test pilot, to ferry four Gloster-built Mark 8s out to Damascus. To get the range it was necessary to go up to 30,000 feet and since none of the aircraft had navigational equipment in them, except a compass, we had to be very careful if we were going to be able to find our destination. We crossed the Channel to Le Havre, picked up the Seine and flew beneath the cloud up to Paris. But the cloud got lower and lower so we had to abandon the attempt to find Le Bourget, climb up through the cloud to 30,000 feet again, and return to Gloster's airfield at Moreton Valence via a series of QDMs. On 3 December we tried again, successfully. Our route was Le Bourget–Nice–Rome–Luqa–El Adem–Nicosia–Damascus. Luqa, in Malta, El Adem, in Libya some 25 miles south of Tobruk, and Nicosia in Cyprus were RAF bases and we could use them for navigational purposes. Elsewhere en route we had to find the destination airfield visually. From Damascus we travelled by road to Beirut and flew back from there. Beirut in those days was just like an Aladdin's cave, full of all sorts of goodies from America, Japan and God knows where else, things still unavailable in the miserable austerity that still prevailed in Britain, with nothing very much in the shops. We used to come back loaded.

'In the Mark 8,' he recalls, 'being a single-seater, it was a job to find any-where to store your kit. We had to use the ammunition tanks'. They also had to carry special hose connections for the three overload tanks, one ventral and two under the wings, and, except when at RAF bases, virtually carry out the refuelling themselves.

In Paris, the pilots' overnight stay was handled by British European Airways, who, Jo says, 'laid everything on for us. We stayed in style at the Commodore Hotel on the Boulevard Haussmann.' That evening they made their way to the rue Pigalle, where they saw a small bar called Fred Payne's and went in, to find only one solitary customer. Jo continues:

This one customer was a chap we all knew, Dick Pendlebury a technical rep. for Dunlop Aviation. So that was our start of the

evening. The bar was a wonderful little place. It had been started by
Fred Payne, I think, after the First World War. He'd since retired, and
the bar was run by his niece, but he used to turn up at some point
in the evening on a motor scooter. They served bacon and eggs for
breakfast on the bar at 4 o'clock in the morning. So whenever we
went to Paris we visited Fred Payne's.

Further deliveries to the Middle East were made in June 1954, when Jo led
three NF.13s to Damascus, and in June and August 1955, when six NF.13s
were delivered to Almaza, outside Cairo, in two batches of three. In connection with the first delivery to Egypt Jo vividly recalls that 'we taxied in
and had to wait for about five minutes with the engines running while two
chaps in uniform almost came to blows about where they were going to
park us.' The Syrian Air Force was better organised, but Jo was told later by
Armstrong Whitworth's technical representative in Damascus that 'after
we'd gone they refuelled one of the aircraft and their ace pilot did a flight
in it, but none of them ever flew again'.

The pilots' reception on delivering the first three NF.13s to Israel could
hardly have been more different, as Jo relates:

When we delivered the first three NF.13s to Israel, we landed at Tel Aviv
and hardly had we got unstrapped before their air force pilots were up
the ladders, peering into the cockpits to spot any differences between
the F.8 and NF.13, which were in fact very little. Before we'd left the
apron they'd refuelled, taken off, beaten-up the airport in immaculate
formation and were heading off to their base. 100% efficient.

In ferrying the Israeli Meteors it was necessary to fly via Greece rather
than Malta and North Africa, and Jo recalls that

at Athens the authorities parked us between two DC6 airliners,
one Egyptian, the other Syrian. Men from the Israeli Embassy were
supposed to meet us, so I left the other two pilots to guard the aircraft
while I went to find the Embassy officials, who were being barred
entry. I managed to get them allowed in and we were well looked
after eventually. We didn't overnight, but left for Nicosia from where,

the next day, we flew to Tel Aviv. In the flight plan I stated we would fly at 10,000 feet but in fact we went straight up to 20,000. I thought perhaps that was the wise thing to do.

The delivery of the second three Meteors was embargoed because of the 1956 Arab–Israeli War and Suez Crisis, but when the aircraft were released for export, the Israeli Air Force elected to collect the aircraft themselves. The result was not quite so indicative of efficiency, as Jo relates:

> Over France they got lost, and one of them came to grief belly landing in a field near Chateaudun. I went out in the Anson with a couple of engineers to check up on the aircraft and I think a working party was sent out to repair it, but we'd only been back at Bitteswell for a couple of days when we got another distress call; another of the aircraft had burst a tyre at Istres, near Marseilles. So I was off again. I went via Lyon and I remember we flew down the Rhone Valley and back again. It was exceedingly turbulent because of the mistral wind and one of our crew was very airsick.

Meteors were also sold to a number of European countries in the NATO alliance, but almost always collected by their pilots. However, in July 1954 Jo flew an NF.11 to Cologne, where various aircraft were being demonstrated to NATO officials. While there he met two of the Luftwaffe's most famous fighter pilots, Adolf Galland and Johannes Steinhoff. He also ran across an RAF group captain whose face he recognised. Hugh Cundall had sat behind Jo in class at Scarborough High School.

The last of the Meteor variants was the TT Mark 20, developed at the request of the Royal Navy, which required a high-speed target tug for shore-based ground-to-air gunnery and guided-missile practice. Accordingly, between December 1957 and February 1965 Armstrong Whitworth converted Meteor NF.11s into TT.20s, with four high-speed radar, or non-radar, responsive targets stowed in the rear fuselage, a windmill-driven winch mounted on the starboard centre section and the rear cockpit converted for a drogue operator. Jo was given responsibility for flight testing the converted aircraft.

About this time Jo had come to the conclusion, as a matter of professional pride and as a potential advantage, that he should acquire a commercial pilot's licence. He writes:

> Before the war, pilots had an A licence and a B licence, one for private
> and the other for commercial flying. After the war this became more
> complicated, with a private pilot's licence and a commercial pilot's
> licence, the latter prescribing the size of commercial aircraft you
> could fly 'for hire or reward'. Beyond that there was the senior
> commercial licence and then an airline transport pilot's licence.
> Strangely enough, for test flying all you needed was a private pilot's
> licence, but I thought I should possess a commercial licence. I didn't
> have to take a flying test, but I had to study and pass tests in aviation
> law, meteorology and things like that, which required taking time
> off to attend the exams in London. Needless to say, Eric Franklin
> was not at all pleased, but he could hardly say no.

In the event, Jo's commercial licence proved useful to Armstrong Whitworth, as he relates:

> Woody Woodhams liked to assist the Coventry Aeroplane Club, with
> which we shared Baginton. We carried out their aircraft's certificate of
> airworthiness inspections and subsequent flight tests. On their annual
> air day we used to put the firm's De Havilland Rapide aircraft at their
> disposal for joy riding, for which they charged. For that purpose the
> pilot needed to have a commercial licence. This made me the pilot
> of choice, since I was the only one in the test pilot team, at that time
> seven strong, who had a commercial licence.

Chapter 12

Armstrong Whitworth:
Sea Hawks, Hunters, Javelins and Argosies

The Sea Hawk, Hawker's first jet fighter to go into production, was a navalised development of the P.1040, which was rejected at the design stage by the RAF because its performance was estimated to be little superior to that of the Meteor, then in production. The Royal Navy expressed interest, however, and it was as a naval interceptor that the prototype P.1040 emerged in 1948. The first production Sea Hawk flew in November 1951, powered by a Rolls-Royce Nene engine developing 5,000lb of thrust, but it soon became clear that Hawker, busy developing for the RAF what became the Hawker Hunter, was overextended, and so Armstrong Whitworth was approached to assume full responsibility for the design and production of the aircraft.

Hawker built just 35 Sea Hawks. Armstrong Whitworth's first naval contract, signed in April 1951, was for 100 aircraft, but when production ceased in 1956, 400 had been built, as well as 90 aircraft to German and Dutch orders. Jo recalls that the Sea Hawk 'was handed over to us still unpressurised with quite a lot of work to do on it', and indeed Armstrong Whitworth was responsible, as with the Meteor, with developing the aircraft through five successive marks.

The first 60 aircraft produced were Mark 1s, identical to the Hawker-built machines, but the remainder of the first batch of 100 were Mark 2s, which had power-assisted ailerons, developed to remedy the aileron flutter that had led to a degree of lateral instability in the Mark 1s. The Mark 2s also had provision for drop tanks, but in the FB Mark 3, the wing structure was strengthened to enable the aircraft to carry two 500lb bombs

or mines. The first flew on 13 March 1954. The Mark 4, which first took to
the air on 26 August of that year, was quite specifically a ground-attack
aircraft, capable of carrying twenty 3-inch rocket projectiles with a 60lb
warhead, or four 500lb bombs. No aircraft were built as Mark 5s, these
being Mark 3s and 4s retrofitted with an uprated Nene engine of 5,200lb
thrust, designed to increase the Sea Hawk's performance, which was little better than that of the Meteors then being replaced by the Hawker
Hunter. The last model produced for the Royal Navy, the FGA Mark 6,
was also fitted with the uprated Nene, and a batch of eighty-seven was
delivered to the Navy in 1956, some of them being successfully operated in
the ground-attack role in support of the Anglo-French invasion of Egypt
during the Suez Crisis that year.

Jo recalls the Sea Hawk as 'a very pleasant little aircraft to fly' once fitted
with power-assisted ailerons, but adds: 'We had quite a bit of development
work to do on it. The first aircraft they sent us was unpressurised, so we
had, perforce, to undertake quite a bit of testing in this aircraft unpressurised. I remember spending some time at 35,000 feet carrying out generator cooling tests and getting a severe case of bends in my right arm and
shoulder. That happened several times.'

At one point the Royal Navy considered using the Sea Hawk as an
advanced trainer, and with that in mind wanted intensive testing of the
aircraft's spin characteristics. Thoroughly out of favour with Eric Franklin, Jo found himself delegated the task of carrying out the entire programme. He comments:

Clearing the Sea Hawks for spinning meant clearing them with
all the variations, which included four turn spins at two different
heights, to left and to right, centre of gravity forward and aft, wing
tanks on, wings tanks off, ailerons power-assisted and ailerons in
manual, inspin aileron held, outspin aileron held. It boiled down
to a permutation of something like fifty-six spins that was finally
decided upon. In the event I quite enjoyed the task. Using the Severn
Estuary it was very easy to count the number of turns, and I had
a 'Wirex' voice recorder installed, from which our secretary, Thea
Yarker, produced transcripts of my commentary. This helped very
considerably with the chore of compiling a comprehensive report.

More pleasant tasks occasionally came Jo's way. One, repeated several times, was to take a Mark 2 down to his old haunt at Boscombe to carry out underwing tank jettison trials. Another in April 1954 also involved a place previously visited, although much earlier, in 1943, when Jo flew a Sea Hawk to Lann-Bihoué, the French naval airfield near Lorient. The hope, unrealised, was that the Aéronavale would order the type. But the demonstration was appreciated, not least at Baginton, as Jo recollects:

> The Sea Hawk was a nice aircraft to demonstrate and one of the tricks I liked performing was to taxi out with the wings folded and time their unfolding so that they locked in place just as I was starting the take-off run and then of course to do the same in reverse after I landed. I got a special phone call of commendation from the managing director when we came back from that. They were pleased, but the French didn't buy any.

While at Lorient Jo took the opportunity to inspect the U-boat pens that RAF Bomber Command had striven so unavailingly to destroy. He found them substantially intact.

Another pleasurable overseas trip was that made by Jo in June 1956 to demonstrate the Mark 6 Sea Hawk to NATO top brass at Wahn Airport, Cologne. The outcome was more favourable for Armstrong Whitworth, in that the German Bundesmarine ordered a total of sixty-eight, thirty-two as Mark 100 day interceptor fighters, and the remainder as Mark 101 single-seat all-weather fighters with search radar. Ironically, the Sea Hawk production line had by then been dismantled, but it was reactivated, the aircraft being supplied the following year, along with thirty-two, known as the Mark 50, supplied to the Netherlands. Jo recalls that he was puzzled by the German purchase, particularly of the Mark 101: 'The Mk.101 was a strange choice for the Germans because it was fitted with a radar scanner in a pod under the starboard wing and the pilot had his visor screen right in front of him. I tried the thing out and found it very difficult to fly the aircraft and search the screen at the same time, there being no autopilot.'

Delivering the German Sea Hawks turned out to be a most enjoyable experience:

We delivered all of the Sea Hawks to Focke-Wulf in Bremen, which was
handling them on behalf of the German Navy, and I must have made
14 or 15 trips, travelling with one or two others. The German Sea Hawks
had a radio compass and there was a powerful NDB (non-directional
beacon) at Spijkerboor in the north-east of Holland close to Eide, so it
made it easy work to track over to Spijkerboor and then to let down
on Bremen. On one occasion when just Martin Walton and I went, the
weather turned nasty and we had to let down through cloud, but we
got QDMs from the RAF Station at Jever, broke cloud at about 800 feet,
right over the airfield, and they steered us on to Bremen.

At Focke-Wulf we were always met by Bernard Plefkar, a huge man
looking a bit like Boris Karloff, who tactfully told us he had worked
for Siemens on radar during the war. He always looked after us very
well indeed and invariably took us out for dinner, accompanied by
his elegant wife, who would embrace each of us affectionately. We
noticed on the train journey from Bremen to Hamburg that the ride
was very smooth and quiet, and were told that was because they
had continuously welded track. At least five years later, British Rail
triumphantly announced to the world that they had an experimental
25-mile stretch of all-welded track! In Hamburg we discovered, and
afterwards always frequented, the Hofbrauhaus, an offshoot of the
famous beer house in Munich. And invariably we got talking to
people on the next table. On one occasion there was a young man
who was obviously having a real ball and we were told that he'd just
managed to escape from East Germany and was out celebrating. On
another occasion there was a table not far away where there were
about 12 young men. They were getting fairly cheerful when suddenly
one of them stood on his chair, pulled his hair down, donned a false
moustache and started taking off Hitler. We thought he was asking
for trouble but everybody seemed to enjoy it.

In 1956, while involved in delivering German Sea Hawks, Jo applied to take
a Fleet Air Arm deck-landing course, was accepted, and instructed to go
down to Ford, a Fleet Air Arm station near Arundel.

There, in preparation for actual deck landings, I had to do 25

'Addles', or Airfield Deck Landing Exercises. The system involved
a special mirror sight, a concave horizontal mirror sight with
a bar across it reflecting lights down the carrier's deck. By this
means you could follow a fixed glide flight path down, a bit like an
Instrument Landing system, such as is still in use today. You held
your descent, maintaining the correct air speed with the throttle,
and just descended until you hit the runway. It's a bit hard to
persuade yourself not to hold off at the last minute, but I did my 25
ADLEs satisfactorily and a day or two later was told to report again
to Ford, where I would be given a Sea Hawk to fly off and land on
HMS Bulwark. However, at Ford they told me that my aircraft was
unserviceable, so I had to drive to Portsmouth where the Bulwark
was still in port. I did that, went aboard and we went to sea. Then I
was told that the aircraft I was going to use had a hydraulic leak, so
I waited around, twice each day donning an immersion suit, which
I found very claustrophobic, getting a tight elastic collar over my
head. The aircraft was unavailable on the first day, and the second,
and on the third I was told that they'd cured the hydraulic leak but
somebody had plugged in an external power supply whilst the hood
closing switch had been left selected in the 'close' position so the
hood had motored itself closed. In order to open it again they had to
operate the hood jettison system and that meant resetting all sorts
of things, so in the end they said it was too late and flew me ashore
in a helicopter, without a deck landing proper at all. It was, however,
interesting to be on the aircraft carrier, watching from the island as
other aircraft were taking off and landing.

Alongside Meteor and Sea Hawk production, Armstrong Whitworth were
also contracted to build the Hawker Hunter. First flown on 20 July 1951,
the single-seat Hunter proved a success from the outset, and was ordered
into mass production as a replacement for the RAF's ageing Meteors. The
first Hawker-built aircraft, an F Mark 1 powered by the highly successful
Rolls-Royce Avon engine of 7,500lb thrust, flew on 16 May 1953. But already,
in March, the Ministry of Supply had placed an order with Armstrong
Whitworth for the construction of Mark 2 Hunters, fitted with the Armstrong Siddeley Sapphire engine of 8,000lb thrust. Both were short-range

interceptor fighters, closely comparable in performance, although the Mark 2 was slightly faster, capable of Mach 0.94 at 36,000 feet. Jo well remembers his first flight in a Hunter, for it caused a stir:

In August '53 Eric Franklin, Bill Else and I went down to Dunsfold to make familiarization flights in a Hunter. I went off last, lateish afternoon and climbed straight up to 40,000 feet in a northerly direction. The weather was gin clear, and I could see Coventry, so I put the nose down and for fun went supersonic, pointing it right at Coventry. Well, the sonic boom scored a bullseye and caused quite a lot of consternation, the local Coventry Evening Telegraph reporting the next evening that 'An aircraft flying through the sound barrier caused the big bang that shook houses in Coventry and was heard in outlying districts at about 6.40 yesterday evening.' It continued: 'The big bang mystified thousands of people and had firemen and police on the alert. Many people described the concussion as like a bomb and some as a double explosion. Scores ran from their homes into the street to see what had happened. One Stoke resident reported, "Our front door was nearly blown in. Coventry fire brigade and the police stood by for emergency calls."'

The following evening, the local paper assured residents that sonic booms were not likely to be heard often in the city, Armstrong Whitworth saying that although Hawker Hunters would be manufactured at Baginton, they would be flown from Bitteswell. The item continued: 'As exclusively revealed in yesterday's Coventry Evening Telegraph, the bang that shook houses in Coventry on Monday was caused when an aircraft broke through the sound barrier near the city. The plane, a Hawker Hunter, was flown by Mr J. Lancaster, one of the test pilots at the Sir W.G. Armstrong Whitworth Aircraft Limited.'

An initial order for 150 Sapphire-engined Hunters was placed with Armstrong Whitworth, Baginton turning out forty-five Mark 2s, one of which Jo flew at the 1954 SBAC show at Farnborough, the balance being completed as Mark 5s, which had a greater internal fuel capacity and underwing pylons for tanks and stores. Production and testing went smoothly, although Jo recalls one tense moment:

The early Hunter had one little defect, firing the cannon at altitude induced engine compressor stall. To overcome this, Hawkers introduced a little gadget that we called fuel dipping, so that when the guns were fired the engine was in fact decelerated. The gadget was wired via an isolating switch on the nose-wheel door. One day, as soon as the undercarriage door closed after take off, fuel dipping came into action through some electrical fault, so that having just got off the ground and the wheels up, the engine suddenly slowed down. I had no idea what it was, but I turned back to the airfield and landed safely. It's a bit alarming when you're only just airborne in a Hunter and the engine suddenly loses power.

Another potential problem was averted, as Jo recalls, but with further strain put upon his difficult relationship with Eric Franklin:

One day when Eric was away, an instruction came through from Hawkers that temporarily negative G during flight tests should be avoided due to a possible failure in a fuel inverted flight device, which could result in fire. I naturally had some misgivings about this, and consulted the Air Inspection Department's Chief Inspector. He agreed with me and grounded the Hunters pending further review of the situation. When Eric returned the following day and found the Hunters temporarily grounded, he was absolutely furious, and promptly grounded me. The problem with the inverted flight gadget was quickly remedied, and everything returned to normal – except my relationship with Eric.

With production of the Mark 5 completed, Armstrong Whitworth began building Hunter Mark 6s, fitted with an uprated 10,000lb-thrust Avon engine, the first flying on 25 May 1955. One hundred of these were followed by a further order placed by Hawkers for twenty-eight. Meanwhile, the Hunter was also being built under licence on the continent by Fokker in the Netherlands and Avions Fairey in Belgium, and Jo found himself briefly testing the Belgian-built Mark 4s:

In 1957 I went over to Avions Fairey in Gosselies, who were building

Hunters under licence. Their test pilot was liable to a fortnight's national service every year and they were pushed, so I went out for a fortnight to help them out. I had quite a busy time there, doing two or three flights a day. I delivered several Hunters to the Belgian Air Force at Chièvres and they drove me back to Gosselies, near Charleroi. Coming back from Chièvres we drove through Mons and I remember seeing names familiar through their connection with World War I.

Jo had no serious problem while testing Hunters, but Martin Walton did. 'He was flying a Mark 6 Hunter at high speed low down,' Jo recalls, 'when one of the undercarriage legs became unlatched and fell down. The force of the air was such that it took the leg right off. Dunsfold was consulted and he was instructed to eject, which he did safely, while the aircraft crashed without harming anybody on the ground.'

As production of the Hunter came to an end, Armstrong Whitworth was awarded a contract to build a second Gloster aircraft, the Javelin. The first British jet designed from the outset as a two-seat all-weather fighter, the Javelin first flew in November 1951, envisaged as the successor to the Meteor night fighters for which Armstrong Whitworth had been responsible. Delta-winged, with the tailplane mounted at the top of the fin, it was fitted with two 8,000lb-thrust Armstrong Siddeley Sapphire engines and was capable of Mach 0.93 at 40,000 feet. The development and testing of the GA.5, as it was originally known, did not go smoothly. On 29 June 1952, while flying at high speed, the prototype lost both elevators following violent flutter. Amazingly, the pilot, Squadron Leader Bill Waterton, was able to land the GA.5 by trimming the variable-incidence tailplane manually, although the necessarily high-speed landing caused the undercarriage to collapse.

Then on 11 June 1953 the second prototype was lost after experiencing super stall conditions with the centre of gravity further aft than had been tried hitherto, the pilot, Peter Lawrence, being killed when he ejected too low for his parachute to open fully. On 21 October 1954 a third Javelin, piloted by Flight Lieutenant R.J. Ross of the RAE, Farnborough, crashed into the Bristol Channel off Weston-super-Mare when he was attempting to recover from an intentional spin at too low an altitude, the Javelin's high rate of descent while spinning giving him no time to recover before hitting the sea. Lastly, on 8 December 1955, a service test pilot, Squadron Leader Dick, was testing a Mark 1 for the A&AEE when the aircraft entered a flat spin during manoeuvres, and although the anti-spin parachute was deployed the spinning could not be stopped, and he ejected. Following this, a stall-warning device was developed and installed in all Javelins and techniques developed for recovery from a spin, which in the Javelin demonstrated unpleasant characteristics, with the nose of the aircraft pitching through some 70 degrees during each turn.

Despite these considerable handling setbacks, the Air Ministry was generally pleased with the Javelin's performance, and the aircraft was ordered into production, the F(AW) Mark 1 entering RAF service in December 1955. The Mark 2 Javelin differed from the Mark 1 only in the type of radar carried, while the Mark 3 was a trainer version. In the F(AW) Mark 4, however, there was a major change, designed to obviate the high stick forces experienced at high speeds in employing the power-boosted elevators, with the introduction of a fully powered all-moving tailplane. Gloster built eighteen Mark 4s, but Armstrong Whitworth were contracted to build another thirty-two, the first coming off the production line in 1956. A contract for forty-four F(AW) Mark 5s followed, these featuring a re-designed wing with provision for four pylon-mounted Firestreak missiles and increased fuel capacity, its limited range being a criticism levelled at the Javelin by the USAF and European air forces that had flown the earlier marks. The Mark 5s were followed by fifty-seven Mark 7s, which were the first to carry Firestreak missiles as standard, alongside two 30mm Aden guns. However, many of the aircraft were modified to Mark 9 standard, often before delivery, by the installation of uprated Sapphire engines with limited reheat capacity, and provision of in-flight refuelling. The last aircraft came off the Baginton production line in 1958.

Jo wasn't particularly impressed by the Javelin, which he thought 'rather gawky-looking', adding that at Armstrong Whitworth it was commonly known as a 'bricklayer's trowel'.

It wasn't a particularly outstanding aircraft in any way though not unpleasant to fly. The Marks 4, 5, 7 and 9 Javelins we built were fitted with full power controls. There seemed to be an abnormally large number of modifications constantly coming through to the Javelin production line and these were quite often to the hydraulic system, which finished up pretty complicated. On one occasion Martin Walton was testing a Javelin, and when he returned to Bitteswell the nose wheel wouldn't lower, but remained fully retracted. Eventually he landed on the main wheels and let the nose down as gently as he could. The Javelin finished up with its radome scraping along the runway but it was made of tough stuff and was just grazed. There was also some shortage of service equipment at the time so we flew them without it, put them off test and flew them down to Kemble, near Cirencester, where they were parked until we brought them back for the equipment to be fitted as available. There was a lot of shuttling to and fro.

I had one Sapphire engine failure on a Javelin, but that was due to a malfunction of a unit in the fuel system, not a mechanical failure as such. For some reason the two Sapphires together made a very distinctive, high pitched whining noise, quite characteristic of the Javelin. As with all the Meteors, Sea Hawks, Hunters and Javelin, part of the production flight test schedule included taking an aircraft to around 30,000 feet and then checking it in a dive up to its limiting Mach number. With the Meteor severe buffeting set in at about Mach 0.81 or 0.82 and in the Sea Hawk at about 0.82 also. With the Hunter and the Javelin it would be just over Mach 1, about 1.01 or 1.02. In neither of them was there any visual effect on the aircraft's control. In the Hunter the stick moved quite suddenly about an inch, but it didn't alter the attitude of the aircraft. In the Javelin there wasn't any stick movement accompanying the transonic stage.

In the SBAC Farnborough displays in the early 50s, aircraft that could go supersonic and make a bang did so. The Hunter, Swift, Javelin and DH.110 would take off a few minutes earlier than their display time and climb up to 30,000 feet. When their time came, they'd start their display off with a supersonic dive and a bang aimed at Farnborough. Everybody loved it and it was all good fun. When Peter Twiss was testing the Fairey FD.2 Delta, in the lead-up to his successful attempt on the world speed record, there were quite often supersonic bangs, but official attitudes to these changed when some character in Bishop's Waltham, Hampshire, heard a sonic bang and decided he'd get his greenhouse repaired. He put in a claim, some stupid government agency accepted the claim and he got compensation. Of course everybody with a broken-down greenhouse or similar was then keen to hear a sonic bang and get it repaired on the government. So that spoilt everything. We were ordered, first of all, to direct our sonic bangs at open country like the Pennines or high ground in Wales, but eventually had to do it over the open sea.

Following Twiss's March 1956 record-breaking run in the FD.2 – raising the world air speed record to 1,132mph (1,811km/h) or Mach 1.73, an increase of some 300mph (480km/h) over the previous record – routine testing resumed, but the Ministry of Supply refused to allow low-level supersonic testing over the United Kingdom, so Fairey took the FD.2 first to France and later Norway for these tests. No claims for damages were lodged in either country.

The failure of the Apollo left Armstrong Whitworth with no aircraft design project of its own, and dependent on subcontract work. The latter was lucrative but the firm nonetheless hankered to develop its own designs. The result was the last Armstrong Whitworth aircraft, the AW.650 freighter, later named the Argosy, design work on which began in 1955. Originally it had been a response to an Air Ministry specification for a medium-range freight-carrying aircraft, but as the prospects of a military contract diminished, the decision was taken to build the aircraft as a private venture civil freighter. With ease of loading and unloading to the forefront, the designers opted for a high-wing layout with tail booms, this allowing for sideways-opening doors at both ends of the fuselage. Four Rolls-Royce Dart turboprop engines were fitted to a wing that was, essentially, that of the Coastal Command Shackletons built by Avro, another of the Hawker Siddeley Group of companies. From the outset it was envisaged that the Argosy would be flexible enough to carry either passengers or freight only, or a combination of the two. The first Argosy, G–AOZZ, left the Baginton factory in December 1958, and flew from Bitteswell on 8 January 1959. Two more trials aircraft followed in quick succession and a comprehensive testing programme was set in motion, all company-funded.

The concept of the Argosy's freight or passenger compartment with doors front and rear made perfect sense, but it brought complications. One was that the fuselage had to be pressurised, and Jo recalls that an elaborate system of some twelve or more separate hydraulically operated locks was installed to ensure full pressurisation. The layout also necessitated placing the flight deck above the fuselage, rather akin to that of the Boeing 747, which took some getting used to. The twin booms also contributed to the individuality of the Argosy, as Jo explains:

> A twin boom layout is fine in something like a Vampire or DH.110, but when you get up to the size of an Argosy it's almost impossible to make it torsionally stiff enough; inevitably there is quite a lot of boom movement in flight. In fact one of the characteristics of the Argosy, even when it went into service, was that on the climb out it would start a little bobbing up and down action. BEA pilots who flew it used to call it 'Noddy' for that reason.

From the first the Argosy displayed generally pleasant flying characteristics, although it had a nasty stall, as Jo recalls:

> The stall in the Argosy was very unpleasant, with severe buffeting and 'kicking' of the ailerons. They were controlled by push-pull rods and on one occasion the rod to the starboard aileron buckled under terrific compression and broke, so that aileron just trailed, disconnected. I had to keep the aircraft level by flying with the port aileron up, which meant having the wheel considerably over to port. We flew gingerly back to Bitteswell, fortunately without more ado.

Until the Argosies were built Armstrong Whitworth employed five test pilots: Eric Franklin, Bill Else, Jo, Jim McCowan and Martin Walton. But the massive testing regime, involving three Argosies, required further appointments. One was Peter Varley, who had been with Gloster at Moreton Valence until it closed. The other was an ex-RAF pilot called Clive Simpson, always known as 'George'. 'He had been at Boscombe Down', Jo says, 'with a handling squadron, which is the unit which writes all the pilots' notes and manuals and he came specifically to do that for the Argosy. For a commercial aircraft the flight manual is quite a tome, covering every contingency in performance and what to do in emergencies. It requires expertise to put it together and that's why Clive Simpson came to us, although he did do some of the flying as well.'

In August 1959 Bill Else, Jim McCowan and Jo, together with a technical and maintenance crew of about twenty-five, took off from Birmingham to undertake tropical trials in the second Argosy, G–APRL. 'We flew out [to] Rome, then Benghazi and Cairo en route to Khartoum', he writes, and 'at Cairo International they were most interested and most pleasant, and told us that ours was the first British civil aircraft to go through Cairo International since the Suez fiasco.'

> The purpose of a tropical trial is primarily to measure aircraft performance, as affected by temperature and altitude. The best way to do so is to measure the performance in conditions of high temperature and high altitude and combinations of the two. The airfield at Khartoum is 2,000 feet above sea level and we needed a minimum ground air temperature of 38 degrees centigrade to get realistic results. That meant that sometimes we had to wait till late morning before it was worthwhile making a start. The weather in the Sudan was almost perfect. There were no sand storms and little cloud, nor a great deal of air traffic, so we were able to do our take-off performance and the other in flight measurements miles from anywhere, with nothing but desert in sight and Khartoum Air Traffic Control merely asking us to call in every 30 minutes to report operation as normal. Good progress was made.

In Khartoum the team stayed at the Grand Hotel, alongside the White Nile. 'It was in a very pleasant position,' Jo comments, 'and in front of the hotel was a big terrace with tables under sunshades. It was enjoyable to sit out there looking out over the river. You could drink the local "Camel" brand lager or imported Dutch fizzy lager, which didn't go down very well. The popular soft drink was Nemoon, which was a pleasant iced lemonade drink.' But while it had once been grand, the Grand Hotel was going downhill. 'The same went', Jo says, 'for the Sudan Club, which at one time had been a great social centre for the Europeans but was also looking a bit moth-eaten. The food at the Grand Hotel was monotonous and everyone suffered a dose of the inevitable 'gippo guts' until their digestive system adjusted. The hotel had only a handful of bedrooms with air conditioning, and they were permanently reserved for Alitalia transit crews. . . . The manager was Egyptian and he seemed to spend most of his time in his office with the door open shouting "Iwa" (yes) in a loud voice down a telephone.'

'I never went very far whilst I was in Khartoum,' he adds. 'In fact there really wasn't anywhere to go, except to Omdurman, which was about 5 miles away on the west side of the main Nile, and had historic connections. They had an interesting museum there, with one of the exhibits a very old vintage car. It seemed a strange place to find such a thing. Many people spoke good English and I found them all pleasant. One old boy with no reason to ingratiate himself with me whispered, "You know, we were far better off under the British." This was after just three years of independence.'

The team spent just over four weeks in Khartoum, during which Jo made thirty-seven flights, then on 3 October flew direct to Nairobi. 'When we arrived it seemed like heaven on earth,' he says:

> For one thing it's 5,000 feet above sea level so the atmosphere is much fresher. We were all staying at the New Stanley Hotel, which at one time had been the best in Nairobi and was certainly very civilized. I was woken every day by a gentleman bringing my morning tea, and greeting me with a cheerful 'Jambo bwana'. At breakfast there was practically everything you could think of – bacon, kippers, devilled kidneys, every sort of cereal, fresh milk. Then in the evening there was the Thorn Tree, an open air bar where you could sit and drink the local Tuscan beer, which is quite good, or gin and tonic. We couldn't understand why the gin and tonic tasted so much better out there. The gin was standard Gordon's, so we concluded that the locally made Schweppes tonic water was the answer. One of the waitresses at the Thorn Tree, an East European, had her concentration camp number tattooed on her forearm, which was food for thought. In the evenings we sometimes went to a little Italian restaurant called Laverinis. They were very friendly and pleaded with us to emigrate to Kenya because they felt that they needed to build up the European population there. And I must say that at that time I was so taken with

Kenya I was very tempted. The main street in Nairobi, then called
Delamere Avenue, was a beautiful sight, lined with Jacaranda trees in
blossom. We didn't have time to stray far from Nairobi, being kept
busy with our work, but twice a bunch of us hired a car and drove
out to Lake Naivasha, lunched in the hotel and watched the flamingos
and the pelicans. The latter amazed me; they looked so ungainly on
the ground but so beautiful in flight.

While at Nairobi's Embakasi Airport one day, the Armstrong Whitworth
team saw Harry Secombe, of *Goon Show* fame, disembark from a BOAC
aircraft. 'From the moment he appeared', Jo recalls, 'he was pulling funny
faces, making silly noises and making funny remarks. . . . I read in the
Nairobi paper afterwards that the airport customs officers, to a man of
Asian origin, were not amused when, asked what he had to declare, he
announced that he was carrying 5,000 busts of Mae West. Later on, on the
first leg of our homeward run at Entebbe, we went to the Lake Hotel and
he was there, in the bar, still making silly noises and funny faces.'

   During his time in Nairobi, Jo carried out forty flights in twenty-nine
days, much of it concerned with take-off and landing performances
at altitude, but for other work the Argosy was taken south, out of the
main traffic lanes, flying over and around Mount Kilimanjaro, which Jo
remembers as 'topped with rather dirty looking snow'. He adds: 'Over to
the north west of Nairobi was Mount Kenya. It had snow on it too but it
always looked cleaner.'

   The Argosy left Nairobi homeward bound on 31 October 1959 and routed
back via Entebbe, Khartoum, Cairo, Benghazi and Rome to Birmingham,
arriving on 4 November. Jo recollects their return for two things. One was
their enthusiastic greeting by the managing director 'Woody' Woodhams
and the chief designer Edward Keen, both well pleased with how the tropical trials of the Argosy had gone. 'I think,' Jo reflects, 'that was probably
the last time I saw Woody, because he retired shortly after that.' The other
memorable moment was an encounter with a customs officer:

   Having given up 40 plus cigarettes a day in 1943 I had become a pipe
   smoker, and when I knew I was going to be in Africa for a couple
   of months I decided to avoid the heavy excise tax by exporting

myself some tobacco. I used to buy it at home in two ounce tins
with soldered-on tops that had a lid with a cutter on it. You cut the
top off and it was always absolutely fresh. I thought that was ideal
for exporting and arranged the export of three pounds through
the British American Tobacco Company, who told me it would be
out in Khartoum within 17 days. After 30 days it hadn't arrived but
while we were in Nairobi it did. So as we staged through Khartoum
on the way back, I collected it. It had, however, been sent not in the
sealed tins to which I was used at home, but in flat screw-top tins,
which had been so battered on the way that practically every tin had
had its lid loosened, leaving the tobacco tinder dry. It was in a very
battered container, so I left it exactly as it was until we got back to
Birmingham, where I presented it to the customs officer, explaining
what had happened. He said, 'Well sir, I can't allow you to import
tobacco without charging you duty on it but I don't know how much
tobacco there is. If you tell me there's one ounce of tobacco I shall
charge you duty on one ounce of tobacco.' So I said, 'There's one
ounce of tobacco there.' To which he replied, 'Right sir, I shall charge
you duty on one ounce.'

Having been away for nine weeks, the tropical trials team had a week off
and then rejoined the testing programme at Bitteswell, where the third and
fourth Argosies were already flying. 'The big aim', Jo notes, 'was to get the
Certificate of Airworthiness for public transport as soon as possible and the
first three aircraft were dedicated to that purpose and instrumented accordingly.' 'It went pretty smoothly really', he recounts, but remembers one nasty
moment experienced by Peter Varley during testing with the autopilot:

Peter had to simulate various malfunctions on the autopilot, one
of which was the sudden application of negative G. When he did
this, very much to his surprise, all four engines suddenly cut out,
and the indicated turbine gas temperatures went right off the clock
because the engine was still under quite a lot of power. Fortunately
they sorted it out quickly by throttling back and unfeathering. The
problem was due to the fact that Rolls-Royce had introduced a torque
switch operated by oil pressure that, in the event of loss of torque,

would feather the propellers automatically. Under negative G, the oil pressure fell and activated the so-called safety device. Rolls-Royce, it turned out, knew all about this but for some reason or other had omitted to tell us.

During the summer of 1960 route-proving tests were carried out; these were simulated scheduled flights in which the performance and engineering aspects were closely monitored. Some were flown from the United Kingdom, but others, in the Middle East, from Beirut. Jo recalls one with a comical side:

> Beirut was a haven for rich oil sheikhs and we were trying to get them interested in the Argosy. The one who seemed almost to own Kuwait had a huge American car that he asked us to fly to Kuwait. This we did, but had a real comedy when they tried to unload it. First they brought a ramp but it was too steep so the car was aground before it got over the bridge. Then they brought a tank transporter but they couldn't manoeuvre it into position, so in the end they took the ramp off the tank transporter and we taxied the aircraft up to the back of the tank transporter and got the car off that way.

During the late 1950s and early '60s, with the aero industry in Britain struggling, the Hawker Siddeley Group aggressively diversified, buying up engineering companies in a range of fields, and Jo remembers how this was reflected in the pocket diary that employees were given every Christmas:

> In the front of this diary all the member companies of the Hawker Siddeley Group were listed, with full details, including a list of the Boards of Directors and Chief Executives. As these new firms were taken over, you'd see them appear in the diary with a list of unfamiliar directors' and executives' names and then the next year the same firm would appear, but all those unfamiliar names would have disappeared, replaced by familiar ones like Tom Sopwith, Roy Dobson, Frank Spriggs and others.

One firm bought up was Brush Electrical, which made heavy electrical gear, and in December 1960 had about 15,000lb of equipment that needed to be delivered to Bahrain urgently. An Argosy was used, but because of the weight of the freight the amount of fuel carried had to be limited, so the journey was made with frequent stops. 'I decided to land at Damascus', Jo recalled.

> In countries like Syria it's sometimes easier to land than to try and explain yourself and suffer a lot of hassle trying to get permission to overfly. By landing, there was absolutely no problem at all. Baghdad, however, was quite eerie. As we approached to land, I told them over the radio that all I wanted to do was to refuel and depart again for Bahrain. Normally, after such a request there would be a chap there to signal us into the parking place and the refuelling tanker would be out to meet us. But nobody took any notice. So I headed for the terminal building, where there were very few people around. The walls were plastered with posters of the President, Abdel Karim Kassem, who had led the insurrection against King Faisal in 1958. But nobody seemed to want to know us and there was very little else going on. I was glad to get out of there.

The high hopes that Armstrong Whitworth had of the Argosy were never fulfilled. Of the original batch of ten, seven went to Riddle Airlines of Miami, at the time one of the largest all-freight airlines in the United States. Riddle bought them for use in fulfilling a contract called 'Logair', running a scheduled bulk freight service for the US Logistics Command within the United States. Riddle's contract ended in 1962 and the Argosies were returned to Armstrong Whitworth, but went on to a long life as freight carriers both in the United States and Britain. Fortunately for Armstrong Whitworth, however, BEA decided to boost its air freight business, and bought the three remaining 100 Series Argosies, the first of which entered service in December 1961. They performed reliably with an impressive rate of utilisation, but never returned a profit, largely because of the Argosy's relatively low cruising speed of 280mph, and modest rate of climb.

Armstrong Whitworth's response was a revamped Argosy 200 Series, which featured a new wing structure to allow the carriage of a greater payload. BEA ordered five of what emerged as the Argosy Series 220, on condition that the manufacturer take back the three Series 100 in part exchange. The new aircraft entered service in 1965, but again BEA was disappointed. The Series 220 Argosies failed to make a profit, and by 1970 all had been sold. Ironically, they and the Series 100s all went on to long and useful careers in such places as Canada's Northwest Territories and New Zealand.

If the Argosy failed to make much impression in the civil market, it did eventually do so militarily, when in 1957–58 the RAF showed a renewed interest in a version of the Argosy 100 Series, eventually placing an order for a total of fifty-six machines. 'Needless to say', Jo comments, 'the RAF wanted quite a lot of alterations.' These included an increased all-up weight, more headroom in the rear of the fuselage to accommodate a Saracen armoured car, the replacement of the side-hinged rear door by doors hinging upwards and downwards, and the removal of the nose door. Jo recounts:

> The RAF had no use for the nose door, so it was replaced by a crew entrance hatch, a toilet and a navigator's position for visually guiding the pilots to aiming points on the dropping zones for stores and paratroopers. The Argosies could accommodate about 90 paratroopers and for their purposes we built a sliding door each side of the fuselage towards the rear. The single-hinged rear door was replaced by two horizontally hinged ones, the lower one acting as a ramp. These were built into the second prototype for initial trials and I had the job of checking them out. The controls were arranged so that the pilot could open or close each door independently to any position, so I had designs indicating the position of each door, and could set them at any position. As I operated them I had Roy Spencer, one of our best flight engineers, down below on the intercom, observing what was happening. The doors worked beautifully. The worry had been that we'd get buffeting over the tail plane, but we tried them at all sorts of speeds and altitudes and every combination of opening and couldn't find anything seriously wrong with them.

Jo was, however, less impressed by other changes on which the RAF had insisted:

In the civilian version we had an excellent system for intercom and
radio monitoring. There was a mixer box, made I think by Ultra, and
by a simple switch you could monitor any of the radio navigation
aids, radios, public address system or the intercom. It was very good
indeed, but the RAF insisted on a more complicated system that didn't
work nearly so well. On the civilian version we also had a very good
central warning system, a series of master buttons on the cockpit
coaming that attracted the pilot's attention by flashing if anything was
malfunctioning. When one started to flash you pulled the button out,
it stopped flashing and you'd look around to see what the problem
was. The RAF didn't like that system, and produced a box with about
20 little windows, all with three letter abbreviations, such as GNR for
generator. It was almost impossible to decipher what all these three-
letter things meant, and was a very retrograde step I thought.

In June 1961 Jo was detailed to take the Argosy C Mark 1, as it was to be
called in RAF service, to Le Bourget for the annual Paris air show, the
equivalent of the Farnborough SBAC show and the world's oldest and
largest. 'I took my faithful flight engineer Roy Spencer with me', Jo says,

> but the day before, a USAF B-58 Hustler, attempting aerobatics at low
> level, had crashed, killing its crew, and the French authorities became
> very unhappy about low flying, immediately imposing a minimum
> height for a flypast of 100 metres. Several pilots, including me in
> the Argosy, got hauled over the coals for coming in lower than that.
> We did several flypasts, including one with three engines feathered
> and the lower rear door wide open and it all went well. Later, in
> September '61, the military Argosy was presented at Farnborough
> again, though I only flew it on one day.

Shortly after the war, Jo had joined the Royal Aeronautical Society (RAS)
as an associate, later became an associate fellow and in 1980 was elected
a fellow. He had also been a member of the Society of Licensed Aircraft
Engineers and Technologists, and when they amalgamated with the Royal
Aeronautical Society became a chartered engineer. 'It was good in the
early post-war years,' he says. 'The RAS used to have garden parties at

various airfields around the country and they were most enjoyable. Now-adays, they're a bit too posh and far too expensive.'

Early post-war, also, Jo joined the Guild of Air Pilots and Air Naviga-tors, and when, in 1956, a test pilot section was established, he was elected as one of two active assistants to the Guild's court. 'This necessitated', Jo comments, 'monthly meetings in London with the full court. I used to travel down once a month and attend the meetings which at that time were held in the Royal Aeronautical Society's premises in Londonderry House at the bottom of Park Lane. Then, in 1960 I was awarded the Guild's Master Air Pilot Certificate, number 325, signed by the Grand Master, Prince Philip.'

In 1960 the British Overseas Airways Corporation were converting to the Boeing 707 and carrying out crew training at Shannon, where traffic was lighter and charges less. When they had to exchange an aircraft, with one coming back for inspection and another going over empty, members of the Guild were invited to go with it. Jo was among those who went along:

The BOAC hosts were Matthew Slattery, the Chairman of the Board, and Basil Smallpeice, the Managing Director. There were many distinguished passengers as guests, including Don Bennett, Sir Francis Chichester, Sir Alan Cobham, Air Chief Marshal Sir Ralph Cochrane, Sir George Edwards, Captain O.P. Jones, Norman McMillan, Sir Frank Whittle, and last but certainly not least Prince Philip himself. The aircraft was full, we sat down anywhere and I found myself sitting next to Sir Alan Cobham, who started chatting about the Bournemouth Symphony Orchestra, which he had a lot to do with and supported. He was charming. At Shannon we were given a buffet lunch, together with abundant Irish coffee – a delicious blend of Bailey's Irish whiskey and cream – and Prince Philip circulated, chatting with pretty well everybody, including me. He, too, was pleasant and easy to talk to.

Most of the time that I was acting as the test pilot assistant on the court, Sir Frederick Timms was the Master. He had been a pioneer navigator but become a civil servant involved in setting up aviation organisations in India and elsewhere. I thought he was serious to the point of being stuffy. Sir Frederick was succeeded as Master in 1956 by

John Lankester-Parker, retired chief test pilot of Shorts, an absolutely
charming man. Also on the Court was the great Captain O.P. Jones
of Imperial Airways. He used to sit through a meeting saying nothing
until a decision was almost signed and sealed and then throw a
spanner in the works, which would start discussion all over again. I
doubt he did it on purpose, but he was a crusty old boy.

When in 1956 the Guild of Air Pilots and Air Navigators became a livery
company of the City of London, Jo automatically became a liveryman
and thus a freeman of the City of London. 'I don't know what my other
privileges are,' he says, 'except that every year I get notices, which I ignore,
to vote for the Lord Mayor. I'm already a freeman of the City of Coventry because anyone who's served a recognised apprenticeship in Coventry
automatically becomes a freeman of the city. In Coventry I believe this
entitles you to graze your cow on the common land. I never got round to
doing that.'

By 1962 Armstrong Whitworth had seven test pilots, but only the RAF's
Argosies coming off the production line and no subcontract aircraft
construction in train. Inevitably, word came through that the number
of pilots had to be reduced. One obvious candidate for redundancy was
'George' Simpson, who had been recruited specifically to write the Argosy
flight manual. A second was needed, and Jo saw this as an opportunity.
'The aviation industry was contracting fast,' he states, 'and it seemed to
be time to get out.'

What should he do? Being an airline pilot had never appealed to him:
'It had always seemed like driving a bus,' he admits. But talking to BEA
pilots he met when they were converting to the Argosy, he had learned
how well they were paid, with their ordinary line pilots' salaries in excess
of what Eric Franklin was earning, and of the generous perks, such as con-
cessionary fares and a handsome pension scheme. Jo was forty-three years
old, and could look forward to fifteen years or so as an airline pilot. For
this, however, he needed an airline transport pilot's licence, which would
involve three months' study at an approved institution followed by exams.
'I went to Lockie,' he recounts, 'who was then Managing Director, and
asked if the company would back me to study for the licence.' Lockwood

agreed, and Jo stayed on salary with all expenses paid for the duration of the course. 'So between April and July 1962', he says,

> I deposited myself on my dear sister Con, her husband Norman and their two children, for about three months. From their home in Highgate I commuted five days a week by Underground to Ealing Broadway, where I attended a specialist school called Avigation. However, I kept my cosy little bed-sit in Church Road, Leamington, to which sometimes I would go for the weekend.

In terms of flying hours, of course, Jo amply met the requirements for an airline pilot's licence, but the specialist courses were a challenge: 'The subjects included navigation and plotting, aviation law, meteorology, climatology, and the theory and use of navigation aids, all culminating in six full days of examinations, morning and afternoon, so it was quite an ordeal. But I successfully sailed through it.'

Jo left Armstrong Whitworth in August 1962, almost twenty-seven years since he began his apprenticeship at Whitley. In appreciation of his long service, on top of funding his licence study, Armstrong Whitworth paid him a year's salary, which he thought generous. He was also given 'a jolly good farewell party' to which Eric Franklin was not invited: 'Everybody else was there.' Franklin's animosity towards Jo never abated. In 1995 Jo organised a reunion of Armstrong Whitworth apprentices. Eleven attended, he says, 'and we had a wonderful weekend at Anstey near Coventry, where most of us who were in the Air Force learned to fly.' Since Eric Franklin had himself been an apprentice, Jo invited him, but got 'a very curt rude response, so that was the end of that'.

Chapter 13

Aerospray (Cyprus) Ltd

While studying for his airline transport pilot's licence, Jo met his former test pilot colleague, Jack Akers. 'I was pleased to meet up with him again,' Jo remarks. 'We had always got along pretty well together and he could be quite entertaining.' For some years Akers had been working for Fisons, then a major chemicals and pharmaceuticals company, which had large contracts involving aerial crop spraying in Africa and South America. Akers had worked in Colombia, Nigeria, Cameroon and the Sudan in Africa, mainly spraying banana and cotton plantations. 'He certainly gave the impression of having done pretty well,' Jo recollects, 'because he was driving a new Jaguar and in addition to a house in Pluckley, near Ashford in Kent, where his wife Vera and three small daughters lived, he had a mews house in Bayswater.'

The set-up, and consequently the opportunity, as Jack Akers explained it, was that Fisons would negotiate a contract, usually with a government department, for crop protection for a whole growing season. Company entomologists would monitor the crops and prescribe the chemicals needed to combat any infestation. Fisons would then supply the chemicals, and also the tankers and other equipment, as well as organising fuel supplies for the aircraft operating on site and any road transport required. The aircraft themselves, together with pilots, maintenance engineers, spares and equipment, would be supplied by subcontractors. 'Jack obviously had made some very good contacts within Fisons and elsewhere', Jo states, 'and was already in the process of setting up a company to carry out the sub-contract crop-spraying.' The company, Aerospray (Cyprus) Ltd, was to be based in Nicosia, and Akers already had one partner, a New Zealand pilot with crop-spraying experience named Ian Taylor. Jo was invited to join them as a co-director and shareholder. 'I must say I was quite intrigued by the prospect of working for my own company,' he says, 'but what really did it for me was the prospect of spending time in Nicosia and Beirut. I had visited them several times during Meteor deliveries to the Middle East and the Argosy route-proving trials and I loved Cyprus and Lebanon.'

Jo accepted the invitation. His stake in Aerospray (Cyprus) was £2,500, which, as he notes, would at that time have bought a four-bedroom detached house. What followed was a busy, interesting and often fascinating three years. 'It could also have been very lucrative,' he admits, 'had we operated together fairly and squarely as a team, but in the event it finished up as a financial disaster for me.'

An early sign of things to come, had Jo recognised it, came when, as soon as he accepted Jack Akers's offer, the latter asked him to move into the house in Queen's Mews, Bayswater. 'He had a good reason,' Jo observes. 'While in West Africa he'd become entangled with a British woman called Etain Boffey, who was now firmly ensconced in Queen's Mews. Jack told me that he was trying to get her to move out and that if I moved in she would go. Well I moved in and she didn't go. She stayed. I didn't like her much and I think the feeling was mutual. She was in effect a live-in secretary and continued to cohabit with Jack.'

When Jo joined Aerospray, early in August 1962, the company already had a subcontract with Fisons for cotton-spraying in the Sudan, starting in mid-September, and preparations were well in hand. Four crated Piper PA18 Super Cubs were en route from the United States. These were taken to Panshanger, a grass airfield near Welwyn Garden City, where under the supervision of Ron Cripps, a licensed engineer, they were uncrated, assembled, tested and submitted for a Certificate of Airworthiness. All bore Cyprus registrations.

Having been granted their C of A, the Super Cubs were fitted with spraying gear, which consisted of a fibreglass ventral tank of 75-gallon capacity for the chemicals, and a wind-driven pump mounted under the engine. For the transit flight to the Sudan, the spray bars, normally mounted below the wings, were taped to the main wing struts, the ventral tank carried aircraft fuel and a 12-volt motorcar fuel pump was mounted on the cockpit floor to top up the main centre-section tank in the wing centre section.

The four pilots were Jo, Ian Taylor, Harry Gandy, a spray pilot already known to Jack and Ian, plus Bruno Brown, whom Jo had met while attending Avigation's ATP Licence course. 'Jack hadn't been able to find another pilot readily,' Jo says, 'and Bruno didn't have a job to go to, so he decided to join us.' Jo was to be the leader for the transit flight and prepared four full sets of maps for the route with the track marked in and all relevant VHF radio frequencies recorded. The Piper Cub had two seats arranged in tandem and in all four aircraft the rear seats were loaded high with aircraft spares, tools and other equipment, leaving little space for personal baggage.

On 9 September the four flew to Southend, cleared customs, filled up with fuel and continued to Lyon. From there the route took them via Nice to Ajaccio in Corsica, Cagliari in Sardinia, Idris (formerly Castel Benito) near Tripoli in Libya, Benina (Benghazi), Alexandria, Wadi Halfa (later submerged by the rising waters of the Aswan Dam) and Khartoum. The longest leg was from Alexandria to Wadi Halfa, a flight of 7 hours 35 minutes. Jo comments:

> It is worth explaining that our aircraft had no blind-flying instruments, which meant that we had to remain in visual contact with the ground virtually at all times. The radios, fitted only for the transit flights, were cheap 'Mickey Mouse' efforts, and the receiver had to be hand-tuned, which meant that you could only tune it whilst the ground station was transmitting. This made things very difficult.

'With the Piper Cubs,' he adds, 'we had the luxury of being able to carry much more fuel than we were ever likely to need, but it got a bit hard on the backside sometimes. The longest trip I flew in a Cub was 8 hours 35 minutes between Corfu and Nicosia.' Jo goes on to say: 'With a basic aircraft like the Piper Cub there was not very much for the pilot to do. We'd set the engine RPM, top up the centre section gravity fuel tank occasionally, and watch the world go past at 90 miles an hour, 500 or so feet below.' Crossing 200 or 300 miles of open sea, however – as between Sardinia and Libya – did lead Jo to 'pay particular attention to the engine and oil pressure and [keep] an ear cocked for any variation in the sweet throb of the four cylinder Lycoming engine, with its 135 horsepower.'

Most of their transit flights were over land, however, and at low altitude there was much to be seen. In particular, Jo recalls

> that on the flight from Benghazi to Alexandria over the Western Desert, I could see what was obviously the mark of tank tracks, characterised by the angular turns. I naturally assumed that somebody's army had recently been out on manoeuvres there, until I noticed that there was scrub growing deep down in the ruts. They were then clearly tracks left by the Afrika Korps or the Eighth Army almost 20 years earlier. On the leg from Alexandria to Wadi Halfa, we had to give Aswan, where the Russians were building a high dam, a wide berth, flying well out to the west. This took us over the rugged Nubian Desert, where everything was red sand or sandstone and there was not a plant or living creature in sight. It was awesome. Further south we rejoined the Nile where it flowed through a gorge not far north of Wadi Halfa, and at low altitude we saw in their original position the figures carved into the stone on the west side of the river at Abu Simbel.

The airfield at Wadi Halfa had three runways, Jo remembers, 'and on one side were the remains of a Vickers Viscount of Misrair, the Egyptian airline, which had come to grief during a sand storm some years previously. They told us at the only hotel, a river boat owned by Sudan Railways, that in Wadi Halfa it hadn't rained for 25 years.'

The four aircraft reached Khartoum on 16 September, with a flying time en route of 43 hours 25 minutes, and were parked in a special area that already accommodated a number of crop-spraying aircraft of different types. They were booked into a small hotel in the city, quite adequate but very Sudanese and very different from the Grand Hotel where Jo had stayed when on tropical trials with the Argosy. 'There was quite an influx of pilots who had been in the Sudan before,' Jo recounts, 'and the favourite meeting place was the bar at the Metropole Hotel, which was run by a Greek couple who tried very hard to produce, from local sources, food which looked and tasted like what most of us were used to at home.' It took a few days in Khartoum to get organised, after which the four aircraft were despatched to Kosti on the West Bank of the White Nile, some 200 miles south of Khartoum. Here they and another team of four aircraft that had arrived from their home base in Nairobi were all in the care of Fisons' local representative, 'Dodger' Green, who was accompanied by his wife and small six-year-old son. The only other non-Sudanese resident in Kosti was another Greek, who ran a general store-cum-post office that most importantly stocked quantities of bottled beer. Mail arrived every four or five days by the train, which continued on its way to Wau in remotest south-west Sudan.

Jo describes the location and living conditions:

During the Korean War somebody decided that in order to feed the troops it would be a good idea to build a bully beef factory in Kosti. To this end they had built about six rather grand European style detached houses complete with mosquito screens for all the windows, very desirable for keeping the millions of flying creepy crawlies out. These were clearly intended for the executives of the proposed meat-canning factory. Then the Korean War ended and the factory was never built. Anyway we were billeted in one of these houses with a couple of Sudanese chaps to cook and keep house. Next to it was a bare earth but quite adequate landing strip where the aircraft were serviced and parked.

He adds:

We were quite comfortable in our house. We had electric light and a plumbing system of sorts. It was kept reasonably free from insects, and a few geckos who seemed to be resident inside the house put paid rapidly to any insects which gained entry. The two house boys kept the place clean and put on a reasonable cooked meal in the evening, while most importantly there was a fridge stocked with a variety of bottled drinks and an icemaker. We each had very large thermos flasks that we had brought with us from the UK, holding about five litres and these we took out with us in the morning, filled with iced drink. The difficulty was to delay as long as possible starting on it, because once this had happened it was difficult to stop.

Along the river around Kosti, wherever the land was flat enough for irrigation canals, cotton was grown. The land was divided into units called schemes, each with a massive pumping station to lift water from the White Nile into the irrigation canals. The land, canals and pumping stations belonged to the Sudanese government but the land was let out in four- or five-acre plots to peasant farmers who grew the cotton and sold it to the government at a price decided by the latter. Entomologists constantly monitored the cotton crop for infestation, which would, if found, be reported to Dodger Green, along with a recommendation as to the chemical to be used to combat it. He would then mark out the area to be sprayed with flags so that the pilots could identify them from the air; he also prepared a sketch map showing the areas to be sprayed and the nearest landing strip, where Fisons' chemical tanker would be positioned, along with aviation fuel.

'Each evening', Jo remembers, 'Dodger would call at the house to tell us his requirements for the following day and we would allocate the areas between ourselves. Sometimes a spray area could be 100 miles or more away. In this case we would set off in the dawn's early light. Navigation was no problem of course because we always had the river.' One such area that Jo visited several times was Um Galala, an hour and three-quarters flying time south of Kosti:

The landing strip there was a dirt road running through a huge field of Dura, a type of millet that grew to a height of eight or nine feet. This strip was only just wide enough to give clearance between the wing tips and the Dura. At one end a space had been cleared large enough to position the chemical tanker etc and to allow the Cub to swing round 180 degrees. This manoeuvre was not helped at all by the inefficient differential wheel brakes on the Cub, which always deteriorated quickly with use. The procedure was to land on the strip towards the tanker, make a 180[-degree] turn and sit there, engine running, while two men refilled the ventral tank with chemicals and then to take off again. This procedure could occur six to eight times an hour until the aircraft required refuelling. While this was happening it was periodically necessary to clean the spray nozzles and the windscreen.

Um Galala was sufficiently far away from Kosti to necessitate occasional overnight stays, so Jo and his fellow pilots always carried food, a camp bed and mosquito net with them. When at Um Galala, Jo shared the Sudanese manager's house with him. He 'used to carry out his prayer mat ritual totally oblivious to my presence,' Jo says, adding, 'the mosquitoes didn't seem to bother him at all either. He didn't need a net, but when, asleep, I inadvertently had any bare flesh in contact with a net they had me at once.'

Jo comments that 'There seemed to be a lot of cooperation between the expatriates resident around there', recalling that 'on one occasion Dodger asked me to deliver something to a chap over near the Blue Nile, some 100 odd miles away. He turned out to be a New Zealander who had "gone bush" as they say, had married a local Sudanese woman, was living in a fairly primitive mud hut and teaching in a little school which he had started.' On another occasion Jo was asked to visit a missionary south almost to Malakal. 'This was well beyond the cotton growing area or any other serious cultivation,' he says. 'I found the airstrip and as I landed an antelope of some kind dashed across in front of me. I taxied up to the end of the strip and stopped the engine. As I was climbing out the missionary dashed up in a jeep, complete with gun, saying "Hello, pleased to meet you. Did you see any antelope on the way in?" When I said that I had, I had to leap in the jeep along with him and dash off to try to find it, without success.' Jo was invited to stay for lunch with the missionary, his wife and another woman who was a nursing sister. The three were running a small hospital for the benefit of the local Dinka people, supported by an American charity, which received supplies and mail monthly when their Cessna aircraft flew in. 'The missionary was Canadian', Jo recalls, 'and a mining engineer. He told me that while working in Australia he attended a talk about the Dinka people and it was just as though God tapped [him] on the shoulder and said I want you for those people. So he went.'

As the cotton-growing season progressed, the need for chemical treatment decreased to a point where Fisons required only three aircraft to operate. 'We thereupon released Bruno Brown,' Jo recounts. 'I became a bit uneasy about him on the flight out when at Tripoli, Benghazi and

Alexandria he got considerably the worse for drink in the evening and was not at all in good shape the next day. In the Sudan, too, he never missed the opportunity to drink and this made him unreliable, so we paid him off, said thank you very much and sent him on his way. I've never heard of him since.'

In 1945 Jo's parents had given up the post office and shop in Eastbury and retired to Lynton, in North Devon, where in 1955 after unsuccessful radiotherapy for breast cancer his mother died. Thereafter his father moved to Norfolk to live with Jo's sister, Margaret. Towards the end of November 1962, Jo received a letter from his sister, Con, telling him that their father was critically ill and suggesting he return home. 'I immediately decided that I should do so,' Jo says, 'and went up to Khartoum. By a great stroke of luck there at the airport were John Cunningham and Pat Fillingham on their way home with a Comet after carrying out tropical trials somewhere. So I got a free lift home with them. Father was in a nursing home at Wells-next-the-Sea in Norfolk, near where my sister Margaret lived, in Binham. I stayed briefly with Margaret and was able to visit father just twice before he died on 3 December, aged 81.'

Jo's stay was brief. 'The state of the work I had left behind in Kosti was such that I felt it imperative that I should get back just as soon as possible,' he states, 'so with the generous blessing of the rest of the family I flew back to Khartoum and was back working in Kosti on 6 December.' In the event the three remaining pilots were hard at work up to Christmas Eve, so on Christmas Day Dodger and his wife organised Christmas dinner for them. 'Interestingly enough,' Jo says, 'quite a few of the locals, although Muslim, joined the celebration and it was interesting to hear Dodger's six-year-old son rattling away in Arabic to some of the local boys.'

The contract in Kosti was completed, and all that remained was to fly back to Cyprus. But with Bruno Brown gone, who was to fly the fourth Piper? Fortunately, Ron Cripps, their engineer, was still with them, and had a private pilot's licence, so it was agreed that he should fly the fourth aircraft back. They left Kosti for Khartoum on Boxing Day, where they were held up for a few days while negotiating transit clearance with Egypt, eventually flying to Wadi Halfa on 30 December and on to Luxor the following day, overnighting there before journeying on to Port Said on

New Year's Day 1963. 'Poor Ron Cripps made a heavy landing,' Jo recollects, 'and cracked his fibreglass ventral tank. We stayed overnight in Port
Said and Ron had to spend hours repairing the tank, always a messy and
awkward job.'

The next day Jo decided that they should head for Beirut, but with no
meteorological office at Port Said he requested a route forecast from Cairo.
When nothing came, Jo determined, perhaps unwisely, that they should
set off without one. Over the sea, however, the eight-eighths cloud base
fell to below 1,000 feet, visibility deteriorated, and Jo became worried,
particularly about the inexperienced Ron Cripps. He therefore led the
others eastwards until about 5 miles off the Israeli coast, intending then
to continue – with the coast in sight – to Beirut. 'Suddenly a pair of Israeli
Mystère fighters appeared', Jo recalls, 'and kept dashing past us rocking
their wings, signalling us to follow them. I was in fact quite relieved. So
we turned in towards Israel and landed at the first airfield we saw, which
turned out to be military.'

There the four were given a meal and told to fly to Tel Aviv, where they
were interrogated at some length, but released when Jo found that the
Air Attaché at the British Embassy was Wing Commander Robin Sadler,
whom he had known in the 1950s at Boscombe Down. He vouched for
Jo and all was well. 'The next day', Jo continues, 'we reached Nicosia from
Tel Aviv and parked the aircraft. We already had a rented house there,
7 Methone Street, off the Larnaca Road, a nice bungalow that was our
headquarters for the next three years. We flew by airline back to the UK,
and one of the coldest winters for years', returning in March to ferry the
four Pipers back to Eastleigh in Hampshire for their annual Certificate of
Airworthiness overhaul and inspecton.

Early in the New Year the decision was taken to make Aerospray fully
self-supporting except for the prescription and supply of chemicals. To
this end, Jo bought an ex-RAF 750-gallon Bedford tanker from a government surplus agent. It required modifying by fitting an auxiliary
engine-driven pump that could suck up water, pump the chemical into
the aircraft or, when doing neither, recirculate the contents of the tank
continuously to prevent the sediment from settling. To do this Jo enlisted
the help of an old friend from Cowes days. 'Jack Stanley, who also had a

flat in Osborne Court, had a flourishing heating engineering business in London,' says Jo. 'He found me a place in Woolwich where friends of his who were Thames lightermen had a workshop, and we took the tanker there to do the work, which was undertaken by a plumber lent full-time for this purpose.'

By the time the tanker conversion was completed, Aerospray had won a contract in Austria with the chemical company Schneider Chemie, so the tanker had to be driven to Vienna. Again, Jo was able to enlist aid, this time from Brian Smith, who had given Jo facilities in his Leamington factory to complete his sailing dinghy. Brian spoke German fairly well following his service in the army of occupation post-war, and had several good friends there. Together they took the tanker across from Tilbury to Antwerp and drove to Vienna, the only mishap a broken fanbelt. In Vienna they found a secure place to park the tanker and Brian Smith flew back to England. Ian Taylor then arrived with one of the Piper Cubs and they set up the operation for Schneider, spraying sugarbeet in the north of the country, on the frontier with Czechoslovakia. 'There was a huge wire fence and frequent lookout posts,' Jo recalls, 'the occupants of which constantly followed us through their binoculars.'

The Austrian contract was followed by one with the Syrian government. This 'was for two aircraft and we would need the tanker for that. Jack and I went out again to Austria and collected the tanker. I well remember driving it through Vienna on a wet Saturday night, its hard tyres not at all good on the wet cobbles. We left Ian to tidy everything up and bring the aircraft back and drove the tanker to Trieste, where we saw it loaded onto a freighter bound for Latakia in Northern Syria.'

To help Jo with the Syrian contract, Aerospray hired an experienced American crop-spray pilot named Bob Turner. At the beginning of July the two flew to Nicosia and thence, at the end of the month, to Latakia where a few days later the tanker arrived. They also had a new long-wheel-base Land Rover with a very large roof rack, which had also been shipped out to Latakia. 'It was loaded with various sorts of camping equipment,' Jo recollects, 'which included much to my disapproval some heavy and clumsy wooden folding camp beds and also an exceedingly heavy and clumsy domestic gas cooker. Much lighter, more compact and efficient camping beds and cookers were available but my objections were overruled.'

The contact within the Syrian Ministry of Agriculture, the director of crop protection, was Rafiq Skarf, whom Jo remembers as 'a quiet and reserved man, intelligent, well informed and easy to get along with'. He spoke fairly good English, and a few years later Jo learned that he had landed a good job with the United Nations, probably with the Food and Agriculture Organization (FAO). Skarf's deputies on field operations were Edmonde Abdelnour and Walid Darkal. Edmonde had attended the Sorbonne and married a Frenchwoman. 'When I was invited to his home in Damascus,' Jo says, 'I was only allowed to meet his young son and in true Arab fashion his wife was kept out of sight. I imagine that French girl must have felt imprisoned for life. Walid was newly married and much more enlightened. His wife dressed European style and travelled with him whenever possible. They had no qualms about showing affection for each other.' Neither Edmonde nor Walid spoke English, and Jo's Arabic was limited to about thirty nouns, but Edmonde spoke fluent French, so perforce Jo had to resurrect his very rusty schoolboy French. 'We managed quite well, but had any Frenchman been eavesdropping, it could have caused a diplomatic furore.'

Aerospray's local agent was George Murr, a Lebanese with one shop in Beirut and another in Damascus, where he was normally resident. Murr had found an assistant, Mohamad Rabbani, a Palestinian living with his mother in Damascus, who 'turned out to be an excellent choice, being a very useful and pleasant young man with some mechanical knowledge'.

Inevitably, Jo and Bob Turner were regarded as potential spies, so they were accompanied at all times by a Syrian Air Force officer, Lieutenant Aziz. 'We never knew his first name,' Jo admits. 'We used to call him Lieutenant. He wore pilot's wings but it was hard to imagine him ever flying an aeroplane. He seemed a bit simple but always pleasant, and when we walked together he always wanted to hold my hand. He did have his uses, however, because every small town in Syria seemed to have an officers' club, to which we had access courtesy of the Lieutenant. These were typical officers' messes, usually well appointed for food and general comfort.'

By the end of July the two aircraft, Land Rover and tanker were assembled at Latakia and ready to start. The location was south of Latakia and on the eastern side of the coastal range of mountains known as Jabal an

Nusayriyah in the valley of the River Orontes. The crew were based at a small town called El Rab, their task spraying the cotton grown in that area. They were given a bungalow but had to fend for themselves domestically. To help with the tanker, though, they hired a local man, Yusef, whom they picked up each morning en route to the airstrip. Says Jo: 'He lived in what was literally a one-roomed mud hut. But he would invariably want us to come in and say hello to his wife and young son and to have a cup of tea or coffee.'

After two weeks at El Rab the team moved via Aleppo to the far north-east of Syria, to Al-Busayrah, about 30 minutes east of the nearest town, Dayr az-Zawr, at the confluence of the Euphrates and a tributary, the Khabur, again spraying cotton. 'It was a pretty bleak place,' Jo recalls, 'very arid and with few signs of civilisation. The midday shade temperatures every day were up to 46 [degrees] centigrade. We all disliked the place very much but strangely enough Yusef seemed to dislike it most of all.' While they were at Al-Busayrah, the Syrian Ministry of Agriculture undertook to keep the team supplied with fresh water, which came in a huge rubber bladder. Only on one occasion did it fail to reach them. 'Things became quite critical, and eventually we were forced to drink the chocolate-coloured water from the Euphrates. I suffered the effects of dehydration for a time, but luckily none of us felt any ill effects from drinking from the Euphrates.'

The stay in Al-Busayrah was mercifully brief, and after three weeks the team returned to El Rab, which, with the daytime temperature at about 33 degrees, seemed pleasantly cool. With only one aircraft now needed, Bob Turner flew back to Nicosia, Jo following him on completion of the contract three weeks later. On arrival in Nicosia, however, Jo found that he and his Piper were required urgently in Sudan. After a brief delay caused by a faulty starter motor, which he repaired himself, he was airborne again for the Sudan, where he joined the team already crop spraying at Wad el Mansi, on the Blue Nile, about an hour's flying time south of Khartoum.

While at Wad el Mansi, following the same routine as at Kosti the previous year, the Aerospray team was offered the use of a Lockheed LASA-60, which was being built under licence by the Italian aircraft manufacturer, Aermacchi, which had in mind to market it as a crop sprayer. A four-seat high-wing monoplane with a tricycle undercarriage very similar in design to the Cessna family of light aircraft, the LASA-60 seemed at first sight suitable, but Jo and the other pilots found it unsatisfactory. 'It had little to commend it,' he comments, 'as the wing loading and wing section were such that it was not docile enough at low speed and it had a six cylinder Continental engine with fuel injection, and microscopic foreign matter regularly got into the fuel, clogging the injection pump. At the time when purpose designed and built crop spraying aircraft were being produced it really had nothing to offer as such.'

Late in December, the Aerospray team left the Sudan for Nicosia again, parked the aircraft there and returned to the United Kingdom, where Jo as a director of the company found himself once again at odds with Jack Akers. He explains:

> To complete our operating equipment I had wanted to get two large horse box type trailers, possibly of the tandem-wheeled type, one for the domestic equipment, with built-in cooking facilities and possibly folding bunk beds. The other would be for aircraft spares, tools and equipment, both to be towed by the Land Rover and the Bedford tanker. Instead, without consulting me or Ian, Jack had bought an ex-army radar trailer, four-wheeled and very heavy. This had been stripped out at enormous expense and fitted with a kitchen, bunk beds and an air-conditioning unit. But it was so heavy that neither the Land Rover nor the tanker could possibly have towed it, so he had bought an equally enormous Scammel diesel towing unit. Mounted on this was an independent petrol driven generator for the air-conditioning which in the event we found so unreliable as to be virtually useless.

The previous year the Pipers had been flown back to the United Kingdom for their annual Certificate of Airworthiness renewals. In 1964, however, it was decided to carry out the inspections in Cyprus. A suitable workshop was rented, and the aircraft, with wings removed, were towed, tail-first, across Nicosia by the Land Rover. A licensed aircraft engineer was brought out from England and the aircraft overhauls were completed. Cyprus had no Air Registration Board, though, and used the British ARB, whose nearest representative was in Beirut, so he was flown over to check and sign off the paperwork. Aerospray was back in business for a further twelve months.

Jo enjoyed Cyprus enormously and feels sad at the way it is now divided into Greek and Turkish states: 'It was a totally unnecessary calamity, which now is seemingly insoluble.' During his time on the island, he came across many individual examples of intercommunal harmony, but was also aware of how ethnic tensions were deliberately being inflamed. Nowhere was this clearer than in the person of Nikos Sampson, former EOKA gunman and owner of an extremist newspaper, *Makhi*, meaning 'Battle' or 'Struggle'. A self-confessed murderer of British servicemen in the years preceding independence, he was a member of the Cyprus parliament and led a flamboyant lifestyle, which included an expensive Jensen car, openly advocated expelling Turkish Cypriots and achieving Enosis, or union, with Greece. The violence he incited erupted while Jo was there, for on 21 December 1963, an armed conflict – since known as 'Bloody Christmas' – erupted. After days of bloody conflict, which left hundreds of Turkish Cypriots, and a lesser number of Greek Cypriots, dead, some 250,000 Turkish Cypriots had been driven from their homes into protective armed enclaves, and the stage had been set for the coup of July 1974, supported by the army Junta in power in Greece, which was aimed at Enosis. In the latter Sampson played a prominent part, becoming president dictator for eight days before resigning when Turkish forces invaded Cyprus and occupied the northern third of the island. Imprisoned for his part in the coup – the only individual to be tried and convicted – he spent years in gaol before being amnestied on health grounds, and died in 2001.

The attempted coup and consequent bloodshed precipitated an immediate influx of media cameramen and reporters, who tended to congregate at one of Jo's favourite watering-places, John Odgers's Bar. 'One,' Jo recalls, 'named John Osmond, tried hard to persuade me to fly him over what was now exclusive Turkish Cypriot territory to see where they were alleged to be building an airstrip.' Prudently, Jo declined. Several other requests from the Cypriot authorities, however, he met. 'The Director of Civil Aviation was an ex-RAF navigator called Hercules Paniatides,' he says,

but his world seemed to disintegrate when all this trouble started. The air traffic controller at Nicosia had taken possession of a Dornier Do.27, a single-engined, five-seat aircraft presented to Cyprus by Germany to mark its independence, but nobody had ever flown it. I was persuaded to supervise its rehabilitation, and even though it had no registration or CFA, I flew it five times to give one of the controllers who had some piloting experience dual instruction. Completely separately, the Cyprus police had acquired a Piper Tripacer and a Bolkow Bo.207, both two-seat single-engined aircraft and built their own airstrip by their headquarters on the Larnaka Road, which runs south out of Nicosia. Once again I was requested to try the aircraft out and give one of their number some instruction, which I did.

Although the intercommunal violence was widespread and bloody, Jo and his Aerospray team were not threatened. But he had several interesting moments:

> One of my favourite leisure haunts was the Harbour Club at Karenia on the north coast, about a 15 mile drive from Nicosia. The club was run by a British couple, the wife having been in her younger days one of my favourite singers of the dance band era, Judy Shirley. We became good friends. When the trouble started there was a Turkish Cypriot village on the road a few miles out of Nicosia and several times I was stopped by a road block manned by a motley gang of armed ruffians. Once I brandished my British passport they were quite happy. On one occasion one of their lot accidentally let off his gun and they all set about him.
>
> On another occasion I had stayed the night in Karenia and was driving back the next morning. I had just passed over the crest of the road over the coastal mountain range, when I ran into a gun fight. Chaps on both sides of the road were leaping about, hiding behind rocks and shooting at each other. I slowed right down and just carried on. They carried on their fight, and completely ignored me.

Meanwhile, Aerospray was still in business and preparing for another contract they were confident of winning with the Syrian Ministry of Agriculture. 'We expected to be rejoined by the American, Bob Turner', Jo recalls,

> but we completely lost touch with him and in his place at the last moment we took on a Canadian, John, whose surname I forget. He

turned out to be a most extraordinary and weird character. Anyway, at the last minute we received a signal from our agent, George Murr, that a Lebanese company had undercut our bid but for £1,500 he could buy them off. Of course this simply stank. But we said okay, not having any intention of paying him for what was obviously a scam.

On 2 July 1964 the Aerospray team set off once again for Syria, returning to Al-Busayrah, where they sprayed cotton for three weeks. 'In the evenings,' Jo reflects, 'we would go to what passed there for a restaurant, the most palatable dish on the menu for me being kidneys and onions. Afterwards we would smoke an aggeeli, or hubble bubble pipe.' In early August, spraying completed, the team moved west to Homs, which Jo recalls as 'a nice little town on quite a substantial river'. His strongest memory of this time, however, was of the restaurant at Hamar, north of Homs, 'where one could sit in the shade and watch a Roman water wheel in action'. He adds:

> Back at Homs we parked our caravan beside an irrigation canal and at nights the canal sparkled with glow worms floating on the water. The night sky was absolutely clear and we were able with the naked eye to see a rocket carcass orbiting. We could actually see it slowly tumbling over and over and could forecast quite accurately where and when it would reappear each time, which was approximately every 100 minutes.

At the end of August Aerospray released their second pilot, the Canadian, John. 'I was not sorry to see him go,' Jo admits. 'He was weird and not very good at his job. I had a strong feeling there was something bogus about him. His surname was very British, but he spoke fluent French and wasn't, I think, French Canadian.'

From Homs the team moved to Tartus on the Syrian coast, where they established themselves on the beach, which they were using as a landing strip. It was a beautiful region, lush and productive by comparison with the stark landscape around Dayr az-Zawr. Just a few miles into the coastal mountains was Safita, a little town dominated by the remains of a crusader castle, built by the Templar order as 'Castel Blanc'. Beyond Safita, Jo found 'lush valleys, where the locals of a Christian sect live an idyllic life alongside crystal clear cold mountain streams, growing almost every kind of fruit and vegetable you could think of.' Jo recalls with amusement that

> it was in those lush mountains that we found a little 'restaurant'
> where the menu was either fish or chicken. If you ordered chicken,
> the restaurateur disappeared behind his shed, you heard a chicken
> protesting loudly and a loud thud. Boiled chicken would appear some
> little time later. If you ordered fish, the restaurateur would wade
> across the river, start up an engine-driven generator, and dangle half a
> pair of pliers on the end of a wire into the water, whereupon a fish or
> two would appear belly-up on the surface. He would collect these, stop
> the engine, wade back and cook them. The food was certainly fresh.

Two other impressive crusader castles were also nearby, one at Masyaf, just a few miles on, in the Orontes Valley, and beyond that was the famous Krak des Chevaliers, the most impressive of all.

While driving in and around Tartus, Jo and the Aerospray team noticed a British-registered VW Beetle and eventually made contact with the driver. She was Honor Frost, a pioneer in marine archaeology who had, in 1959, been the first to recognise that a wrecked ship off the coast of Turkey at Gelidonya – which contained a rich cargo of copper and tin ingots together with personal possessions of the crew – dated from the late Bronze Age and was early Phoenician. 'It was fascinating to hear her on the subject,' Jo recalls. 'She spoke some Arabic and was of small build, but in the water she just went off like a torpedo, a marvellous swimmer.' On one occasion Jo took her aloft in a Cub for a low-level reconnaissance along the coast. 'The water was calm and translucent, you could see rocks on the bottom and she was able to identify all sorts of things which were of great interest to her. We were airborne for nearly 3 hours.' Jo met up with her again later in Damascus, where she gave him a copy of her recently published book, *Under the Mediterranean*, inscribed 'Ruad October 21st 1964, to Jo Lancaster, the pioneer of aerial marine archaeological photography. Very gratefully, Honor'.

The spraying from Tartus completed to the Ministry of Agriculture's satisfaction, Aerospray's one remaining aircraft was released and on 8 November Jo flew it back to Nicosia. Then he returned to Damascus to wind up the contract, deal with George Murr, and, most importantly, be paid. 'I decided first', Jo says, 'to deal with George Murr and the £1,500 he was expecting. I wrote a letter to him dispensing with his services as of that moment and explaining why. Before giving it to him I went to see Mr Skarf and told him the whole story, about which he made absolutely no comment.'

Then there occurred an incident that turned out well in the end, but occasioned Jo some concern at the time. 'During my protracted stay in Damascus', he writes,

I had befriended an American pilot called Al Temple who worked for the UN's Food and Agriculture Organization (FAO). We had been staying at Cattans Hotel, a 3 star hotel conveniently placed in the centre of the city, but decided to move to a pleasant but more moderately priced one. One morning, very shortly after meeting Mr Skarf, I was awakened about 7 o'clock by a worried hotel manager. He told me to get up immediately, which I did, and in reception awaiting me were two scruffy-looking chaps who wanted me for questioning. I told the hotel manager to tell Al Temple what had happened, got in their Land Rover, where I had to sit between them, and was driven off to an inconspicuous house, which turned out to be the headquarters of the Deuxième Bureau or secret service. I was taken into a room where another scruffy chap sat at a desk on a raised platform and we sat there looking at each other for about an hour. Eventually a presentable, well-dressed young man who spoke reasonably good English arrived and took me down to the basement. On the way down I caught a glimpse in another room of a woman prostrate and motionless on the floor. The young man was very calm and polite and started to question me about all sorts of things. I had no problems. I had a clear conscience and simply told him the truth. In due course I was returned to the upstairs room again for about an hour or so and then the questioning was repeated. It didn't seem to follow any particular line and I couldn't make out what they were expecting to learn from me. Having been offered neither food nor drink all this time, I was eventually allowed to leave at about four o'clock. There was no Land Rover this time; I had to find my own way back to the hotel. Al was there, greatly relieved to see me. He was just on the point of going to the British Embassy to tell them what had happened.

'We never heard from our friend George Murr again,' Jo adds. 'I wonder whether he got a going over by the Deuxième Bureau too. He never got his money anyway.'

During his final sojourn in Damascus, Jo was told that the Ministry of Agriculture had bought two Piper Cubs, which were in their crates at Damascus airport, and was press-ganged into assembling one of them. 'I protested loudly that I was not technically qualified to do such work unsupervised,' Jo says,

> but they would have none of it. They provided me with an assistant, I think a Syrian Air Force chap in mufti. In a small hangar on a remote part of the airfield we uncrated the first aircraft. Fortunately, the fuselage in the crate was complete with engine centre section and undercarriage and all we had to do was fit the propeller, wings and wing struts, the tailplane, fin and rudder, connect up all the control cables and charge the battery etc, and there we were. When I declared the assembly was complete they demanded I carry out an air test. Poor old Lieutenant Aziz turned up to act as passenger, or perhaps to prevent me from fleeing the country. Anyway, we did a successful air test, everybody was happy – and they didn't ask me to assemble the second aircraft.

'Whilst all these things were going on,' Jo adds, 'I was paying daily visits to the Bank of the Middle East, trying to extract our money. In true Arab style, each time you made one small step forward it was "bardin bukkra", which means "later on" or "tomorrow", and you could then get absolutely nowhere until the next visit.'

Leisure time in the evenings, and there was plenty of it, was almost always spent in Freddy's Bar, owned no longer by Freddy but by an elderly Syrian, who sold a good brand of local beer. 'It was a place to meet other ex-pats,' Jo remembers, 'and one evening I remarked that there were no less than eight nationalities in our little group. One chap who always included himself was a Syrian who spoke very good English. No one knew exactly who he was or what he was supposed to be doing. It was generally accepted, however, that he was planted as an intelligence officer, trying to find out what all we potential spies were up to.'

Jo finally left Damascus with about 5 inches of snow on the ground, and flew to Nicosia, where he was joined by Ian Taylor, who was to fly the second Cub back to Britain.

The team Jo took to Syria had included an engineer named Bill Trollope, but he had returned to Britain with health problems. In his place Aerospray hired an Indian, Mark Ambat, 'a genial, outgoing chap who told everyone that he spoke like Peter Sellers, so he had a sense of humour'. Ambat was a capable and fully licensed engineer, but while they were operating from the beach at Tartus Jo observed a small problem: 'When carrying out his routine engine inspections, Mark would remove small parts, nuts and bolts etc, and put them straight on the ground, sometimes subsequently walking over them. Very tactfully I found some items to use as trays and he took the hint.' A much greater problem, however, Jo did not know of until it was too late. Operating from a sandy beach made an efficient carburettor air filter absolutely imperative. But when replacing the air filter after inspection on one occasion Ambat had not positioned it properly. 'Locating it could only be done by feel', Jo says, 'and he couldn't see the mounting base. The result was that he didn't get it located properly. It was on a flange instead of grounded, and the result was a big leak and the engine ingesting sand, causing cylinder wear and excessive oil consumption.'

The obvious solution was to remove the engine for a complete rebuild, but Mark Ambat was not qualified to do that, so the only option was to fly the aircraft home. But the oil loss was so great by the time the two Cubs had reached Athens via Rhodes, that Jo felt he had to devise a solution to the problem. 'I went shopping and managed to buy a large brass syringe and some plastic tubing. I then went to Olympic Airways' workshop and got them to drill a hole in the oil filler cap and connected that to the plastic tube with the syringe in the cockpit. On the rest of the journey home I would periodically fill the large syringe with oil from the can which I kept on the floor of the cockpit and then inject it into the engine. It was very slow hard work, but it worked, although everytime I did it I got absolutely soaked in oil.'

Back in Britain things started to unravel for Aerospray (Cyprus) Ltd. Jo takes up the story:

It emerged that Jack Akers had been travelling the world, admittedly mostly looking for business, but the dreaded Miss Boffey had been accompanying him, including on a trip to the United States and back on the Queen Mary. I had not been receiving any salary at all, and I had spent much of my own money in support of the company's operations. It was now time for reimbursement but there was none forthcoming. We had completed five successful crop-spraying contracts but there seemed to be nothing to show for it. Then I learnt that Jack Stanley and Brian Smith, the two friends of mine, had not been reimbursed for their out-of-pocket expenses incurred when, as a personal favour to me, they helped us out with the tanker. To make matters worse, I found that Jack had started another company called Aviation Agencies, of which he was the sole director, and that much of Aerospace Cyprus's funds seemed to have been routed via that company. Finally it emerged that Jack's house in Pluckley, which he had been renting, had had to be put on the market and that he had bought it with company funds.

Ian Taylor, the other director, and his wife were by then running a firm called Auto Tours, specialising in cheap European motor tours for students and it was doing well. 'Ian became preoccupied with that,' Jo says, 'and seemed not to want to be involved in aerial spraying anymore or sorting things out.'

Jo's relationship with Jack was by now very bad, and he decided he too would get out of the firm. 'I didn't have a regular solicitor so I went to Roy Dollimore, who had been a Technical Officer at Boscombe Down during the war and now had a practice in Mayfair. I told him of my predicament and he advised me to resign as a director. This I later learnt was about the worst thing I could have done.' Proceedings dragged on for about five years until Aerospray (Cyprus) Ltd was wound up and Jo, who had pumped thousands of pounds of his own into the business while drawing no remuneration – and was owed more than £7,500 – eventually received just £400 to help pay his solicitor's fees. 'It was such a tragedy,' Jo says, 'that we built up a nice little business, well equipped and with a good reputation, and it was all wasted.'

Chapter 14

Meridian Air Maps

In March 1965, Jo's financial situation was parlous. He had very little money left in the bank, having sunk thousands into Aerospray (Cyprus) Ltd over the previous three years while drawing no income. He had high hopes, ultimately dashed, of recovering the £7,500 he believed he was owed, but in the meantime needed a job. Fortunately he had many friends and former colleagues in aviation, and it was to them he turned for information and possible tips as to job opportunities.

One of those former colleagues was Charles Moss. A wireless operator on Jo's flight at Boscombe Down, he was now a rostering officer with British United Airways at Gatwick and in a good position to know what jobs were available. There were only two that he knew of, recalls Jo. 'One was flying a Dakota to Düsseldorf and back every night with the newspapers. This job I declined. The other was flying a DH.125 executive jet for the Managing Director of the Rank Organisation, John Davis. He had a reputation for being very demanding and difficult. I got as far as an interview for this job with one of his minions, but probably cooked my goose when I told him in response to his description of the job that I had no intention of becoming an errand boy.'

Fortunately, there was another option. A small company called Meridian Air Maps was advertising for a pilot. Based at Shoreham Airport, near Brighton, Meridian had recently been formed by three cartographers who had been working for a major air survey company, Hunting Air Surveys Ltd, but had decided to go it alone. 'I went down to Shoreham for an interview, was offered the job on the spot and accepted. For my part at this time I regarded the job as a stop gap until I could find an airline post.'

Jo promptly gave up his small flat in the basement of a friend's house in Leamington, which had been his UK base while working for Aerospray, and sought accommodation close to Shoreham. 'I was lucky,' he says, 'to find a comfortable bedsit in a large house on the outskirts of Worthing that had been converted into about six bedsits. All the other residents were elderly ladies, not financially hard-pressed but perhaps dumped there by their families.' The landlady, with whom Jo got on well from the start, was a Mrs Curzon, a very gracious old lady who informed him that she had been Lady Curzon.

Later that year Jo became a homeowner for the first time, having purchased a bungalow in Fulking, a tiny village tucked into the north side of the South Downs, just north of Brighton.

Hitherto, Jo had never given a thought as to what was involved in aerial survey work. Now he would find out. Almost all Meridian's contracts involved producing large-scale maps of very high accuracy, usually required for civil engineering projects such as new roads. The data from which the maps were produced was derived from stereoscopic pairs of prints, nine inches square. These were set up in a very complicated and expensive plotting machine made by the same company as the camera, Wild of Switzerland, large and heavy at about 150lb, made mostly from cast steel and costing nearly as much as the aircraft. Three cassettes were carried, also cast steel and each weighing 70lb.

The flying operation involved a crew of three: pilot, tracker and camera operator. Jo's task, as pilot, was to fly level, maintaining a predetermined height and following the required run line as directed by the tracker, who was sitting alongside him. The tracker's job, before take-off, was to prepare a map with the required photographic area marked on it and to draw over this the run lines required to cover the area adequately, suitably spaced so as to give a minimum of 10% lateral overlap between adjoining runs. He also had to mark in the required height of each run. In the air using a downward-looking optical sight the tracker would direct the pilot using voice or hand signals to position the aircraft in order to fly directly along the required track line and to instruct the camera operator sitting behind him when to turn the camera on and when to turn it off again.

The camera operator had a sight within the camera and, through this, by reference to the ground passing beneath, he would adjust the camera to compensate for any drift that the aircraft might have in a crosswind. He would also set and continuously monitor the sequencing controls to maintain a minimum of 60% overlap on successive frames. As well as this he monitored the shutter speed and aperture according to light conditions.

'The three founder-directors had built up a reputation for first-class map production,' Jo says.

But nobody in the firm had any idea about aircraft operation, although one or two thought they did. Flying operations had started with a Miles Aerovan, which had been replaced by an old ex-RAF Anson. They probably got it cheap but it was too big and much too expensive to run. When I got there they had fortunately just acquired a Piper Aztec which was much more suitable. It was currently undergoing the major modifications necessary to accommodate the survey camera. The directors had never employed a regular pilot but had relied upon any odd bod they could find to do the flying, mostly airline pilots living locally who had a bit of spare time. But this was clearly not the way to take full advantage of the all too few weather opportunities.

'By far the greatest problem was always getting the right weather conditions', Jo says.

Ideal conditions were when there was full cover of thin high cloud which gave good diffused light with little or no shadow. Cloud below aircraft level was obviously no good because it would appear on the photography and obscure the ground. The cartographers did not like hard shadow on the ground, cast by broken cloud above the aircraft level, and obviously visibility had to be good with little or no air turbulence and the light had to be adequate. In the UK in winter, even in good conditions, there were only about three hours around midday when there was enough light.

'With so few weather opportunities', He continues:

> It was absolutely vital that no mistakes be made because this might
> entail waiting for days for a chance to repeat. Occasionally, the camera
> operator would be careless and lose the required overlap or something
> else perhaps. But most mistakes were down to the tracker, who might
> leave a gap between runs or lose the lateral overlap somewhere, which
> didn't become apparent until the films had been developed and
> plotted. The tracker's job was not easy. Some got the knack and did
> a good job, but others were hopeless. When I joined Meridian they
> were using an ex-RAF drift sight, which gave a very limited view of
> the ground beneath the aircraft. I eventually persuaded my masters to
> invest in a purpose-designed sight made by Zeiss. It was expensive but
> it rapidly paid for itself by easing the tracker's job and cutting down
> his mistakes.

'I felt that they needed me,' Jo says, 'and I became very involved in reorgan-
ising things, although it was very hard work at times, particularly when
convincing them to spend money. The upshot was that I got so engrossed
in all this that age-wise I passed the point of no return so far as an airline
job was concerned and settled for a career in aerial surveys instead.'

In due course Jo was given the title of aviation manager and the aircraft
fleet grew to two Aztecs, two turbo-supercharged Piper Navajos, a Cessna
210 and a Dakota, the last two inherited from Spartan, a Canadian company with which the managing director had been associated. The Dakota
was brought to the United Kingdom on completion of a contract in Africa
and parked in the open air at Marshalls of Cambridge, as Spartan had
arranged. Jo comments:

> As we had no immediate need for it I wanted to take it to Lasham,
> where Dan Air had a maintenance base and were willing to inhibit the
> engines and store the Dakota under cover for a very modest charge.
> I could not persuade my masters to do this. Instead they let stand
> the arrangement which Spartan had set up, whereby the aircraft was
> to be parked in the open air and Marshalls would run the engines
> every month. This was not cheap and when as frequently happened

moisture got into the ignition systems they charged much more to rectify this. No other maintenance whatsoever was undertaken and eventually the aircraft was in such a sorry state that it was sold for £1,500. This was much less than had already been paid out in parking fees and maintenance, such as it was. This whole episode was just one of a number of stupid and costly episodes. Another occurred when it was decided to get rid of the Cessna 210. I managed to sell it to Michael Bishop, now Lord Glendonbrook, and then Chairman of British Midland Airways, for a decent price. He was going to refurbish it and use it as his own personal aircraft, but when it came down to the formalities our company secretary managed somehow to upset Bishop and he pulled out of the deal.

Although much of Meridian's work was in the United Kingdom, as the business expanded contracts were obtained for survey work in Guyana, Belize, the Caribbean, South Africa, East Africa, Nigeria, Cameroon, Egypt, Cyprus and, closer to home, Portugal, France and the Republic of Ireland. For this work, Jo declares, it was crucial that the self-contained team of three was led by a pilot who was competent, confident, resource-ful, self-motivated and determined to lose no opportunity to get the work done at all possible speed. 'Operating aircraft was very expensive', Jo recalled.

> So unnecessary flying had to be avoided. It clearly followed that a really competent team, and in particular the tracker, would almost always complete a job satisfactorily on the first attempt. Any gaps in the photo cover or other mistakes meant that the aircraft had to repeat the flight, wasting both money and probably favourable weather too. Yet in all my 19 years with Meridian I never succeeded in persuading my masters that it would be money well spent to induce the really good ones (and we had some) to stay. The directors' tight-fisted approach was false economy.

'I had lots of applications for a pilot's job', Jo says.

Mostly from young chaps who had just qualified for their commercial

licence and needed a flying job to build up their flying hours and
experience before applying for a senior commercial or air transport
pilot's licence. Some of them were very good indeed. I also had
applications from ex-airline pilots who for various reasons were not
operating as such.

We had one ex-airline pilot who felt his rank so much that he
refused to dine with the other two chaps even when they were out
in the bush. Another I subsequently learnt, had been dismissed after
sexually assaulting a stewardess. A third had an Algerian father and
a French mother. He spoke English very well, was very good-looking
and had a great way with the ladies. He was quite a good pilot, too,
but in Nigeria he pulled a knife on someone and his two colleagues
had a delicate and difficult job resolving the situation. It was quite
a crisis at the time. A fourth one, of Czech origin but working in
the UK, was foisted on us by one of the directors for some political
reason. He was to fly one of the Navajos from Nigeria across to Kenya,
but instead of taking the approved route he went via the Central
African Republic, where I believe he had a friend, but where the
correct grade of aviation fuel was not available. So he filled up with
ordinary automobile petrol and was very lucky to arrive in Kenya at
all. Both engines were ruined and had to be replaced. It was all due to
stupidity and lack of intelligent planning.

'The most successful and satisfactory pilots for overseas work', Jo comments,

were all the young newly qualified pilots. They generally did a good
job and logged the flying hours which they needed to progress
to much more lucrative airline work. I wished that I could have
persuaded some of them to stay, but I couldn't get them a salary to
make it a worthwhile deal. So I wished each of them good luck and
sent them on their way with a glowing reference. One of them has
stayed in touch with me to this day and when I went to Canada and
the US some years ago, to show his gratitude he provided me with
several free airline tickets.

'There were no serious accidents while I was Aviation Manager,' Jo reflects, 'but one very sad incident. I was short of a pilot, picked an application form out of the pile and called the number. It was answered by his mother, who told me that just minutes earlier she had received a telegram to say that her son had been killed in a flying accident in Canada.'

While teams were working worldwide, Jo's task in the UK included providing everything required by aircraft and crews operating abroad, including aircraft spares, of which he had to maintain a comprehensive stock under lock and key. 'Communication was always difficult in those days,' he recalls. 'A telephone call sometimes could take days to get through and when you did get through you mightn't hear properly.' Sometimes, using his contacts, he was able to persuade flight crews on one of the scheduled airlines, against the rules, to take out spares or messages, but the work was always time-consuming.

Besides catering for teams working overseas, Jo was also involved in a UK-wide surveying programme, which, he says, 'we never ever were able to fully catch up on'.

> Suitable weather conditions as always were what we lacked. The job was seven days a week and from first light we had to start checking the weather. There was a civil aviation VHF radio service called Volnet, which gave the weather conditions at about 20 UK airports, updating every 30 minutes, and we could ring the 24 hour Met. office at Gatwick or elsewhere, but their information was useful only as a guide because what was excellent flying weather to most people was not by any means always suitable for air survey photography.

Most of the work in the United Kingdom was for major civil engineering contractors or local government authorities. The latter, Jo was told, were bad payers, sometimes taking over a year, without good reason, to pay up, and making it abundantly clear that if they were pressed too hard further contracts would not be forthcoming. 'There was always pressure,' he admits, 'which could be very frustrating and exasperating, especially if, as something they undoubtedly did, our sales people offered over-optimistic and unrealistic delivery dates.'

The United Kingdom flying programme involved work all over the country, and particularly during the summer months the survey weather often came first thing in the morning, before convection cloud started forming. It was therefore necessary to be based at an airfield near the photo area. 'We got well known at some of these airfields,' Jo says.

> Most of them didn't open until about 7 or 8 in the morning and we needed to be airborne earlier than that. In some cases we were able to sign a form of indemnity and then they were happy to allow us to operate outside normal operating hours. Others wouldn't allow this, so we'd be sitting on the tarmac, engines running and on the radio to them on the stroke of opening time.
>
> If we were lucky we would get two or three hours' photography in before the cloud forced us to stop; usually there was no chance of any more work that day. So after landing we would refuel and reload the film cassettes, then make for some little café and feast on eggs and bacon, satisfied with having achieved something worthwhile.

The hotels at which they stayed were usually cooperative about early morning departures. If there was a night porter, he might be persuaded to produce tea and toast and Jo recalls that at least one place they were told to go into the kitchen and help themselves. 'One of our favourite hotels,' he recalls with amusement, 'was the Grange in Harrogate, close to Leeds Airport. The night porter there would always gleefully greet us with the words, "Ee, you'll do nowt today."'

Several times Jo led a team working in the Republic of Ireland, twice staying at the grandly named, but probably two-star Waldorf Astoria Hotel, very conveniently positioned in Dublin facing the river. 'We were made very welcome there,' Jo recollects.

> In the bar, which was in the basement, one night I finished up acting as barman. On another occasion we stayed at Malahide, about 10 miles north of Dublin at the Grand Hotel, which had clearly been grand about 50 years earlier. There again, the bar was in the basement and one evening our visit coincided with the remnants of a wedding reception. One very happy little chap greeted me affectionately,

insisting that I was his old pal Paddy Sale, who was apparently a Dublin bus driver. He simply wouldn't be persuaded otherwise. Again at the Grand, before retiring one night I entered a request for morning tea in a book left on the reception desk for the purpose. Having at times been provided by the night porter with very weak morning tea, I added in brackets, 'strong'. It arrived punctually but totally black and undrinkable. I imagined the night porter gleefully muttering, 'So he wants his tea strong does he?'

Jo had a markedly different experience when, based at Teeside Airport, the team stayed in Durham, a city known not only for its wonderful cathedral, but also for its large prison. 'We went out to a local pub in the evening and the landlord looked at us and said, "Are you cops or screws?"'

His work as aviation manager kept Jo in the British Isles most of the time, but he did roster himself in 1971 for a six-week stint in Portugal, flying one of the Piper Aztecs. 'We lived in the Cibra,' Jo remembers, 'a holiday hotel at Estoril, about 10 miles west of Lisbon, and flew from a small private airfield just north of there. I took my favourite tracker with me, Roger Bouchet, a Frenchman who spoke passable Portuguese. I was amazed how rugged that country is up in the north and it was altogether a very pleasant interlude.'

In 1976 Jo again rostered himself for an overseas stint, this time six weeks in Greek Cyprus, flying one of the company's Navajos. 'I wasn't going to miss a chance to go to Cyprus again,' Jo says. 'Nicosia Airport was still closed, so we operated from Larnaka, commuting each day by car from the Kennedy Hotel in Nicosia. I was instantly recognised and warmly welcomed by both Andreas Ashakolis, my erstwhile grocer/bar keeper and by Michael Perides, owner of the famous John Odger's Bar. It was another very pleasant interlude.'

Besides survey photography Meridian occasionally undertook other less usual jobs. One was testing sidescan radar equipment for EMI. 'Their technical man was a very practical chap called Mr Kingston,' Jo recollects.

His equipment required liquid nitrogen and a 250 volt power supply. So together we went out and bought a small petrol-driven 250 volt

generator and a length of flexible metal pipe. The radar equipment
was mounted over the camera hole in the floor of the aircraft and
we mounted the generator beside it with the flexible pipe taking the
exhaust fumes down and out through the camera hole. Mr Kingston
sat behind the equipment with a large insulated flask of liquid
nitrogen which, when required, he poured into the equipment for
cooling purposes. If the Air Registration Board or our insurers had
ever known what we were doing they would have gone berserk.

Another contract, which Meridian's sales team concluded with British
Gas, very much against Jo's advice, was to photograph large sections of
their underground gas pipeline from very low altitude to check for potential hazards. Jo felt there were many practical difficulties in doing this with
a fixed-wing aircraft and finally persuaded management to subcontract
to another company, operated by Chris Foyle, a junior member of the
bookshop family. Shortly after, Foyle took the obvious step and employed
a helicopter.

One major problem that cropped up from time to time was mapping in
controlled air space, i.e. the control zones surrounding major airports and
airways, or flight corridors. It was illegal to enter these areas without being
in radio contact and with the permission of the ground controller, who
coordinated all activity within his area. 'In 1965,' Jo states, 'it was sometimes possible to call up on spec. and get permission to enter controlled
air space to carry out a detail, but air traffic density increased so rapidly
that it became expedient to call up the air traffic centre and make a request
to the duty supervisor beforehand.' Even this had its problems, however,
since it was difficult to explain over the phone exactly where the survey
crew wanted to fly and what flight pattern was involved. To overcome
this Jo devised a proforma application, which he submitted, together
with a map providing detailed information, and sent it in advance by
post. The air traffic supervisor then allotted a special flight number. In
this way, when a weather opportunity presented itself, Meridian could
ring up, quoting the special flight number, and the supervisor – with the
information he required in front of him – could decide whether it was
feasible, in view of the airline traffic density, to permit the flight. 'The
situation greatly improved when eventually our aircraft were equipped

with transponders, which identified each aircraft on the controllers' radar screens and indicated its height and heading.' Eventually, the air traffic authorities laid down a special procedure for work such as Meridian's, which was termed Non-standard Flight Procedures.

It was evident to Jo that some supervisors were relaxed and cooperative dealing with Meridian, while others regarded its activities as unimportant and a nuisance. 'I did have some sympathy with the duty controllers,' Jo says, 'because there were undoubtedly a few pompous airline captains who if they spotted another aircraft, especially a light aircraft, near them, would complain loudly and bitterly to air traffic control.' Jo, however, found it interesting and even fun: 'For instance, I carried out all the survey work for the western end of the M25 before they built it. This involved making frequent runs across the take-off and landing path very close to Heathrow and at 1,500 feet.'

In the late 1970s Jo went to his optician for a routine eye test, to be told that he had a cataract in his right eye that would almost certainly be followed in due course by one in the left eye. This was naturally a matter of concern. From the age of forty commercial pilots are required to have a six-monthly medical examination conducted by an approved aviation medical practitioner. In his case, for many years Jo had been seeing Dr Ian Perry, who had his rooms in Sloane Square, London. 'When I next went to him for a medical,' Jo recalls, 'I said that I had been told that I'd got a cataract. "I could have told you that a couple of years ago," he replied. But even though the sight in one eye became gradually so bad that it was like being in a room full of steam, he kept on signing me out as fit to fly. I kept on flying, and had no difficulty in doing so.'

After each medical exam by the aviation doctors the results are routinely sent to the medical department of the Civil Aviation Authority. In 1981, aged 62, Jo received a letter from the CAA Medical Department, saying that they were not altogether happy about some aspects of his most recent medical examination and asking him to attend CAA headquarters for clinical tests. He did so, was interviewed by three doctors and then spent a long session on the treadmill wired up to recording equipment. 'The treadmill gradually became steeper,' he says, 'and I think faster, but the only discomfort I felt was in my legs, which weren't used to so much activity.'

The doctors found nothing amiss and Jo was cleared for further flying. But the CAA episode prompted him to act on something he had been wondering about for some time, which was how his fellow survey crew members felt, flying with a pilot in his sixties. Were he to become incapacitated while they were in the air, he thought, they would be quite unable to do anything about it. Did it worry them? It seemed an ideal opportunity to sound them out, which he did. He recalls that when he asked them how they felt, 'they just looked at each other a bit blankly, shrugged their shoulders and shook their heads at my question. Clearly they had no problem with me, thank goodness.'

After retiring Jo had the cataract in his right eye removed and was fitted with a contact lens, implants at that time being in the early stage of development, and fitted only to those who could not manage a contact lens. But Jo found that he was one of those who had difficulty inserting and removing the lens and eventually gave up using it. 'I seemed to be able to drive okay without it,' he says. A year or two later, however, he received a phone call from a Warrant Officer Paul Smooker at the RAF hospital at Ely. He had been researching the history of the hospital's gate guardian, as the RAF calls an aircraft standing at the main gate. It was an Armstrong Whitworth Meteor 14 night fighter, in which Jo had carried out its initial flight. 'We had a wide ranging chat,' Jo remembers, 'and the subject of my cataracts arose somehow.' Smooker asked why Jo did not have them operated on at Ely, and there and then obtained the approval of his CO, Wing Commander Jordan. Implants in both eyes, the right eye redone when the first implant did not anchor itself correctly, eventually gave Jo almost perfectly restored vision.

By mid-1983 Meridian Air Maps' financial situation had begun to deteriorate critically. 'We had been a group subscriber to BUPA, a private healthcare company,' says Jo, 'but that was discontinued. We had had a pretty good pension scheme and that too had to be wound up. Shell ceased to honour our fuel credit card, so when funds were available we had to operate with a great wad of banknotes to pay cash for fuel, which I found rather embarrassing. And then pay cheques started to bounce.'

The main cause of the cashflow crisis was the company's heavy commitment to work in Nigeria, where not only were there contracts already completed and others under way, but time and money had been committed to preparatory work for promised future contracts. 'I don't know why,' Jo recollects, 'there was no complaint about the work that had been carried out, but the Nigerian clients withheld payment totalling something like £250,000.' The managing director flew to Nigeria twice to try to resolve the situation, but without success. Meanwhile, in the United Kingdom a lack of cashflow began to bring everything to a standstill. Key personnel left, and having, on 4 February 1984, reached the pensionable age of sixty-five, Jo retired. 'I had hoped to continue flying for Meridian for a year or two longer on a freelance basis, but now there was no chance of this.' He did, however, return for a few days to help sort out and catalogue the considerable quantity of aircraft spares, listing and then packing them and arranging to sell them back to the suppliers at a reasonable price.

A few months later, Meridian Air Maps went into liquidation, owing Jo something of the order of £2,000 in expenses and allowances. He put in a claim as a creditor and eventually received a small payout, but lost about £1,800. As with Aerospray (Cyprus) Ltd, what had been a challenging and (in flying terms) rewarding career, had ended badly in financial terms.

Epilogue

Jo retired in February 1984, comfortable in his cottage in Clappers Lane, Fulking, which he had bought in 1965. It had been arranged that he would continue to fly for Meridian Air Maps on a freelance basis, but with the liquidation of the company his flying days ended. In 1994, with almost all the public amenities in Fulking discontinued, he moved to Hassocks just 5 miles away. He lives a quiet life, beginning each morning with the *Daily Telegraph* cryptic crossword, and is disappointed if within an hour he has not completed it. But as one of the now fast-diminishing band of Bomber Command veterans, he and his local group of geriatric 'Terror-fleigers' attend print and book-signing charity events in aid of the Bomber Command Memorial Fund, for which they have now raised more than £60,000. He is also consulted by authors working on aspects of Bomber Command's war, as by one working recently on yet another book on the Wellington.

Jo has also been in demand over the years as the first ejectee using a Martin-Baker ejection seat in an emergency. The company has invited him to many functions, including Sir James Martin's funeral in 1981, celebration dinners at Park Lane hotels and Sir James Martin memorial lectures, followed by dinners at the Royal Aeronautical Society headquarters in Hamilton Place. The highlight, though, occurred in October 1999, when the Martin-Baker Aircraft Company Ltd hosted a major PR occasion in Washington, to mark the opening of their new service and repair facility in Johnstown, near Pittsburg. Jo recalls his trip:

I flew first class from Gatwick to Baltimore Washington International (BWI), and thence by stretch limo to the J.R. Marriott Hotel on Pennsylvania Avenue, Washington DC! The official proceedings were a large reception, addressed by the then Martin-Baker Chairman, Denis Burrell, during which I was introduced as Exhibit A, followed by a dinner served in the foyer of the Smithsonian Aviation Museum, with the original Wright Flyer, 'Spirit of St Louis' and Bell X-1 suspended above our heads. Later I spent several hours in that fascinating place. Before leaving the UK I had bought a 30 day 'go anywhere on United's domestic routes' ticket, which included Canada. When the official proceedings were over I visited friends in Pittsburg, Miami, Nassau, Seattle, Vancouver Island and Toronto ('Queen City of the Empire'!), and had a wonderful time.

Capping all these events was one that occurred in 2013, when, rather mysteriously, Jo was invited to lunch by Andrew Martin, during which the subject of the Rolex watch, presented to Jo by Sir James to mark the first emergency ejection, was brought up. Jo explains:

> I told Andrew that I had been burgled in about 1975, and that the watch had been stolen, whereupon he produced it from his pocket, still in its rather battered presentation box. I was, of course, astonished. It turned out that the company had received an email from an individual in New York who had made the connection through the inscription on the back. Someone from Martin-Baker's American operation identified the watch and bought it back, cost undisclosed. The then 'owner' was apparently a rather dubious Italian-type character, who would not explain how it had come into his hands.

Nor was that all, for earlier in the meal, Andrew Martin had produced from his pocket what Jo describes as 'a rather sophisticated Bremont watch of which possession would be limited to Martin-Baker ejectees'. 'These had to be bought,' Jo continues,

> but in my case they said that they would buy it for me, have it duly inscribed as No. 1, and then auction it, the proceeds to go to the

Bomber Command Memorial Fund – a very generous gesture. Just before leaving it occurred to me that I would like to include the Rolex in the same sale. Their response to that was to offer to buy the watch back for £5,000, that sum to go into the Bomber Command Memorial Fund on my behalf, and the Rolex to remain in Martin-Baker's own museum.

'I wondered whether I would miss flying very much,' Jo says, 'but the answer is no. There have been so many things on the ground to take my interest.'

First and foremost of his interests is his family. Graham, now retired, and his wife, Margaret, have two children, Richard and Charlotte – both now in their twenties and well established – while Jenny – born in 1967 to Jo and Jill Derracott, to whom he was briefly and very unhappily married – and her partner Ollie produced a daughter, Jean, in 2006 who brought a late, unexpected, but delightful further dimension to Jo's life.

In nearly forty-seven years Jo accumulated a grand total of 11,000 hours on some 150 different aircraft types. In airline pilot terms, 11,000 hours is not remarkable, but Jo points out that almost all of those hours were under manual control, radically different from airline flying. Another way of measuring his career as a pilot would be to count how many take-offs and landings he had made. 'I had a year of circuits and bumps on Wellingtons,' he says, 'and when the Armstrong Whitworth production runs were in full swing, an average test flight on a Meteor was 17 minutes and you could carry out up to eight flight tests a day. When crop-spraying, you could easily be doing eight or ten trips in an hour.' His take-offs and landings, therefore, must run into the thousands.

Does he envy those who still fly? 'When I was invited up front in a British Airways 757 in mid-Atlantic at 37,000 feet,' he responds, 'it certainly was a beautiful sight, and I could envy the two pilots sitting there, relaxing with a cup of coffee. But it's when I book a flight or on pension day that I envy them most.'

Endnotes, Sources and Bibliography

Chapter 4: **1.** David Gunby, *Sweeping the Skies*, p.165. **2.** *Ibid*, p.166. **3.** *Ibid*, p.167. **4.** Martin Middlebrook and Chris Everitt, *The Bomber Command War Diaries*, p.209.

Chapter 5: **1.** Chorley W.R., *Bomber Command Losses, Volume 7*, p.167.

Chapter 6: **1.** Martin Middlebrook and Chris Everitt, *The Bomber Command War Diaries*, p.344. **2.** *Ibid*, p.353. **3.** *Ibid*, p.360. **4.** *Ibid*, p.366. **5.** *Ibid*, p.368. **6.** *Ibid*, p.371. **7.** *Ibid*, p.371. **8.** *Ibid*, p.382.

Chapter 8: **1.** Tim Mason, *The Secret Years*, p.149 **2.** *Ibid*, p.109. **3.** *Ibid*, p.7. **4.** *Ibid*, p.7. **5.** *Ibid*, p.8. **6.** *Ibid*, p.9. **7.** *Ibid*, p.9.

Chapter 9: **1.** Rawlings, John, and Hilary Sedgwick, *Learn to Test, Test to Learn*, p.12. **2.** *Ibid*, p.12. **3.** *Ibid*, pp.13–4. **4.** *Ibid*, pp.14–5.

Chapter 11: **1.** Oliver Tapper, *Armstrong Whitworth Aircraft Since 1913* (London, 1973), p.296. **2.** Quoted in Derek Collier Webb, *UK Flight Testing Accidents 1940–1971* (Tonbridge Wells, 2002), p.97.

Sources: J.O. Lancaster. Flying Logbooks. Recorded memoirs. Operations Record Books for 12 and 40 Squadrons.

Bibliography
Chorley, W.R. *Bomber Command Losses, Volume 2*: 1941 (Earl Shilton, 1993).
Chorley, W.R. *Bomber Command Losses, Volume 3*: 1942 (Earl Shilton, 1994).
Chorley, W.R. *Bomber Command Losses, Volume 4*: 1943 (Earl Shilton, 1996).
Chorley, W.R. *Bomber Command Losses, Volume 5*: 1944 (Earl Shilton, 1997).
Chorley, W.R. *Bomber Command Losses, Volume 7*: *Operational Training Units 1940–1947* (Hinkley, 2002).
Gunby, David. *Sweeping the Skies: A History of No. 40 Squadron RFC and RAF 1916–56* (Bishop Auckland, 1995).
Jefford, Wing Commander C.G. *RAF Squadrons. 2nd Edition* (Shrewsbury, 2001).
Mason, Tim. *The Secret Years: Flight Testing at Boscombe Down 1939–45* (Aldershot, 1998).
Middlebrook, Martin and Chris Everitt, *The Bomber Command War Diaries* (London, 1985).
Rawlings, John, and Hilary Sedgwick, *Learn to Test, Test to Learn* (Shrewsbury, 1991).
Tapper, Oliver, *Armstrong Whitworth Aircraft since 1913* (London, 1973).
Webb, Derek Collier, *UK Flight Testing Accidents 1940–1971* (Tonbridge Wells, 2002).

Index